10.50

IMMORTAL SHADOWS

IMMORTAL SHADOWS

A BOOK OF DRAMATIC CRITICISM

BY

STARK YOUNG

OCTAGON BOOKS

A division of Farrar, Straus and Giroux

New York   1973

Copyright, 1948, by Charles Scribner's Sons

Reprinted 1973
by special arrangement with Charles Scribner's Sons

OCTAGON BOOKS
A DIVISION OF FARRAR, STRAUS & GIROUX, INC.
19 Union Square West
New York, N. Y. 10003

Library of Congress Cataloging in Publication Data

Young, Stark, 1881-1963.
  Immortal shadows. New York, Octagon Books, 1973.
  Reprint of the ed. published by Scribner, New York. 290 p.
  1. Theater—New York (City)—Reviews. I. Title.

PN2277.N5Y6   1973   792'.09   73-7662
ISBN 0-374-98844-7

Printed in USA by
Thomson-Shore, Inc.
Dexter, Michigan

To the memory of Doris Keane in *Romance,* where the effort and exhaustion of the artist went toward the projection of what only was beautiful, lyric, passionate and witty; so that she became not so much the elusive, remarkable darling of her public as their idol. She was as it were all music and security of outline, like a swan on water, and something we long to believe can never cease.

PREFACE

THIS volume does not by any means assume to be a chronicle of our American theatre. It is simply a selection from my reviews written for various stage events over the years, with for the most part a certain time order, but without insistence on that point. Many of them deal with a period that is now one or two decades ago. There are two reasons for this:

First, there is the fact that in the 'twenties and early 'thirties there was a remarkable movement in our theatre. Mrs. Edith J. R. Isaacs, who as editor of *Theatre Arts Magazine* made an admirable contribution both to the record and the success of this period, has said a profound thing about this. She said that not only was the period remarkable, but those of us in it at the time knew that it was remarkable.

Second, after the death of Herbert Croly, who as Editor-in-Chief of *The New Republic* had a profound understanding of the place of all the arts in our society and of the problems of critical writing, the editorial policy of the magazine gave less and less authority and concern to the arts in general, so that with the proper urging my articles got shorter and shorter. This state of things finally reached a climax where it was more than apparent that there would be neither room nor encouragement on my part for any article of any length that in my opinion would have done credit either to the paper or myself, not to speak of service to the theatre. I, therefore, resigned from *The New Republic* in July, 1947. I may add that this volume represents the last writing that I shall do on this subject of the theatre.

For permission to reprint the articles I am indebted to *The New Republic* and in the case of "The Little Clay Cart" and "Caesar and Cleopatra" to *The New York Times,* on which I served as Dramatic Critic for the season of 1924–1925.

STARK YOUNG

CONTENTS

	PAGE
TRANSLATIONS	1
THE TORCH BEARERS	5
HAMLET	8
THE MOSCOW ART THEATRE	15
QUEEN ELIZABETH'S PLAY	20
IT IS THE LARK	25
DUSE'S IBSEN	29
THY WILL BE DONE	33
ITALIAN, RUSSIAN	37
THE PASSIONATE PILGRIM	41
THE MIRACLE	45
THE PIRANDELLO PLAY	48
THE LITTLE CLAY CART	52
CAESAR AND CLEOPATRA	57
THE GREAT GOD BROWN	61
HABIMA AND SOREL	67
AN AMERICAN TRAGEDY	72
THE SILVER CORD	76
THE BROTHERS KARAMAZOV	80
PIRANDELLO'S COMMEDIA	84
IN ABRAHAM'S BOSOM	88
DYNAMO	91
MACBETH	96
THE KINGDOM OF GOD	101
STREET SCENE	106
JOURNEY'S END	110
MEI LAN-FANG	114
THE GREEN PASTURES	119
THE PHILADELPHIA LYSISTRATA	123
THE SHADOW OF WINGS	127
EUGENE O'NEILL'S NEW PLAY	132
KING JAMES IN CHINATOWN	140

CONTENTS

	PAGE
SORROW'S SHARP SUSTAINING	145
FOUR SAINTS IN THREE ACTS	150
MOLIERE KINDERGARTEN	153
LUREATE BRAINS	159
VALLEY FORGE	165
SPANISH PLAYS INDEED	169
NOCTIS EQUI	174
MISS LORD'S DAY	178
THE COUNTRY WIFE	181
HIGH TOR AND HIGHTY TIGHTY	185
ETERNAL REINHARDT	189
CANDIDA, CANDIDA, CANDIDA!	193
RICHARD II	196
THE SEA GULL	200
HEARTBREAK HOUSES	206
THE WHOLE TRAGICALL HISTORIE	211
SAROYAN THEATRE	215
TWELFTH NIGHT	218
BOOK BASIS	223
OLD WINE, NEW BOTTLING	227
OTHELLO	230
A GENTLE MRS. STOWE	236
SO DIVINE AN AIR	240
BOSTON LIMITED	243
THE TEMPEST	246
THE GLASS MENAGERIE	249
MID-SEASON	254
MISS CORNELL'S ANTIGONE	258
THE OLD VIC	263
THE OLD VIC OEDIPUS	266
THE ICEMAN COMETH	271
WEBSTER	275
MARTHA GRAHAM	278
INDEX	283

IMMORTAL SHADOWS

TRANSLATIONS

The Birthday of the Infanta. A pantomime with music and scenario by John Alden Carpenter, décor by Robert Edmond Jones. The Manhattan Opera House. February 2, 1922

AFTER *I Pagliacci* with its hot loves and fierce dramatic lyricism, its tawny and blue and crimson world, and its tawdry and mediocre setting, *The Birthday of the Infanta* brought a strangely different atmosphere. Against the passion, laughter, revenge and death of those strolling players, it set up the thin and innocent life of a little princess of twelve and her court in the midst of the rich, hard magnificence of the circumstance about them. We see first the garden courtyard of the palace. On either hand the high walls rise, flat spaces with long heavy moldings, grey varied to darker and more ashen tones. To the left at the head of a flight of steps a door, very high, with an inspired touch of greyish white in the baroque metal awning across the curve of the top; and dark red curtains showing through the glass at the sides. Across the middle of the scene and between the two walls, a sort of raised terrace and balustrade connecting them, and to the back a high iron screen through which appear the Spanish mountains, a violet silhouette hardening to blue against the cold grey-rose of the sky. It is all grave and austere and cruel and lovely, elegant, rich and superb, this place where the child princess and her court will make their festival. And the music meanwhile in that opening moment is austere, a little thin; it is innocent, lonely, continuous; and now and then it hints at the grotesque and the poignant and the frail tragedy to come.

The Infanta enters through the great door; her court surrounds her. They bring in gifts; a chest with a gown, brocade banded with galloons of gold; a huge silver cage with strange birds; a painted casket with a doll in a green farthingale. There is a birthday cake with lighted candles, there are mock rope-walkers, jugglers, and a mock bull-fight, when the ladies have taken their places on the terrace to see. And then last they bring in the Grotesque. He is Pedro the dwarf and hunchback. He looks strangely around him, crooks his head, and begins to dance about for the court. He is perplexed, a lonely, vague, ashen little figure amusing the fine company, and clinging to the balustrade as he reaches out his hand to the princess above him. The Infanta and her court withdraw. And as the scene ends Pedro eludes his guard, gets his crooked legs through the door just in time, shuts it in the guard's face, and escapes into the palace.

The curtain rises then on the palace vestibule, lofty, with a high door looking out on the same cold-rose sky as before, across a terrace promenade. The scene there in the palace is crimson and grey, dull rose, gold, black. Candlesticks with their huge candles stand ten feet high, and there are two mirrors higher still. The dwarf, Pedro, enters; he is awestruck by the splendor around him, and then he sees the mirrors. Then, as in Oscar Wilde's story, he sees himself for the first time in all his ugliness and deformity; and dances a frenzied dance until he falls dead. After a little the princess comes in, touches him and calls him to dance for her. But he does not waken and she sees that he is dead. She lays her red rose on his cheek. They draw her away as the merrymakers from without appear in the door.

All this innocent and grotesque, sombre, ornate gaiety Mr. Carpenter expressed, so austere is his music at times, so macabre, so hauntingly elaborated, so wistful, and so finely withdrawn. This music of *The Birthday of the Infanta* has none of the fury of sex in it, for the lives that it reveals have an ironical innocence and formality; but in them and in their music as well there is the shadow of what will mature into passion. In spite of Mr. Van Grove's rather thin conducting, especially in the first part; in spite of the miming and dancing, which lacked mass rhythm and emphasis; and in spite of Mr. Serge Oukrainsky, whose Pedro had no pathos or dramatic magnetism, the imagination of the music constantly appeared. It was not Stravinsky—and who is except Stravinsky, with his prodigious invention and celestial mathematics?—but it sustained a modern quality throughout; it had the excitement of poetic sincerity, and it carried the whole piece toward something that was inescapably drama.

TRANSLATIONS

Mr. Robert Edmond Jones' contribution to *The Birthday of the Infanta* is as distinguished as anything he has done so far, it seems to me. And it is, moreover, a fine illustration of the fact that the art of the theatre is not a mere combination of any particular things, setting, actors, recitation, literature, for example; it is a distinct and separate art. It may be composed of many things, but it is none of them. Nothing that goes to compose this art remains as it was before becoming a part of it. The art of the theatre has ultimately its essential character; and differs from painting, literature, architecture and all its contributory arts as they differ from one another in the essential character that sustains and perpetuates each one of them. But what that separate art of the theatre is, can be more easily illustrated than defined. As an illustration of it, then, in one single respect out of the many involved, take the setting for the *The Birthday of the Infanta*.

Nowhere in Spain have I seen buildings like these. But I have seen in Spain that character of sterility, of color and mass. I have seen that barbaric and cruel barrenness of sheer walls emerge, though any amount of rococo and baroque or plasteresque ornamentation had been superficially laid on to soften the aspect of it. And I have seen in Spain this cold elegance pushed to the romantic; as in the Escorial, where Philip's simplicity becomes at length a glowing and sinister affectation. The character of Mr. Jones' settings, then, perfectly expresses the Spanish instinct, into which the actuality of buildings has been translated by the artist. But that is not the important point just here. So far they have indeed become art, it is true, but not necessarily the art of the theatre. The important thing to be said here is that this is not architecture in Spain or anywhere else, but a translation of architecture into theatre terms.

The same is true in a region even more difficult perhaps, and certainly more elusive: the costumes. These costumes in *The Birthday of the Infanta* were not particularly interesting as reproductions of Spanish fashions toward the end of the seventeenth century. I have seen much better copies than they were or tried to be. And they were not mere clothes such as we used to see in a careful Clyde Fitch production, or garments that were costly enough and exactly borrowed from history, as in the usual Belasco or Winthrop Ames productions. None of these things. These costumes for *The Birthday of the Infanta* were distinguished because they were Spanish seventeenth-century costumes seen superbly in terms of the theatre. They would suffer heavily—as they ought to do—if taken out of their present employment. They are inseparable from the whole, and in themselves they are moving and exciting.

There are three high spots dramatically in *The Birthday of the Infanta*. The third and last of them is at the death of the dwarf, the very end of the play; and here the scene subordinates itself; it only envelops the action in a towering, rich shadow, and leaves the moment to the music, whose language best suits its poignant necessity. But the drama of the two others is almost entirely created by the setting. It is the décor here that conveys much of the dramatic idea. One of these places is where against those iron bars and the hard mountains beyond them, the princess and her ladies in their citron color, their crimson, blurred saffron, rose and white, gold, silver and black, sit on the balustrade above the courtyard, and the little hunchback below in his pallor and drab and green reaches up his lean hands toward the dazzling splendor of them. And the other and still more dramatic incident—and more simply achieved—is that earlier moment when the little princess enters that great door, and stands there under the height of it and at the top of the steps leading down, a figure like a doll in all that relentless magnificence and order, and a symbol of the tragic puppetry of all life in the midst of time and the world's vastness. And, meantime, her grave and delicate little body is borne along in those billowy, great skirts as her heart is borne on the waves of the music.

Finally this achievement in the décor for *The Birthday of the Infanta* illustrates remarkably how in the art of the theatre precisely as in other arts, say music, painting, poetry, the reality must be restated in terms of the art concerned before there is any art at all. It must have the charm of presence and absence, as Pascal said of portraits. An element must be there which was not there before. It must be incredibly translated into something else; it must be the same and not the same, like the moon in water, by a certain nameless difference born anew.

THE TORCH BEARERS

The Torch Bearers, by George Kelly. Forty-eighth
Street Theatre. August 29, 1922.

IN *The Torch Bearers* a group of people are bitten with the little-theatre idea. At the leading lady's house the husband returns to find a rehearsal of the play going on, directed by Mrs. Duro Pampinelli—so well played in a high-horse, lady-group style by Miss Alison Skipworth. This directress is a rapt egoist whose stage promise has been blighted by a husband. The star part in the play has fallen late to a new member, because of the fact that the sudden death of the first leading lady's husband had removed her from the cast. The husband of the new member, as the first had done, falls in a faint when he sees his wife act. He resolves not to attend the opening. But in spite of this the rehearsal goes on; art is art, as Mrs. Pampinelli sternly insists. The night of the play comes round, the cues are wrong, half of a mustache falls off, the actors stumble on the door strip, and finally when they are taking their calls the curtain breaks loose and drops. But there are mounds of flowers and all the actors in the cast agree that they didn't think the audience noticed anything; it was a great success. In the last act the husband—who has seen the performance after all—the wife and the directress fight the question out; the wife renounces acting and art and the husband promises eternal devotion.

All this, of course, touches on farce; it has at times the exaggeration and the speed of farce, and admirably so. And farce, almost as well as high comedy can do, may carry with it an expert material of human living, a sharp eye and a nose for essences. Mr. Kelly has got hold of something in our American life, and we can see that often he has seen it for himself and not as Broadway expects him to see it. In the same way most of his characters talk for their own and not their Broadway selves. And he has moments of real wit; as when, for example, that unseen directress, the votaress of a high and selfless art, cut off from making her bow to the audience by a broken rope and fallen curtain, goes running about among the screens and properties in her frenzy to meet with her share of the applause, and then, baffled in that attempt, pitches into the stage manager and thunders at artistic incompetence; or when Mr. Twiller comes off the stage with his half mustache and stands pouring out his aesthetic theory about the acting he has just done; or, better still, when Mrs. Sheppard, three weeks a widow, who at the first had had the leading part, and who had been sitting in the audience heavily veiled, standing at the rear to watch the performance, comes backstage, knowing amid her tears that Fred would have wanted her to come and all, he would have understood. She wants to congratulate the company, to tell them how she too felt what it all meant. Everyone is bowing to the audience, flowers are raining on to the stage. Why does she too not go on, the directress asks. "Do you think they would understand?" she moans, eagerly. And a moment later she comes off radiant, with an armful of crimson roses, not entirely out of it after all. That one stroke turns the whole mania inside out, the incongruity, the egotism, and the head-on will to show oneself. It carries the theme of the play to a quintessence, and it is as brilliant as anything I know in all satirical comedy anywhere. It has about it, in its due field, that supreme dramatic invention in which the incident, the character and the comment are all together at once completely revealed.

But *The Torch Bearers* is not yet written into a play. It has few of the fundamental virtues that can make Broadway comedy vigorous and hearty. It shares some of the faults; in its humor, for one instance, which is sometimes cheap, too much the expected Broadway brand; or in the husband, who has too much of that stupid, blunt, forced and vulgar repartee that passes on our stage for the typical droll American male. And the structure of *The Torch Bearers* breaks down for lack of any frame to carry it through. As it stands it is really matter for a forty-minute piece. Molière fell in the same way once on a larger scale. In *The Misanthrope* he had superb material, dear to him, the portrayal of great charm, culture, distinction made socially impossible and absurd by a jealous egotism. He set this out with poignant and delicate understanding, a just scale of social values, a sweet daylight humor, a loving, grim tolerance, and with style and wit and elegance. But *The Misanthrope* was in its day and has been ever since a failure when played. It is not quite theatre. Molière saw this so clearly that no play of his after *The Misanthrope* ever lacked its sure framework to go upon, a pattern of resolving tangles and cross purposes. In this respect Mr. Kelly, if he tries, may learn the same lesson. It is unkind to put a playwright up beside Molière of course. But in a way he has had a training not unlike Molière's, for where Molière trouped in the provinces those twelve years, Mr. Kelly trouped in vaudeville over the country. Vaudeville is a dead art now, but in its time it was the best school that we ever had for the theatre.

Of the two sensuous avenues by which the art of the theatre is apprehended, the eye and the ear, the eye at present is the one that we travel most importantly. Gesture, movement, scenery, even the actors' appearance to the point of likeness or duplication—casting for type in sum—these go a long way toward conveying to our audiences what stuff of life is to be conveyed. But for a theatre where there is fullness of resource and culture, the ear is no less important than the eye. Its region in the theatre involves that region of our nature that music draws upon; a part of the same fundamental response and excitement is involved, the same underlying essence of our experience with its register of familiar tones out of our round of ordinary American life. Mr. Kelly certainly has a better ear and gift for reproducing than most of our playwrights have, when it comes to everyday American speech. What's more, he knows how to increase this naturalness of effect by sharp attention to cueing and timing—the quick timing now aimed at, he may, in fact, before he knows it, overdo.

There are signs in *The Torch Bearers* of concessions to the audience' opinion that may or may not promise well. Concession to people's opinion in a mind like Molière's is one thing, for its basis is reason, balance and a due acknowledgment of the duty of the drama to give pleasure. But concession in our Broadway minds is apt to be cruder in essence, often hit or miss because of loose foundations. The result of it remains always to be seen. The chances are that Mr. Kelly if he remembers what is joyous will be our best writer of comedy. If he tries the serious he will be floored by the bad translations we have of Ibsen and by Ibsen's would-be disciples, and will produce plays that are neither flesh, fish nor fowl, but serious prose drama that could not be taken too seriously.

HAMLET

The Tragedy of Hamlet.
Sam H. Harris Theatre. November 20, 1922.

MR. JOHN BARRYMORE seemed to gather together in himself all the Hamlets of his generation, to simplify and direct everyone's theory of the part. To me his Hamlet was the most satisfying that I have seen, not yet as a finished creation, but a foundation, a continuous outline. Mounet-Sully's Hamlet was richer and more sonorous; Forbes-Robertson's at times more sublimated; Irving's more sharply devised and Sothern's, so far as we are concerned strictly with the verse pattern, was more securely read. But there is nothing in Mr. Barrymore's Hamlet to get in the way of these accomplishments also, with time and study. And in what he has done there is no inherent quality that need prevent his achieving the thing most needed to perfect, in its own kind, his Hamlet; I mean a certain dilation and abundance in all his reactions. This Hamlet of Mr. Barrymore's must give us—and already promises—the sense of a larger inner tumult and indeed of a certain cerebral and passionate ecstasy, pressing against the external restraint of him. He needs the suggestion of more vitality, ungovernable and deep, of more complex suffering, of not only intellectual subtlety but intellectual power as well, all this added to the continuity of distinction that he already has, the shy and humorous mystery, the proud irony, the terrible storms of pain. Mr. Barrymore brings to the part what is ultimately as necessary to a fine actor as to a fine singer, the physical gifts that enable him to express his idea. He has a beautiful presence, a profound magnetism. His English, much of which is but recently acquired through the teaching of the remarkable Mrs. Margaret Carrington, is almost wholly reborn from what it once was, and is now almost pure, even and exact, though not yet wholly flexible. His voice, also to a considerable extent Mrs. Carrington's production, is not supreme. It is not a rich and sonorous volume such as Mansfield had, but is capable of high, intelligent training, and is already in the middle tones highly admirable.

With such an artist as Mr. Barrymore has risen to be, one cannot escape the matter of the technical means by which he fills out and develops the kind of truth that he sees in his rôle, or confuses and prevents its realization. His chief technical triumph, I think, lies in the absence from his work of all essentially theatrical faults. There are no idle tricks of the voice, no empty display of actor vanity and professional virtuosity, no foolish strutting, none of the actor idol's way of feeling his oats. There is no egotistical intrusion on the play, no capricious distortion of the truth in the service of histrionic exhibitionism. Throughout the performance the technical method is invariably derived from the conception of the part and never allowed to run ahead of it.

Mr. Barrymore's important technical limitations at this stage of his achievement seem to me to be two. The first concerns the verse. The "resistant flexibility," to use an old phrase, that is the soul of fine reading, he has not yet completely acquired. Much of his reading is excellent; but now and again in his effort to keep the verse true to its inner meaning and to the spiritual naturalness that underlies it—and because, too, of a lack of concentration on his projection at times—Mr. Barrymore seems to be afraid to admit the line for what it is, verse. Sometimes he allows the phrases to fall apart in such a way that the essential musical pattern of the verse—which is a portion of the idea itself—is lost. In the line—to take an example—

Why, she would hang on him,

he put a heavy stress on the word "hang" and almost let the "him" disappear; a useless naturalism, for the same effect of sense emphasis can be secured and yet the verse pattern of the lines preserved, by sustaining the nasals in "on" and "him" with no more actual stress on them than Mr. Barrymore used.

For one more instance out of a good many, take the line

Must, like a whore, unpack my heart with words.

Mr. Barrymore let the phrase "like a whore" fall out solid from the verse, which then began anew with "unpack." But there is a certain sustained unity to the line; "must" and "unpack" have a resistant connection together—to be secured by the tone—which the intervening phrase does not break off. And, as a matter of fact, everywhere in Shakespeare the long, difficult, elaborate and complex passages depend above everything on their musical unity to recreate out of their many details that first profound unity of emotion from which they sprang. Without this unity these details appear to be—as in fact they often are, in the earlier plays especially—mere images and ornaments thrown in, whose artificiality is only embarrassing.

The other technical limitation that I feel in Mr. Barrymore is in his rendering of decreasing emotion. To be able to rise successfully to emotional heights is one measure of an actor's art; but this declining gradation is a no less sure test of it. For an illustration of what I mean, take the passage in the closet scene where the Ghost vanishes.

> HAMLET: Why, look you there! look how it steals away!
> My father in his habit as he lived!
> Look, where he goes, even now, out at the portal!
> QUEEN: This is the very coinage of your brain;
> This bodiless creation ecstasy
> Is very cunning in.
> HAMLET: Ecstasy!
> My pulse as yours doth temperately keep time,—

Mr. Barrymore repeats the word and goes on with the speech in a reasonable and almost even tone. But in such places a part of the effect of preceding emotion appears in the graduel lessening of it in the actor's manner and voice. This speech of Hamlet's is reasonable, yes, but the calm in the thought precedes the calm in the state of emotion; the will and the idea are to rule but only after conflict with the emotion.

I cannot admire too much Mr. Barrymore's tact in the scenes with Polonius. Most actors for the applause they get play up for all it is worth Hamlet's seemingly rude wit at the old man's expense. But Mr. Barrymore gave you only Hamlet's sense of the world grown empty and life turned to rubbish in this old counselor. And, without seeming to do so he made you feel that Polonius stood for the kind of thing in life that had taken Ophelia from him. How finely—even in that last entreaty to Laertes for fair usage—Mr. Barrymore maintained an absence of self-pity in Hamlet, and thus enlarged the tragic pity of the play! What a fine vocal economy he exercised in the scene where Horatio tells him of his father's ghost! And what a stroke of genius it was, when by Ophelia's grave Hamlet had rushed through those mad lines, piling one wild image on another, and comes to the

> Nay, and thou'lt mouth,
> I'll rant as well as thou

to drop on that last, on the "I'll rant as well as thou," into an aspirate tone, hoarse, broken with grief and with the consciousness of his words' excess and the excess of irony in all things!

And I must admire the economy of business—not all Mr. Barrymore's, of course, but partly due to Mr. Hopkins, Mrs. Carrington and Mr. Jones—all through the part. The nunnery scene with Ophelia was done with a reaching out of the hands almost; the relation of Hamlet to his mother and through her to the ghost was achieved by his moving toward the ghost on his knees and being caught in his mother's arms, weaving together the bodies of those two, who, whatever their sins might be, must belong to each other at such terrible cost. There were no portraits on the wall with a ghost stepping out, as Hackett used to do it in the sixties. There was no crawling forward on the floor to watch the King during the play, as so many actors have done; and none of Ophelia's peacock fan for Hamlet to tap his breast with and fling into the air, as Irving used to do. About all this production there were none of those accessories in invented business; there was for the most part, and always in intention, only that action proceeding from the inner necessity of the moment and leaning on life, not on stage expedients. The inner limitations of Mr. John Barrymore's Hamlet are both less tangible and less amendable perhaps. They are in the direction of the poetic and human. With time, meditation and repetition it will gain in these respects no doubt; but it needs now more warmth, more abundance in all the reactions, more dilation of spirit. It takes too much for granted, makes Hamlet too easy to understand, and so lacks mystery and scope. It needs a larger inner tumult, more of a cerebral and passionate ecstasy pressing against the outward restraint of the whole pattern. It needs more of the sense of an ungovernable vitality, more complex subtlety and power. It needs more tenderness and, above all, more, if you like, generosity.

Miss Fuller's Ophelia could not dominate the longer speeches in her first scenes. But in the mad scenes she sang her ballads with unheard-of poignancy; and the mere slip of her white, flitting body was itself the image of pathos. Miss Fuller sharpened the effect of madness by putting into it a hint of that last betrayal that insanity brings to Ophelia: indecency. Miss Yurka, though she subsided at times out of the part when she had nothing to do, read her lines admirably; and contrived to suggest without overstating it the loose quality in this woman that subjected her to the King. Mr. O'Brien's Polonius was good, simplified rather far, perhaps, but with a certain force of truth that rendered what Polonius, despite his fatuity, has: a kind of grotesque distinction. Mr. Reginald Pole brought to the Ghost's lines a fine ear and an exact method of reading the verse that you gratefully detect before he is three lines under way. The Laertes of Mr. Sidney Mather is the only very bad performance in the company. The role is extra difficult because of its Renaissance approach, through character and reality, to the flowery gallantry and lyric expedition required; though the bases of Laertes' feelings and actions seem to me fresh, accessible and human. The fact remains, nevertheless, that unless the actor gets the manner and flourish of Laertes, the expression of his vivid, poignant and decorative meaning cannot find its due outlet. Mr. Tyrone Power's King—superb in voice and metre—was admirable. He suggested not mere villainy but rather a tragic figure of force and heavy will. Mr. Power's King gave us also the sense of great charm exerted upon those around him that is attributed to the character in the play.

It is in the scene where Hamlet catches the King praying and does not kill him—the climax of the play—that the method of production employed by Mr. Hopkins and Mr. Jones is reduced, it seemed to me, to its most characteristic terms. The King enters through the curtain, already used a number of times, with the saints on it. He kneels, facing the audience. He lifts his hands and speaks to heaven. Hamlet enters through the same curtain. He debates the fitness of the time for the King's murder, decides against it, withdraws. The King says

HAMLET

> My words fly up, my thoughts remain below;
> Words without thoughts never to heaven go.

and rises and goes out. One man is here, one is there. Here are the uplifted hands, there the sword drawn. Here, sick conscience, power, and tormented ambition; there, the torture of conflicting thoughts, the irony, the resolution. Two bodies and their relation to each other, the words, the essential drama, the eternal content of the scene. No tricks, no plausible business, no palace chapel. And no tradition.

Tradition of conception there is now and again, of course; but throughout the entire production there is very little concern about external tradition. And what of it? If we had some kind of Théâtre Français, a conservatory where a classic like *Hamlet* would be seen from time to time as a star returns on its course; or if in our theatre we had a succession of rival Hamlets, as was once the case, the question of tradition would be more important. Under such conditions a certain symbolism of stage business might develop, full of deep significance, familiar and accepted, and not to be abandoned too readily. But in the American theatre today the disregard of Shakespearean tradition is easy and commendable. To pursue it doggedly is to block the way with dead husks of forms once full of meaning. It only thwarts the audience and Shakespeare's living matter with a kind of academic archaism and, even, with a certain fanaticism; which consists, as Santayana says, in redoubling your effort when you have forgotten your aim. Messrs. Hopkins and Jones and Barrymore have, for the most part, let sleeping dogs lie. Nothing could be easier than not to do so; hence their eminence.

Mr. Robert Edmond Jones has created a permanent setting of architectural forms and spaces, bounded across the stage, and down two-thirds to the front line of it, with a play of steps. Within this, easy variations are possible to indicate the changes of scene. The design of the setting cannot be conveyed in words, of course, but it is princely, austere and monumental. It has no clutter of costumes or elaborate variations in apartments, but instead a central rhythm of images, of light and shade innate to the dramatic moment. The shortcoming of this bold and eloquent setting is that it either goes too far or does not go far enough. In this respect the limit was reached when the time came for the scene of Ophelia's burial,

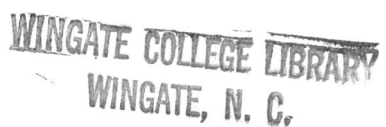

where the setting was at least enough like a palace to make the grave toward the front of the stage—and therefore the whole scene—appear to be incongruous if not absurd. A greater vastness of imagination was thus required of the designer. In his defense it should be said, however, that our theatre does not easily allow for repeated experiment, with the discarding and choosing and the expense involved.

This production of *Hamlet* is important and is out of class with Shakespeare production from other sources. This is not through any perfection in the field of the Shakespearean so called; but because it works toward the discovery of the essential and dramatic elements that from the day it was written have underlain this play. The usual Shakespeare production, however eminent, goes in precisely the opposite direction. It does not reveal the essential so much as it dresses up the scene at every conceivable angle, with trappings, research, scenery, business.

Such a production as this of *Hamlet* could not hope to be uniformly successful. But in its best passages, without any affectation of the primitive or archaic, it achieved what primitive art can achieve: a fundamental pattern so simple and so revealing that it appeared to be mystical; and so direct and strong that it restored to the dramatic scene its primary truth and magnificence. For a long time to come this *Hamlet* will be remembered as one of the glories of our theatre.

THE MOSCOW ART THEATRE

The Moscow Art Theatre. Jolson's Fifty-ninth Street
Theatre. January 8, 1923

MR. OLIVER SAYLER'S admirable book, combined with the most intelligent and effective publicity in the course of our theatre, had made us familiar with the Moscow Art Theatre before we ever saw it. And twenty years of criticism have established the main qualities and theories of this group of artists; everyone knows that their method is the representational, which professes the intention of ignoring the presence of spectators and of producing an effect of life as life would be seen going on if the fourth wall of a room were removed; everyone knows by now the phrase "spiritual realism," implying a selection among realistic details that can bring out the inmost spirit of the actual matter. And everyone knows about the exhaustive search for right particulars, the last perfection of illusion in make-up; the spirit of the group working together under Stanislavsky; the competent training that makes it possible to exchange rôles among the actors; and the sincerity of approach to the meaning of the dramatist. About the Moscow Art Theatre these are all by now the merest commonplaces; one may see these players through phrases at least if not through the eyes. So that, even more than usual, criticism is free to be a personal affair.

Well, for my part, if I had seen the Moscow company in nothing but their historical poetic drama, *Tsar Fyodor,* I should have been very much disappointed. In this performance I saw that Moskvin was a very fine actor, with an art that was fluid, continuous, pathetic in the deepest sense. I saw that Mme. Knipper-Chekhova was a highly competent actress, and that everyone in the company played carefully, freely, well. The costumes too were superb and evidently correct so far as history goes, the jewels likewise. The palace rooms were plainly authentic canvases of rooms to be found somewhere in Russia, very rich and entertaining. The ensembles were astonishing; as individuals and as a mass the actors in them were convincing and lifelike. And over the whole stage there was—that seven days' wonder of stage directors—a complete air of human beings living there in the familiar ways of men. All these virtues were easy to see in the performance; but, except for bits of pathetic acting and for moments of pictorial beauty of figures and garments, I cared nothing about it. I have no interest in poetry taken as prose, and almost no interest in history taken, but for its mask of antique trappings, as contemporaneous human life. For the truth of history seems to me to be a combination of actuality and remoteness. Of this sixteenth-century matter of men, equipage and event, the reality to me is the *idea* of it, and this includes the vista of time as one of its chief elements. In other words, in the performance of an imperial ancient story like this of the *Tsar Fyodor* I should like the style of the acting to achieve not the studied naturalness that we take daily as the ways of men but the form, the magic of distance and scope, the conscious arrangement, the artifice and logic, that would create in my mind the idea. And with jewels and arms and clothes I can see the merely correct history of them in museums if I choose; what I want on the stage is these things translated into stage terms, restated with that lustre and relief, to use Coquelin's phrase, that would make them art. In sum, I wanted through all the play less of what that sixteenth-century situation may or may not have been and more of what to me it really is. Chaliapin in Boris, then, yes, that was another school of art, that had great style, simplification, removal, magnificent idea; it remained in the mind like music, like great poetry, great abstractions; it was independent of every concern outside its moment, complete in itself. But for this Moscow Art Theatre's fine producion of Alexis Tolstoy's historical poetic drama, I was professionally attentive, admiring, but quite unmoved, indifferent. The effort and theory of making the past as natural as if it were the present seems to me only a deficiency in cultural perspective.

As to the décor for *Tsar Fyodor*, I should say that though the device of lowering the richly colored palace ceilings in order to heighten the effect of tallness in those burly knights was a clever one, the décor in general of *The Birthday of the Infanta* knocked this Russian enterprise into a cocked hat. This Russian culture, warmhearted and adolescent, and for us too sweated out with theatre publicity, is not to be taken too seriously.

Of Gorki's play, with its mixture of the dregs of the world, the fallen baron, the fallen actor, the cynical philosopher, the old prostitute, Anna the dying woman, Luka the pilgrim, and the crowd of others, and its remarkable achievement of a kind of heightened and violently crude poetic actuality, the performance seemed to me not wholly convincing but more satisfying than that of the *Tsar Fyodor*. There were passages of fine directing and fine acting all the way through—that last scene of the play, for example, where the lodgers left in the place talk together, with its haunting fervor and ironic desolation; or the scene in the courtyard where the old man and his young wife talk from the window above to the group below, incomparable moment of pure theatre, glittering, bitter and pagan and gay, like two colors laughing together; and most of all the beautiful, faultless scenes where Luka the pilgrim ministers to the dying woman. Fine moments and some fine acting, Moskvin, Mme. Knipper-Chekhova and Kachalov, and stretches of extraordinary poetic realism; and now and then a vast, compelling mood over all, these were the achievements of the Gorki play. But what let me down and left me dashed and disappointed was the broken quality of the performance as a whole. Too often it separated into parts. Character after character stood out to the eye, heavily accented, without a blur. Stanislavsky's Satine was the worst of these—and on this general point there can be no argument, someone was wrong, either Moskvin or Stanislavsky, since Moskvin was exactly the contrary to Stanislavsky. The picture he conveyed was a complete blend without obvious accentuation. Satine's coat, his waistcoat, his shirt, his socks, his shoes, his cap, his beard, he could not turn or move but I ran into more shreds and patches, white stitches, ragged edges, everything insufferably scored—as his speeches, for all their great intelligence, were scored—like the work of a brilliant amateur. And too many of the events in this performance stood as brightly apart as the characters: Alyosha's entrance, for one example, where he danced into the room so delightfully in his rose-colored togs, was quite as much a "number" as anything ever seen in vaudeville. All this spotting and separate rhythm and glare would be well enough so far as I am concerned; I like the effect of pure theatre frankly played as such; and I like the presentation of Gorki's play as high theatricality, which it essentially is rather than naturalism;

but the possibilities in this direction were crippled by the Moscow production's working in the opposite, they worked on an assumption of exact realism, and so mixed matters up. On the whole I came away, when the performance was over, stirred and swept and shaken in my memory as after certain great numbers on a concert program, but with no sense of any deep mood or of one single, profound experience, either of art or of poignant life.

The two Chekhov plays were another matter! Here was that rarest of events in the theatre anywhere, the combination of acting, producing and dramatic writing, one proceeding from another and all illuminating one idea. Some of the players were manifestly past their prime—it is only intelligent to recognize that—but it mattered very little; what they did seemed forever right and fine. I saw there on the stage Chekhov's characterizations, so whimsical, pitiful, keen, exact; I saw Chekhov's art come true, all the strange, incessant flux of it, its quivering and exposed humanity, its pathetic confusion of tragic, comic, inane and grotesque. I saw more than ever the likeness between Chekhov's method and Shakespeare's. Shakespeare starting with a fundamental emotion or state of mind, finds facet after facet for the surface of its expression; he makes images, comparisons, ornaments, elaborations of musical cadence, all of them springing from one source and all taken together revealing it. Shakespeare allowed himself every freedom in the poetic method, to use any flight or exaggeration or happy impossibility to secure his end. Chekhov uses only words and actions that are possible in actual daily life that are seen and heard by the eyes and ears. As Shakespeare uses his poetic details Chekhov uses these actualities, throwing together item after item, often seemingly incongruous things, weeping, kissing the furniture, calling on memory and God, asking for water, reproaching a man for trimming his beard, in order to convey the fundamental emotion from which they sprang and which they must reveal. Without using any means that might not be perfectly possible and actual, Chekhov contrives to give us the utmost shock and centre of the life he portrays. Shakespeare's scope and power make another discussion; but, though in such diverse regions, this similarity of method between him and Chekhov is full of significance; and it appears unbelievably in the Moscow Art Theatre's interpretation. And out of this modern and realistic art I got something of the same thing that comes off from Shakespeare: the tragic excitement, the vivacity and pathetic beauty, the baffling logic of emotion, the thrill that comes from a sense of truth.

What the visit of the Moscow Art Theatre means to the New York stage seems to be clear enough. It is not that this school or method of production is a new genre; this is in fact what we have had on hand for a generation or more, and tend of late to depart from. It is not that the drama these players bring with them is in any sense new; Chekhov differs only in depth and technical perfection, not in kind, from Clyde Fitch. It is not that we have seen no acting so good as this on our own stage; in single scenes at least I have seen Jefferson, Pauline Lord, David Warfield, Laurette Taylor and others do quite as good realistic acting as any of these Russians. It is not that the scenery of the Moscow Art Theatre can teach us anything; in their present state these settings are battered and much mended, and would, I am sure, have been cast off long ago if the company's finances had permitted; and this scenery belongs to the school that we have seen exhausted by producers like Henry Irving and Belasco; and as exact realism or illusion it has, moreover, been infinitely surpassed by such settings as the Robert Edmond Jones actual bar-room in the first scene of *Anna Christie*.

What the Moscow Art Theatre means to our stage—apart from our delight in mere proficiency—is something that is more moral and ethical than aesthetic, in so far as morality can be distinguished from the aesthetic. Chekhov's plays carry realism to an honest and spiritual depth and candor and to a relentless, poignant perfection and truth. These actors can act not only one scene or one play but, through humility and long labor at learning the technique of their art, they are equally competent throughout many parts. They represent a group of sincere artists, created by their art, rich by their intense living in it, and sure of all art's importance and duration. They are artists that have been working together thoroughly and through many years, in an organization, and under a distinguished and sympathetic leader, and for a devoted public. And, most significant of all, they possess a racial or popular life from which they can draw their belief and idea.

QUEEN ELIZABETH'S PLAY

Will Shakespeare, by Clemence Dane. National Theatre.
January 8, 1923

MR. NORMAN BEL GEDDES' setting for *Will Shakespeare* has somewhere between his studio and the theatre run into a mishap. As the scenes progress we get the curious impression that they were created by an artist of much invention and then lighted by a stagehand. One has only to look to see that the lighting used could not have been intended by the designer, who obviously would have spared himself the trouble of devising this remarkable variety of planes and structural lines if he could have known that his work would be half wasted in that wholesale, meaningless glare.

In the scene backstage, for example, the glowing spot on the wall that the lantern throws, where Anne's mother will plead with Shakespeare to come to his dying son, where Marlowe and Mary Fitton will talk, and where later Shakespeare and Mary Fitton will be so passionately swept together, this glowing spot and its dramatic point is all lost in white light. The scene in Shakespeare's cottage is lit to the very top; its fire on the hearth, the day fading beyond the window, everything is lost in a paperish daylight proceeding from nowhere but drying up all. And so on, scene after scene, this electrical platitude proceeds. In cold blood one can see that Mr. Geddes' idea is striking and carefully searched, one can see the fine doors and recesses and subtle nuances of varied spaces; but over most of it the confusing and idle light spreads like a flock of geese turned on a garden. And so the performance, save where Miss Wright takes it in hand, is cheated of its mood. She provides an instance of this curious thing about acting when it is really at its best: it can suddenly and sharply supersede everything else present in the theatre; by its closeness to life itself it can be the life and the resurrection of all that is involved; it can come into its own purely by its peculiar intensity, singularity and wholeness of impact.

In an odd sort of way this use of light on the production is a parallel to Miss Dane's use of the poetic style on the play.

Will Shakespeare is strictly an invention, Miss Dane is careful to remind us. It does not wholly stick to such facts as we happen to know them. The story of the play is tepid, arbitrary and weak. *Will Shakespeare* on his farm at Stratford-on-Avon is married to a woman seven years his senior. He has never loved her but has been betrayed into marrying her by a lying tale of the coming of a child. Meanwhile we get the refrain, familiar in the weaker type of English poetry, of hedgerows, birds, spring and the may. Henslowe, quaint Elizabethan that he is—played with such conscientious quaintness by Mr. John Shine—comes by and entices Shakespeare with tales of the Queen and fame and fortune up to London. Shakespeare discovers his wife's trick and is free to rush away. Then we have London. The Queen wants a great tragedy of this young poet. She sets her Mary Fitton to snare him and to rule his life into greater depths of creation. *Romeo and Juliet* is played. When the boy actor gets a fall, Mary Fitton takes the part of Juliet. She rushes out into Shakespeare's arms. Afterward she forgets him again for her own light ways. She loves Marlowe. Shakespeare and Marlowe have a struggle in the Deptford Inn; Marlowe falls on his own dagger. Mary Fitton is banished to the country, the Queen sets Shakespeare to work, for the glory of England.

There is moment after moment in this play where Miss Dane shows the same theatrical sense that she brought to her *Bill of Divorcement* last season, in spite of that play's forced situations and frequent hollowness of dialogue. Some of the first scene, where the poet is drawn away from his old ties, has a good dramatic thrust to it. The scene backstage where Mary Fitton, shaken by the power of the lines she has said, is lifted to the poet's own passion, is brilliant theatrical motivation. And the whole idea of the last act, where the Queen claims the great poet for England and her reign and shows him how her life and his are under the same magnificent and tragic necessity, is one of the finest inventions in modern drama anywhere. But through all these scenes—though far less in the last—the poetical babble goes on. You have a great artist driven to follow his destiny, you have a man's passion making him forget his art and his dying son, you have the torture of great creation laying hold of a great artist, you have, in a word, Miss Dane conjuring up situations that are terrible in their human implications, that draw on terrible depths and heights of the human soul, and you ask yourself how she can dare to venture on them without being sure that she will pay the price of them, jot by jot, in terrible depths and torture of her own imaginative soul, and in the last truth of words, emotions, dramatic revelation. But what happens is that one passage of her play is good perhaps, the next bad; one is imaginative, the next is prettified, poetical, extraneous. At the wild moment when Shakespeare finds out his wife's trick and reviles her for her deception, one of her condoning arguments runs thus, speaking by the way of the little beasts in the field:

> What shall their pensioners
> Do now, the rustling mice, the anemones,
> The whisking squirrels, ivies, nightingales,
> The hermit bee—

sweet and zoological and good in a pageant written by an Oxford don, but for a dramatic moment beneath comment. Miss Dane, like most of the writers of our so-called modern poetic drama, tries to lard the play with poetic sauce. But dramatic poetry is not the dramatic situation poetically expressed; it is the dramatic expression of the poetic that lies in a situation. The glow and darkness and the revelation of the poetic meaning can come not from the obvious source of some method or style, but only from the depths and lines and spaces, from the mystery too, of the characters' actions and souls. Quite as the light on Mr. Geddes' settings dilutes and strips off their intention, Miss Dane's poetical additions too often weaken the effect of the play's actions and ideas. She might, in fact, be said to be rich in jittery boredom.

And so Miss Winifred Lenihan, in that first scene where she struggles against losing the man she loves, has a hard time. She is a young actress with sincerity; she secures her effect of the moment's intensity, its sick distress and insistence. But her work in the end leaves us not so much pleased as uncomfortable, partly because she is still young in her art and its blending of tones, and partly because of the dramatist's imposition of pretty twaddle on to the reality of the situation. Miss Lenihan is at least better suited to reality than to twaddle. Another way to say some of this is to say that, like the rest of our younger players, she has not the technical groundwork on which to take a rôle not too well set out by the dramatist and more or less to force it into shape regardless.

To act the rôle of Shakespeare is naturally a trying venture. And the author makes the rôle more trying with her own languors and sympathies and with her lady-novelist conceptions of the sorrow and soul of a genius—a dear, full approach of tell-me-where-it-hurts-and-I'll-kiss-it. The rôle is rendered less attractive by creating a man who is not so much a part of a pressing and universal necessity of life as he is a hard egoist and moongazer. Mr. Otto Kruger as Will Shakespeare is no worse than many another actor with no idea of what the whole thing meant would be. His eyes at least and their make-up look remarkably like the Droeshout portrait, smudgy as it is.

It is Miss Haidee Wright—in that last act, which is largely hers—who is the star and triumph of the piece.

This last act of Miss Dane's, wholesomely cut for this production, has a fine idea, an inspiration to use the Renaissance and the share that princes had then in the progress of great art. Now and again in this act the lines fall into pseudo-poetic messing, but much of the thought is really poetic in its passion and truth. But whether the lines are true or false, they are compelled by Miss Wright's art into an essential truth; they are by her force driven home to whatever source in truth they may have, however blurred and remote and superfluous the author has left them.

Miss Wright's qualities are, first, wit—a happy, swift recognition of points as they arise—and then style—an unfailing personal distinction in the expression of her idea. She sits there looking like a Zucchero of the great Queen and yet not like it either. She rather makes herself, her manner and her gown, a re-creation, fresh and in terms of her own art of acting, of Queen Elizabeth's portrait. She appears to give us not something imitative so much as a witty inspiration. With this comes—and partly due to history and the dramatist's ideas—a kind of gorgeousness of mind and humor that piques and astonishes and thrills us; and a mingling of Renaissance pride and caprice and intellectual audacity, and splendor of humanity, that lifts the scene out of itself into a great era. We are moved constantly by the breath of fine poetry that fills now and again her lines and always her delivery of them; our minds are exhilarated by that sense of exactitude and light that poetry conveys. And through this Miss Wright leads us into a deep pathos, at once poignant and lofty; and gives us a sense finally of what she is most bent on creating in the scene: the beauty, solitude and fatality of great natures.

IT IS THE LARK

Romeo and Juliet. Henry Miller's Theatre. January 24, 1923

IF YOU talk of whether a theatrical performance—or the design for a production—is great or not, you might very well be expected to suggest at least what the word *great* in such a case implies. In the performance of *Romeo and Juliet,* then, the achievement will be great in so far as it is inclusive, in so far as there are lines in it that draw from large spaces of living and run on from the single occasion into those spaces again, in so far as there is brought to bear on this single instance the light of a wider human living and truth. In the balcony scene, to take an example from the play, besides the technical ability to recite the verses, we should have the idea of youth, the access of passionate love, the eager calling one another back to speak of love again, the romantic and wistful poetry of the moment, the point that lies beneath the verse and its ornament and elaboration. These are necessary qualities before the performance of the scene can get anywhere to speak of at all. And even then it would approach being great in so far as there appears beneath all these necessary qualities a sense of the depth of all life and passion, of what it means to have this moment pass, and of the shadow that lies around this flame.

Greatness here will imply a recognition of the fact that at such a moment, and for the moment, we hear the rumor of the blood in the veins, that we look to no reality outside of human life, which becomes incandescent, complete in itself. In so complete a moment of living there exists a harmony with all natural things, the human element becomes like light and trees; and that is why the speeches of lovers show how they feel themselves one with the place, the hour and the season; and why the lovers' thoughts and their pretty images turn so frequently on the stars, the moon, the birds and the dawn. In the last act of *Romeo and Juliet* the necessary details for the actors will as a matter of course include a grasp of the idea of young grief and hot impulse, of the romantic expenditure of life, the pathetic story of lovers. But greatness in this scene will only come as there appears in it something about life and time that spreads beyond the single moment or the disaster that befalls these two particular persons; something that is not only pitiful but also tragic; something that conveys the surprise of truth and the happiness of it, however bitter it may be; something that, after the scene ends and the curtain is down, remains and fills the mind, as the mind is filled—though strangely—with a kind of luminous abstraction after music has been played.

How far Shakespeare himself achieved all this range and truth might be debated. *Romeo and Juliet* is an early play. But it seems to me undeniable, as I listen to the lines, that, though the young dramatist is yet full of the ornate manner of his epoch and is sometimes overheavy and diverted with sixteenth-century surface detail, the emotion underlying the progression of the scenes is absolutely secure and true.

The performance of *Romeo and Juliet* at Henry Miller's Theatre could not be called great, if one itches for that threadbare word. But we have no particular right to demand greatness every time Shakespeare is tried out; if we get greatness once in a century we may thank our lucky stars. Nor need we pick the bones of actors merely because they venture into Shakespeare when otherwise in lighter efforts we let them off so easily. But, great or no, this new *Romeo and Juliet* is a performance full of fresh and persuasive life.

The production, so far as settings go, is not well lighted for the most part, and lacks on the whole a single stamp of invention or idea. Capulet's House is the worst, with an unfortunate shallowness and an inexcusably lean and trivial central doorway. Juliet's chamber with its purple and red; the fine yellow wall in Mantua, and the shadowy crypt with its effective stair, are better.

The ensembles generally are only indifferent good; the part of the page, of the parents and friends and cousins, are more or less fair, the nurse tart, so so, though it could be a telling rôle. Mercutio, that indestructibly happy part, comes off agreeably, if a little thinly, at Mr. Dennis King's hands; who, nevertheless, has a touch of poetry and a well-bred diction and approach worth watching. Mr. Rollo Peters has made a good start with Romeo; and Romeo, when everything is said, is one of the most troublesome parts in our theatre, so closely does he skirt on being a mere fool of a lover, a romantic blunderer reciting his head off. Romeo, I think, has to be imagined as a human vessel through which pours the passion of love, as the wind comes out of space and blows through the boughs of a tree; he has to be seen as an extravagant abundance and excess; he has to be seen as a piece of young life identical with the violent beauty and heat of living. Mr. Rollo Peters as an actor is not always flexible yet, and not by any means secure or evenly designed in his performance, but his idea is excellent. In the Mantua scene, to take examples, where the news comes of Juliet's death, he has the verse, the pose, rather than the bottom of the tragic moment; in the balcony scene he reads the very difficult and elaborate lines beautifully, with genuine poetic understanding and a fine variety and precision of cadence and a deep emotional naturalness beneath the intricate surface of Shakespeare's words.

Miss Cowl's Juliet is beautiful, first of all, to see. She is a child, a tragic girl, a woman convincing to the eye as few Juliets ever have had the good fortune to be. She has quiet too and naturalness and a right simplicity of method. Her readings are often, as in the speech about waking among her great kinsmen's bones and plucking the mangled Tybalt from his shroud, quite traditional—which is nothing against them—but well studied and made into her very own. Her weakest spots are toward the first of the play, those with the nurse especially, where more poetic transmutation must be wrought and more of the beautiful necessity discovered. Some of this is due to the play itself, which has its difficulties in getting started, and some of it is due to the costuming that has been provided for Miss Cowl's Juliet: her gown is too loose and easy, a tighter and more formal effect in the cutting would help enact the dramatic idea that this girl is imprisoned within the family patterns and the feudal conceptions that go along with them. But in all the actress' conceptions meanwhile the mind is lovely.

And meanwhile, regardless of all else, we have the sense that the actress herself would give her whole heart and soul to the moment, whatever it may be; and this is a part of Miss Cowl's lovely approach to the rôle. What time and study and thought may do to extend into the deeper beauty, and into more of that kind of impalpable distinction that would make Miss Cowl's performance a great one, remains to be seen. But at present her Juliet manages to avoid entirely any intrusion of actor egotism or trivial novelty; the conception behind it appears to be flexible and eager and gentle; within its present range it is a sweet and sincere beginning. Miss Cowl has had many millionaire successes and so now could, if she liked, be doing a play of great commercial value no doubt. She has done instead, during these last seasons, a number of parts, from *The Quinteros Brothers* and otherwise, where the range is wider and the problem less easy. The reward for that in our theatre is what it may be: people and critics who can take the silliest works are suddenly alert when ambitious projects are shown; and opinions, foolish or right, drown the rattled theatre air. And so it is a lovely thing for Miss Cowl to give us a Juliet, a lovely thing for a popular actress to dream thus of a finer and brighter theatre.

    The whole occasion of this *Romeo and Juliet,* in fact, seems to have a bright and pitiful, happy and young life shattering down upon it. The players are mostly not very tall personages, Juliet, Mercutio, Romeo; they all look fresh and slight and alive with something going on in them that is their own, a romance of youth and energy that might induce you to forgive them much more than there is to forgive. In sum—unless you ponder longer on the depth of meaning that Shakespeare wrought into his golden scenes, you could well believe that there on the stage were young people who had written their play for themselves.

DUSE'S IBSEN

La Donna dal Mare, by Henrik Ibsen. Metropolitan
Opera House. October 29, 1923.
Ghosts, by Henrik Ibsen. The Century Theatre.
November 6, 1923.

WHAT strikes me most in Duse's *The Lady from the Sea* is the way in which she adds idea to the play. Ibsen set forth a story of a woman now married to a doctor but once promised to a man who came to her from the sea. The longing of her days when she lived in her father's lighthouse returns to her after the death of the child whose eyes had been the eyes of the first lover; and Ellida, haunted by all these and feeling some great power drawing her to it, refuses to live with Wangel as his wife and dreams of going away. All this happens in the midst of the little affairs of daughters and lovers; and much of it is dependent on coincidents which in the midst of the realistic, scientific elements of the play, seem highly improbable and dragged in. In the end the stranger comes to keep his vow and take Ellida away; her husband at last gives her perfect freedom to choose, and, with the responsibility and the complete freedom, she chooses, sends the man away, and comes to Wangel at last, with a full and happy love for him. We have here turns of psychology, biology, romance, poetry and homely comedy, beginning rather stalely, running into a region with no little dream and fascination to it, and winding up in a poor muddle of pseudo-scientific and moralistic explanations, manias, obsessions, freedom of choice, responsibility and the like, out-dated now and always rendered by Ibsen without imagination or unifying power. A great deal of *The Lady from the Sea* is in fact, mere Nordic rubbish; and it remains to be seen whether the Mediterranean, which has given us most of the thoughts we have of any basic value, has something to add to Ibsen's Scandinavian concepts.

What Duse does is something that she has done before with many other pieces in the theatre. She enlarges the meaning and quality of the play until it goes beyond anything the author had imagined for it, and beyond what he could have imagined.

When Ibsen's Ellida comes on the scene, with her restlessness, her hunger for the sea, her sense of the stranger's power drawing her, we get some touch of mystery, no doubt, but also a strong suggestion of explanation; obviously the woman is neurotic, suffering from an obsession. When Duse's Ellida comes on the scene what we get is poetic idea, a thing free and eternal in our minds, caught there like a light in the momentary shell of a human body. The woman is neurotic if you like, sick, obsessed with a state of mind, just as she is Wangel's wife, speaks with a voice, in the words of a language. But that has little to do with the point, which consists in the wonder of this thing felt, the singleness and purity of this mood, this dream of freedom, this infinity that affrights and allures. The woman before us is only the vessel for this. It is this that is permanent and beautiful and that drives forever toward the immortal; that is both poetic and —and here with Duse is found the right place for the science—biological. The truth that Duse discovers for *The Lady from the Sea* has the oneness of life at its depths and heights, which art only at its best moments can achieve, and which Ibsen in the midst of his fuddle of serious purpose, prose details, poetic symbolisms and ethical farrago fails to achieve.

As Duse progresses with the play she comes, passing the little sterilities of the daughters, the young man with the flat chest, and the various remarks and observations on living, to the final idea. The Stranger reappears, Ellida is free to choose. What Duse creates then concerns love and freedom. A complete and limitless love, she tells us, is as vast as the sea and as infinite, and is itself the ultimate human freedom. The body of Wangel stands between her and the body of the Stranger who has come to take her away; the love defeats the power that has haunted and destroyed her soul. And because this love is boundless, and wild and inexhaustible, it even more than the sea allures and affrights her and feeds and consumes her life. This love even more than the sea can become her mystery.

With that conception and illumination, so outside the scope and statement of the play, as Ibsen understood or stated it, that Duse brings to the theme of his drama, the whole is lifted into poetry. She has done to it what would have happened at the hands of a great poet. She has thrown light upon it, dilated it, discovered in it what is most significant and essential, and given to the whole of it an existence of its own. She has discovered for it a right relation of the concrete to the ideal, of the phenomenon, the accident, to the permanent, the essential. And she has created for this idea a form that is inseparable from it.

After that has happened with Duse, the conclusion of Ibsen's play, with its little solutions and resolutions, and bringing in the children, and helpful suggestions to restless, sick spirits, seems to limp itself out to the last speech, stolidly and without inspiration, like a dry assistant in a laboratory trying to explain the nostalgia of the hills out of his notes on nerves and entrails and the habits of white mice, or some stubborn Northern provincial conscience trying to preach and prove itself the source of some action whose sheer rightness and happy truth have already, in its own due clime and condition, brought it about.

Take, for an instance, the first act in *The Lady from the Sea*. Ibsen has written it, so far as the portrayal of Ellida goes, with much success. Ellida comes in from her daily plunge in the sea, she finds the flag out and garlands, she meets the tutor of the children, an old suitor of hers, she discovers that the celebration is for the first wife, she receives the mistaken young man's birthday offering of flowers, she falls lightly and charmingly into the situation and puts good sense into what might be an awkward strain. You must watch Duse through a scene like that and then, when it is over, review and sum up what she has accomplished, if you would realize her quality. There are many actresses who can express this emotion or that, or this and that reaction, can create this or that phase of the dramatic moment, can move and convince us with the human life they exhibit and enact. But the great artist appears—over and above the mere actress—in the general sum of the scene, in the emphasis of the parts, the relation of all of it to life; in short the gradation that will express what is to be its final truth at the artist's hands. To this first act of *The Lady from the Sea* Duse, when she has finished it, gives something so right that the full content and possibility of it may not appear to us for days. Then we may see how on Ibsen's scene and the idea that she had filled it with, how on the whole and each part,

Duse has exercised her imagination and culture and wise humanity and beautiful grace of spirit.

THE end of Ibsen's *Ghosts* as given by Duse's company was not well thought out, fixed; it showed the lack of sufficient rehearsals and planning and performances together. There was evident also in her supporting players a certain lack of cultural understanding, as it were, which, of course Duse could do nothing about. But provided you understood the language spoken—in this case Italian of course—that first act of Duse's was a technical and spiritual marvel. The first act of *Ghosts* as Ibsen wrote it, has an undercurrent of fine dramatic power and a sharp edge of truth. But in the course of the writing, a provincialism and drabness of mind more than once appears; Mrs. Alving and the dramatist are now and again insistent and parochial and without imagination. Duse has no great opinion of Mrs. Alving, for one reason because, as she said to me, Mrs. Alving is a liar, to herself and to others. But Duse from her very first entrance put distinction into the part. She was a great lady, moving exquisitely and delicately, a sensitive strong being. She showed too a mind and mettle that could dilate and grow, and that could touch and go, lightly, swiftly, securely. Ibsen's Mrs. Alving now and again falls into platitude, stubborn and firm. Duse turns such passages into what is not obvious platitude but passionate memory. And what in Ibsen's lines is but half placed, culturally, his reflections on life, debates, analyses, Duse easily established in its right relation to a wide culture and insight. Meanwhile she sets forth the idea that is so clearly to dominate the play as she conceives it: the idea of maternal love and of a being whose body and whose love are interposed between her son and universal law. Technically, the variety of Duse's reading, the tone, the pressure, the ictus, the vitality, of it; the stillness with which she could imbue the quieter pauses in the emotion; the marvels of rhythm that she brought to the lines; the scale of values by which she sorted and unified the many reactions in thought and feeling; and finally the continuity of motion that she gave to her presence on the stage, were almost past belief.

THY WILL BE DONE

Così Sia, by Gallerati-Scotti. The Century Theatre.
November 13, 1923.

COSÌ SIA—So Be It, in the English translation put down as *Thy Will Be Done*—the play by Gallerati-Scotti that Duse is just now presenting, is at best a single, simple line, the story of a mother and her son. It is without D'Annunzio's genius, without the astonishing fecundity of image and color and those almost physical subtleties by which he penetrates and reveals such details of life and character as interest him, and without the defect of this excellence also; but it aims at D'Annunzio's kind of glowing analysis and D'Annunzio's ardent and often false allusion and imagery. And it follows D'Annunzio in its singleness of interest and mood.

In the first act a mother sits beside the cradle of her dying child. The doctor, seeing that no more can be done, leaves. The father, a bull merchant, comes in; he is sorry to lose his son but tells the woman bluntly that such things must happen, no need to go mad over it. If she loves the child more than she does him, there are plenty of other women. He is off to the market. She is to remember to order a suitable funeral for his son, such as befits his father's position. The neighbor woman advises the mother to pray, to ask God to save the boy; and, if God seems too far, to ask Mary the mother of Jesus. Left alone, the mother, who has almost forgotten how to pray, offers the Virgin all her money, her silk dress, her jewelry. That is not enough. She will go in sack cloth to the shrine on the mountain, every year till she dies, creeping there on her knees. That is not enough. Very well then, she will give up the one, secret, dearest thing, her lover. She will never speak to him again, never go to meet him in the lanes, never wait to see his smile and his white teeth. Presently the child awakes and calls out to her.

In the second act, twenty-three years later, the mother comes in on her way to the shrine at the top of the mountain. A neighbor tells her that her son has returned from America and is coming now from some nearby tavern with some girls and young fellows. It is two weeks since he landed. The son enters with his companions. He does not greet his mother. Finally when he starts away she calls to him. He sends the others off and turns to her. He recognized her at once, he says, but her rags disgrace him and the family. And he tells his mother that he knew of her lover, he had heard him beneath the window and had seen her weeping. Weeping, yes, his mother cries, but no more than that. He will not believe her and says that his dead father stands now between her and him. The son goes away.

The third act is in the sanctuary on the mountain. The old woman has crawled there to die. She stays when the door is shut for the night. She has nothing left now to offer, but she prays Mary to save her son's soul, whom she loves now more than ever, for now he has more need of her. She seems to hear the image speak to her, and she smiles as she sinks to the floor and dies.

That is the single, simple story of the play, about which, as Duse knows as well as anyone, there is no great artistic merit, but which is worth setting down only because it indicates the framework on which Duse rests her deep and universal conception of the whole idea of the maternal passion in woman and of all love in general penetrating all things, and around which she lives for those two hours on the stage so radiant and terrible a revelation of life. This little play is worth while, too, as a vehicle for an actress who is now close to sixty-five years old and is thus limited in her choice of roles. The great Bernhardt at seventy-five would at the drop of a hat have played Marguerite Gautier or L'Aiglon, and at that, for all the incongruities, put marvels into what she did. But Duse is a different kind of talent and a different kind of egotism. She is more sensitive to the chance of absurdity, and less armed with what in Bernhardt was, within its special limitations of course, an invulnerable, if restricted, technical craft.

Duse does not exemplify the art of acting so much as she illustrates the fundamentals of all art. All art, obviously, is concerned with the expression of life. To this purpose the artist is the first means, and after the artist the medium, color, words, sound, whatever it may be, that he works in. Duse's art illustrates first of all the principle in art of the necessity of the artist's own greatness, his sensitivity and power in feeling, in idea, in soul, in the education and fine culture of all these. Her art illustrates the necessity for a fierce and subtle and exact connection between the artist's meaning and his expression of it. It illustrates the universal problem of rhythm in art, of line, emphasis, mood, all rhythm. It illustrates supremely the nature of the poetic as it applies not only to poetry but to every art. And it illustrates the nature of realism in general, especially of that best Italian realism which, as it occurs most of all in sculpture, is so capable of rendering by means of only actual or possible external details the inmost idea. Duse has a strong mimetic gift, which gives her a secure foundation for acting; but she never uses it to reproduce or counterfeit. Everything she presents has a certain removal and restatement.

You constantly hear and read of the sadness of Duse's art, of the tragic element that is said to be always present in it, and that is admired or resented by the spectators as the case may be. It might very well be more profitable, I believe, to think of this quality in Duse and her art as not deriving so much from sadness as from a certain impression of finality. In her art the thing presented, the action, the thought, takes on the pathos of finality, it is carried so far into a kind of ultimate grace and purity that it seems to us poignant and sad; there is in it for us somehow a nostalgia, a tragic sense of beauty and completion.

And so it is that you cannot easily get from Duse's acting a pure acting delight. She is not the actor's actor, as Velasquez is the painter's painter, or Spenser the poet's poet. That is to say you cannot delight in her performance as supreme craft, something that delights whether it is deep or flitting, delights because of the perfection of its brush, its tone, its manner, because of its competency, because of its happy application of the art and the possibilities of pleasure in it by reason of its sheer technical purity and perfection, independent, so far as that is possible, of everything in life outside itself. And it is difficult to take any academic delight in Duse's acting. Something in you withholds you from saying what a beautiful gesture that was, what a tone, what a contrivance in that scene, what reading in this, what technical facility. All these things are good in themselves, of course; they too may be almost in themselves a kind of art. They are means of speaking, dialects for ideas; and, after all, art is art, not life. Style, however, in the sense of an added elaboration and distinction of method, of something in itself creative and separable, style in that separable aspect of technical felicity or skill or tact, Duse rarely has. Style in the sense of a medium which, like a glass over a laboratory experiment, disappears before the matter which it isolates and exhibits, Duse is never without. It is only slowly and almost unwillingly that Duse's art will allow you a stylistic or academic enjoyment. It will not allow that separation of the craft from the meaning; it will not yield itself to the mere choice judgments of a sophistication in taste. Duse will not grant you that kind of appreciation. It is as if she would accept no love but the love for all herself and the cost that follows.

It is only slowly that you see what labor and skill has gone to make up that creation of Duse's soul in the outer forms of an art. You see her bending over the child, you see her carry the pilgrim's staff, the lines of her long garment, the pity of her hands, the wandering of her hands among the lights on the altar. You see suddenly that dumbness, and then that flutter of life through the body. You see that the entire moment has revealed itself to you. You see what this woman knows; and you wonder whether such a knowledge of the human life and soul resolves itself in her finally into tears or into light. But it is only slowly that you perceive this artist's years of study of the lines of statuary—and especially of sculptors like Mino da Fiesole and Desiderio da Settignano and those more delicate realists of the earlier Renaissance—to discover the inevitable lines of grace and meaning, to learn how to study the rhythms of the form in order to free them of all but that last beauty of its own characteristics. And you gradually observe that Duse suggests perpetually a state of music which must have come from a long love and study of that art. And most of all you will see that such a gradation of emphasis throughout the play and so fine and so elusive but unforgettable a comprehension of the entire meaning of the character and theme could come only from a remarkable ability and association with culture and ideas, combined with a poetic and reflective nature, with a courage of mind, and, finally, with something throughout the personality, quiet and taken for granted, a kind of untouched and unstressed and constant spiritual audacity.

ITALIAN, RUSSIAN

La Locandiera, by Goldoni. Jolson's Theatre.
November 21, 1923.
The Brothers Karamazov, Scenes from the novel by
Dostoyevsky. Jolson's Theatre. November 19, 1923.

GOLDONI'S *La Locandiera* began with the Moscow Art Theatre in a scene that was charmingly painted, the table, the walls, the upper gallery, the doors. A charming place but, considering the nature of the play, too loud. The gentlemen began to talk, in very full voices, to swish and move around. The mistress of the inn herself —Olga Pizhova—came in; her face, her carriage, her voice were lively and hard. She laughed, a laugh that was engaging, if you like, but fairly mirthless and certainly not sunny or sweet. More talk followed, and a good deal of noise, together with much energy. It was clear that the company had set out to give us a lively occasion and that their conception was to turn Goldoni's comedy into a farce or shall we say a hearty, sure-footed harlequinade. The cues were wonderfully taken: the extraordinary ensemble of the Moscow Art Theatre appeared; every crossing on the stage went off in due time; and every individual, pair or group was perfectly disposed of. Much effort in the long training, much thoroughness, were apparent everywhere. There were energy, movement, loud voices, busy limbs, active eyes and animated lips. And yet with it all there was not much joy. Judged by itself the performance was amazingly thorough without being very infectious.

Judged by itself that was. Judged by the quality of the play it was pretty much all wrong. One does not ask a Russian company to give us something that is Italian, any more than one expects from an Italian company a Russian surface to Chekhov. But Goldoni's play has a characteristic quality and point of view, which is there even when the more immediately Italian elements are set aside, as they should be by any foreign company. What the Moscow Art Theatre missed in *La Locandiera* as a play was about everything that distinguishes it from a lively farce. What they missed about it as a piece of life was about everything that makes it civilized, light, suave, sweet and full of gay dignity. They took a play that comes out of an old civilization, a gracious and cynical tradition of social culture, and made it lively, empty, laborious and a little boorish. They had noise rather than joy, and they translated into mere animal activity what in Goldoni is the flower of good temper and high spirits. Madame Chekhov was infinitely laborious but heavy and ungraceful. Stanislavsky's Ripafratta was a great fellow who had done with women, boorish and heavily laid on. Tamiroff's Fabrizio was not warm, not simple, not lovable. And Madame Pizhova's Mirandolina, mistress of that inn, perpetually forced; she acted in spots, with little continuity. She was only crackling and shrill where she was meant to be shining and human. As expert acting the players were all good, busy, careful, well trained. As creations they were all slightly harsh and never lovable, gracious or quick-witted. They lacked that certain easy noonday, as it were, of an ancient, easy civilization. First-rate craftsmen and second-rate artists.

How different from Goldoni, Papa Goldoni, with his invulnerable cheer, and his sweet delight, his comical decorum and eighteenth century hint of formality! *La Locandiera* is one of those things in drama that move in a kind of super life; it takes its people and events and sets them in a smiling air, far up above the necessities of our familiar humdrum lots; it creates a happy flowing logic of living; it shines and struggles and laughs; it bristles with secure, unwounding epigrams; and deals out retributions and fates at last that coax us toward sanity and fair humor. And Ripafratta is a gentleman, however provincial, who descends from an old cynicism and grave art of getting through life. His dislike of women comes out of this, not out of crude manners and impetuosity. And Mirandolina, the mistress of the inn, is a sweet wild creature, impish, untouched, in and out among these pursuing gentlemen like a glancing shrewd light. She has her own logic, her own methods of managing men, but at the same time she has her own busy, kindly life, the pressure of her own simple affairs. She is, I remember Pirandello's saying to me once, all women. And above all she has a dignity on which her charm may rest. Mirandolina is one of those rôles that any actress who is barely passable can play. But at the same time the shining life set forth, the bustle, the charm, the folk poetry and blunt purity in the part commend it also to great artists. Duse used to play it, as everybody knows, and many another actress great and small. To see it so cut down, as it is in this Russian performance, to activity, technical skill, engaging effort, hard laughing and artful minx, it to see the whole play lost, however lustily it may go roaring on as a rather conventional farce with an old and obvious situation. Twenty years ago I am willing to believe that the Moscow Art Theatre players were closer to Goldoni's comedy. I have no doubt that the idea of Goldoni that this company pursued was once more fair and flexible and warm, though even then, more than likely, it was never really right. What they give us now in *La Locandiera* lacks, at that centre from which the whole performance must radiate, fragrance of idea, comic joy and gravity, and the grace of civilization.

But if the company of the Moscow Art Theatre in Goldoni had proficiency and skill without grace or light, in Dostoievsky they exhibit an understanding, a perfection of ensemble and an inexhaustible study and elaboration of the characters, that must certainly be unequalled in theatres anywhere. It is clear that the dark tenderness and power of this Russian art of Dostoievsky's is true and close to the players. They seem to prosper best when they can undertake the character from its individual centre outwards. They find with infinite thought and suffering and effort the very soul of the man to be portrayed. They worm into him, pity him, carry the glowing life from him into themselves. Their attack on the rôle plainly becomes selfless, becomes absorbed only in the truth of the character, its nervous and spiritual intricacies and its external mannerisms, its sum of life and passion. And when this is done, the several characters are brought together into the play, the proportions of the scenes are found, the ensemble brought to perfection. You will scarcely anywhere in a lifetime see a scene—a very long scene too and very complicated and crowded—brought off so wonderfully as the scene was in the inn where Grushenka and her Polish lover sit drinking, Dmitri comes and the peasants, and finally the officers to arrest Dmitri on the charge of murdering his father. Leonidoff—though plainly a tired actor now—played Dmitri with immense variety and pathos. And though Katchaloff's scene where Ivan imagines himself in the presence of the devil is one of the great things of the Moscow Art Theatre, I thought Alla Tarasova's playing of Grushenka even more extraordinary if that could be possible. What she did was in every scene beautiful and exact and wonderfully graded, one of the three or four great performances in our theatre this season.

If you watch, scene after scene, the progress of *The Brothers Karamazoff* as the Moscow Art Theatre gives it to us, you will see something that may comment more or less on the failure to understand Goldoni. Each of these Karamazoff scenes and the whole evening of them draws from a terrific and vivid life that is at the core of their matter. They are pitiful, vivid, truthful, violent. They spring out of the mysterious light and shadow of individual souls, happy, tortured, passionate, resigned, crafty, insane, whatever the case may be. All this that we see portrayed has about it sincerity, fervor and a kind of mystical realism and truth. But it lacks order and a social mind; it lacks suavity and rule and idea. It has no outline but only violent points and quivering details. It is at heart essentially barbarous. Not that this is bad necessarily; what you decide about that depends on your conception of life and society. Shakespeare at the heart of him is also unordered and private and barbarous; though the manifestation of his art, his morality and his beauty achieved in general its form and order. But that does not affect the point, which is that with the Russian players Goldoni was missed by a defect of that excellence by which Dostoievsky was perceived. You see the truth of Dostoievsky as when you look out from the darkness and fire of your heart into your dreams. You see Goldoni's truth as you see the light resting on a landscape.

THE PASSIONATE PILGRIM

The Merchant of Venice. Lyceum Theatre.
January 1, 1923.

THERE are, as Shakespeare's pilgrim sings, certain signs to know faithful friend from flattering foe. But it is worth while, nevertheless, if you are a lover of Shakespeare, going to *The Merchant of Venice* to see Mr. David Warfield. You will see an East Side father, an old, tired man, pathetic, pious, hopeless but not stupid, bitter, suffering. Mr. Warfield's impersonation of Shylock lacks power and lacks variety and range, but it has humanity and infinite, patient pathos. Within these gentle, deep limits of his, Mr. Warfield's technical means are exact and admirable. He gives us a very fine and convincing piece of realistic acting.

Anyone interested in Shylock as a racial portrait or commentary must, however, think twice over this result that Mr. Warfield achieves. For my part, measuring it by the range of values in human character, quality or endowment that seem to me most significant and important, I find this comment of Mr. Warfield's, however well meant, more distressing than that of the more traditional Shylock that he avoids. Shylock even in the most exaggerated Elizabethan conception of him has in him power, magnificence. He has an endowment of fire, feeling, mind, avarice, malignity, will, that rises to the superb, to a consummate abundance of living human stuff. He stirs the imagination with his elemental force, as earth, air, water and fire may do. But Mr. Warfield substitutes for the elemental forces a tamer range of values; mild ideas of right and wrong, of justice and conduct, the middle-class necessity for approval. This Jew of his has only pathos, solitude, life driven inward, poisoned, suffering.

And, moreover, such a Shylock as this of Mr. Warfield's throws the artistic quality of the play quite out. In Shakespeare we have—whether he be good or bad, or comic or tragic—a Jew rich with the Renaissance, with the nearby Orient. What Shakespeare's Shylock is, sets up a fight that balances the contending forces of the play. I have seen few things so off, so wrong, as Mr. Warfield's Shylock in the trial scene, that little, bent, heart-breaking figure of the Jew, with his pious, suffering eyes, fawning, relentless, sharpening his knife, in the midst of that glittering court and in the face of the silly and delightful legal rubbish that the young lady lawyer with her winning glances has to spring on us. I watched Mr. Warfield and was moved deeply, as I have been sometimes when I saw some old, ragged father on the East Side who stood on the corner peddling to the people he despised in his heart trifles that he scorned and who had in his eyes so much goodness, unapproachable fanaticism, patience, tragic silence and distress. But I felt also that the wrong involved was not so much a matter of the play as of life, a part of the tears of things. And what happened to Shylock in this scene seemed not a legal but a kind of natural justice. Biologically, even, it seemed right and necessary that such a creature—no matter what his wrongs may have been—should be defeated. On the side of the Venetian gentlemen, these senators, these lovers and friends, there was gorgeous vitality, beauty, happiness, open love and the desire for happiness, there was generosity, brave passions and prodigal, abounding life. They might be cruel but they were no more cruel after all than the animal world, no crueller than nature. But this creature that they destroyed so gaily, as birds kill one of their kind sometimes—it was not wholly his fault, but the fact remained that he had no dignity, no taste, no style, no health, no beauty, no volume of creative life, he had only pitiful defeat, thwarted mind and purpose, sick wrongs, and dumb, profound, unwholesome intensity. Shakespeare in the riotous, golden brutality and romance of this scene meant nothing of the kind. Shakespeare meant to supply a fight between powers, not a humiliation of humanity.

For that matter, of course, Shakespeare never meant the trial scene to be heavily serious, or the mercy speech as a legal and ethical harangue. This is a fact well known to many cultured persons, but apparently very hard for the intensities of the theatre mind to receive. If the trial scene were as serious and tragic as it is usually played, the last act of *The Merchant of Venice,* that fifth act with all its poetry and charm, would make no sense; it would be out of tone with what goes before. (Some producers have actually cut the whole of it!) The mercy speech is to be taken not as a sermon; it is in the nature of an aria, and any other way is merely platitudinous, spouting and out of place.

It is worthwhile, too—almost as one goes to a museum—going to *The Merchant of Venice* to see the brocades, the incomparable splendor of the textiles that the actors wear, and to see the reminiscences of Titian, Tintoretto and Veronese in some of the figures on the stage. In themselves—whether they are dramatically wise or not—all these are magnificent. As for the accuracy of the Venetian atmosphere afforded, the results of laborious days on the spot at great expense et cetera, one may put one's tongue in one's cheek. It might easily be passed over as of minor importance in the art of the theatre; but when so much has been said of it, to the sad confusion of the real artistic issue, one may point out that these scenes have no particularly inspired Venetian quality at all; those streets for anything they achieve might as well be in the older quarter of Padua, in Vicenza or even in an Umbrian hill town like Cortona. The column of St. Theodore looks very odd moved into the Doge's Palace. The furniture for the clerks' use belongs to sixteenth century Venice, not early Tuscan or Bolognese; and the stalls and the rostrum of the Council Hall should be painted not walnut but Venetian Red. As for the dazzling costumes, they range over a hundred years or more, though that does not matter of course; and even if it did, we might easily forgive it for the sake of seeing Mr. Philip Merivale, who not only reads his lines and bears himself so that Bassanio seems intelligent and distinguished, but looks exactly—head, steel corselet, clothes and all—as if he had walked out of a fresco by Gozzoli, and even knows how to hold his right knee like the young man in Botticelli's *Primavera*.

But scratch the Shakespeare here and you will find Belasco; and that is really the best thing about the occasion. Good, bad or indifferent, it means at least a certain fullness and genuine theatricality. Whatever else, it will have exuberance and he will have taken every care within his capacity and perception. Mr. Belasco has long been a kind of landmark in our theatre, and the course of his career has many meanings.

The theatre trick, the contagious presentation of the matter to be shown, is more or less the same in all epochs. One epoch plays up the romantic, one the social-serious, another sexual audacity, and so on; but in all epochs and all theatrical talents this instinct for persuasion, magnetism, diversities in glamor, whether low or superb, persists and is the basic element. Mr. Belasco will snatch at any or all of these preferences and elements, with whatever taste, or lack of taste, understanding or what not possible to him and will push them as far into theatricality as he can get them. As a whole, as something taken seriously by the largest number of people of the sort one could take seriously, his position was at its zenith in the nineties and on into the early years of this century. As time went on he kept a secure public, but one that was less and less notable. The newer gods in drama, acting, production and décor were not in his direction; and some of the laborious shine and *réclame* of his position faded from him. As time went on, it became rather distinguished to flout his achievements. Critics showed their sophistication by pointing out the tosh and hokum of his stuff. Often in doing so they themselves indulged in a certain intellectual hokum as it were; for the simplest chambermaid would have known that this business of Mr. Belasco is all a game and all too easy to see through. Theatrical rivals arose as always, and directors who could teach their companies very little could at least teach them to despise the Belasco spectacle and craft.

It goes without saying that Mr. Belasco has no supreme gift of any sort. As a showman he has an eye for effective plays and effective moments. His taste, though luxurious and enthusiastic, is uncertain, to say the least; uncertain to the point of vulgarity—some of which anyhow is merely a matter of being out of style—at times. As to the acting, the play, and their relation to sincerity of purpose and artistic aim, he stands on no high, impressive plane. Amid the new movements, foreign influences, themes, et cetera, he has kept his ear to the ground, his eye on the theatrical chance. What he has not learned was not in his nature to learn. At least one kind of sincerity cannot be denied him, and that is theatrical sincerity. Events, people, passions, the arts, his private and personal experience, his joys and sorrows he can see in only one light; without footlights, in sum, without footlights he is blind. He trembles all through his being with a thousand echoes, despairing silences and warm applauding hands, invisibly awaited. And this in the theatrical faculty is a kind of genius.

THE MIRACLE

The Miracle, staged and created by Max Reinhardt, book by Karl Vollmoeler. Century Theater. January 15, 1924.*

THE MIRACLE taken as a theatrical event is one of the most conspicuous things that have been seen in our theatre for years. Beginning with the house itself transformed into the semblance of a Gothic cathedral and going on through the amazing management of crowds and the inexhaustible array of costumes and groups and movements, *The Miracle* is one long exercise of skill, energy and money. The distances and elevations of the theatre, of the stage itself and the auditorium, the resources of light and the multiplication and variety of events and motivations and incidents, are drawn upon to their very last possibility by practised hands. And there is a succession of scenes, handled with an energy and detail that astonish anyone almost, and most of all a worker in Reinhardt's profession.

Taken as art, *The Miracle* does not fall so easily into place. The first scene up to the intermission seemed to me in many of its moments beautiful and moving. The columns rising in the cathedral choir, the statues, the people coming with their sorrows and supplications, the blind, the maimed, the halt, peasants, lords and every class, banners and pilgrims' branches and spears and halberds, under Mr. Geddes' lights and the color he laid on the masses and individuals there, all this had its great beauty and emotion. And the Madonna of Lady Diana Manners lent to the scene a gentleness and quietude and unchanging patient love.

After the first scene *The Miracle* seemed to me to grow less interesting and except perhaps for the mass triumphs of the mob scene, less achieved. To my mind the directing violated one of the simplest necessities for the security of effects in art; I mean that incident after incident arrived, entrance after entrance, movement after movement, before what was in hand had a chance to live itself, before it could flow out of its beginning and pass into what followed it. One thing

---

* It may be an interesting comment on Reinhardt himself to note his reaction to this review, so severe in contrast to the high praise *The Miracle* had from so many critics. As reported to me by several persons present when it was shown to him, he said it was all true and that it was the only review that he was taking back to Europe with him.

piled on another until a kind of barbarism of interest began to be encouraged—mere multiplication. And motifs like, for instance, the death shadow with his dance, if they had ever a possibility of excitement and depth in them, lost everything by their suddenness or by the crowding of other motifs upon them. The story, partly for lack of this same security in duration of time, began to muddle itself; I began to grow indifferent to what happened; and the arrival of the coronation scene, done with such a volume of movement and costumes and properties, found me looking at the pangs and ironies enacted there with little interest at all; I watched it with less ardor or penetration than I might give to a circus number. I ceased to be moved; the nun's story flowed into Reinhardt's career and his astounding willingness to work in numbers and quantities; the grotesque and poignant world enacted seemed to me no longer concerned with its own life or power but loaded and vulgarized into a kind of theatrical exhibitionism.

Finally, what *The Miracle* most lacks is line; it needs to be more consummate. It is obvious that in general *The Miracle* intends to work its end in terms of crowds and immense quantities of color, invention, detail, a perpetual flux and heaping up and subsiding of characters, emotions, happenings and things. But a difference in the quantity of the material in which it works does not alter the principles involved nor lessen the need in a work of art for a final purity and certainty of intention. And however many or however few the people or incidents in *The Miracle,* they need to be forced into idea that is purer, more final, unescapable, and less confused. The scenes and the motives need constantly to be freer of what are not essentially their own characteristics. In fact the only two things in the evening that took hold of me securely and seemed consummate and pure were, for one thing, those beautiful slender columns rising into the mist of the choir and giving permanence and flight to the changing light that was sent among them. For the other, the procession in the first scene, the people, the suffering, the splendor of the banners, the tilted spears and lances; that—though it must be said that some of this is due to the very nature of a procession, which is composed of these things—had throughout itself line and power and progression.

Mr. Norman Bel Geddes' contribution to *The Miracle* exhibits an enormous energy and invention and variety, a robust independence and almost violence in choice, and a large technical talent. As a whole, nevertheless, I felt a certain crowding of mind in Mr. Geddes' idea as a whole, and sometimes a quality of sheer arbitrariness, as if for him, as for the directors, *The Miracle* often had no single and clear meaning or centre.

The acting in *The Miracle* presents, obviously, a very difficult problem. It is not drama but pantomime; and its importance as art will increase as it establishes a style that is not mere unspoken acting but is essentially pantomimic. The excuse for pantomime—as for any other art or kind of art—consists in the extent to which it expresses something that could not quite be expressed in any other way. To get, without years of schooling, a group of actors who could do this, is plainly impossible. Nevertheless a fair excellence in this direction was achieved in *The Miracle*. The leading rôle, certainly lived superbly up to any requirements. Mr. Werner Krauss is a fine actor, with a fine style. Through the entire part of the Piper, who is the force of life itself, who is Pan, drawing toward happiness and finding grief and death, Mr. Krauss, apart from the magnificent mediaeval intensity of the moment of the healing, carried always a tortured irony, a dramatic precision and a kind of acrid poetry that should be at least a stylistic lesson on our stage. Mr. Rudolph Schildkraut with a less marked style was admirable. Miss Rosamond Pinchot has, of course, cruelly laid upon her a part which she cannot do and which few actresses even of more experience could touch either technically or in spiritual understanding; but in the lighter and more physically active moments of the rôle Miss Pinchot has sincerity and a young charm. All the acting individually, however, was secondary to the crowd action; and in the crowds the range of the director's ability most appeared.

The Miracle is a remarkable milestone on our theatrical road. But every piece of art must in the end rise out of its special field and live itself with all art and all life. At present, so far as *The Miracle* is concerned, the necessity under it, the pressure out of which it arises, seems to me wholly a theatrical one. It has ability, effort, opulence; but the living substance of it is managed, marvellously engineered; there is no hurt, no finality, no inevitable hunger, no wound. *The Miracle* to be great art needs behind it some unifying necessity or spiritual passion, the sense of something through it that is believed.

THE PIRANDELLO PLAY

The Living Mask (Henry IV) by Luigi Pirandello, translated by Arthur Livingston. Forty-fourth Street Theatre. January 21, 1924.

THE Pirandello play at the Forty-fourth Street Theatre is important not by reason of any display or novelty or foreign importation but through the mere occurrence on our stage of a real intellectual impact, a high and violent world of concepts and living. So far as the practical end of it goes Pirandello's *Henry IV* is difficult for our theatre. Its range and complexity of ideas are made more difficult by the presentation that it gets now and that it would be almost sure to get one way or another from any of our producers.

The play is fortunate in its translation, certainly; Mr. Livingston's rendering is both alive and exact, and especially in the second act, where the thought is more involved, Mr. Livingston achieves an unusual quality of distinction. Mr. Robert Edmond Jones' two settings —save for the two portraits in the first scene, which obviously should be modern realistic in the midst of the antique apartment—are ahead of anything Pirandello would be apt to get in Italy, more precisely in the mood and more beautifully and austerely designed. Otherwise the trouble begins with the acting. Bad Italian actors would, congenitally, if in no other way, be closer to this Italian play and its necessities than many actors of our own would be. The actors in the opening moments at the Forty-fourth Street Theatre could not even cope with the necessary delivery of the words. They not only could not whack out the stresses needed for the mere sense of the lines, but had no instinct for taking the cues in such a manner as would keep the scene intact. All that first part of the scene Pirandello means to keep flowing as if it were taking place in one mind; and the actors should establish that unity, speed and continuity by taking fluidly their lines as if from one mouth. Miss Lascelles' portrayal of Donna Mathilde is not definite or elegant enough; it is muffled and it is not full enough of a kind of voluptuous incisiveness. Mr. Louden's Doctor is wrong, too flat and narrow; the part is rough and tumble—out of the old commedia dell'arte very nearly—and a satire on specious scientific optimism and incessant explanation. And Mr. Korff's troubles with the language make his lines, which are hard enough already to grasp, confused and elusive.

Much of the meaning of *Henry IV* will depend of course on the actor who does the central character. Mr. Korff is a very good actor indeed in a certain style. He has a fine voice and a good mask in the manner of the Flemish or German schools of painting. But his portrayal of Henry IV lacks most of all distinction and bite. It is too full of sentiment and too short of mental agitation; it has too much nerves and heart and too little brains. The average audience must get the impression from Mr. Korff that we see a man whose life has been fantastically spoiled by the treachery of an enemy, that the fall from his horse began his disaster, which was completed by the infidelity and loose living of the woman he loved. But this weakens the whole drama; the root of the tragic idea was in the man's mind long before the accident; Pirandello makes that clear enough. The playing of this character which is one of the great rôles in modern drama, needs first of all a dark cerebral distinction and gravity; the tragedy, the irony, the dramatic and philosophical theme, depend on that. Mr. Korff has theatrical power and intensity, but too much waggling of his head; he is too grotesque and undignified vocally; he has too little precision and style for the part; and not enough intellectual excitement and ideal poignancy. And the very last moment of the play he loses entirely by the rise that he uses in his voice and by the kind of crying tumult that he creates. Pirandello's idea cannot appear in such terms as Mr. Korff's. Pirandello is concerned first and last with a condition of life, an idea, embodied in a magnificent personage, not with personal ills and Gothic pities.

A man dressed as Henry IV of Canossa fame rides beside the woman he loves, who goes as Mathilde of Tuscany. His horse is pricked from the rear and lunges; the man when he comes out of his stupor believes himself to be the real Henry IV. For years the river of time flows past him; his beloved marries and has a daughter, she becomes the *amante* of his rival. He chooses, when his reason returns, to remain in the masquerade of the character that for an evening's pleasure he has put on. Life has cheated him, made a jest of him; he gets even with life by remaining permanent in the midst of everlasting change. All men play a part in life; he plays his knowingly. And the people who come out of life to him must mask themselves before they are admitted; he makes fools of them. The woman he has loved comes with his nephew and the doctor to see him, bringing also her *amante*—well played by Mr. Gamble—with her and her daughter, who is the image of what she herself was in her youth. They are the changing Life brought now against the fixed Form in which the supposed madman lives. Driven by the sense that years have passed and are recorded on these visitors from his past and that he has not lived, he tells his attendants of his sanity and his masquerade. They betray his secret. In the end he sees that in the young daughter alone can he recognize his renewal and return to life. There is a struggle when he tries to take her, and he kills the *amante*. Necessarily now, after this crime, he remains shut up in the mask under which he has masqueraded.

With this the Pirandello theme appears—the dualism between Life on one hand and Form on the other; on the one hand Life pouring in a stream, unknowable, obscure, unceasing; on the other hand forms, ideas, crystallizations, in which we try to embody and express this ceaseless stream of Life. Upon everything lies the burden of its form, which alone separates it from dust, but which also interferes with the unceasing flood of Life in it. In *Henry IV* this man who has taken on a Form, a fixed mask in the midst of flooding, changing Life, remains in it until the moment when his passion and despair and violent impulse send him back into Life. But only for a moment: the impetuous violence of the Life in him expels him into his masquerade again: in the struggle between Life and Form, Life is defeated, Form remains.

Nothing in town is to compare to Pirandello's *Henry IV*—well or badly done—as worth seeing. If there is a tendency in many of his plays to think, talk, analyze, without embodying these processes in dramatic molds that carry and give them living substance—and I think that is one of Pirandello's dangers, his plays too often when all is said and done boil down too much to single ideas—this fault cannot be laid on his *Henry IV*. In this play Pirandello has discovered a story, a visual image, and a character that completely embody and reveal the underlying idea. This drama has a fantastic and high-spirited range in the spirit of the Italian comedy tradition; it has also a kind of Shakespearean complexity and variety; and in the second act, at least, something like a poetry of intellectual beauty.

THE LITTLE CLAY CART

The Little Clay Cart, a Hindu play in eight scenes, translated from the Sanskrit by Arthur William Ryder, directed by Agnes Morgan and Irene Lewisohn: settings and costumes by Aline Bernstein. The Neighborhood Playhouse. December 5, 1924

A FEW DAYS ago the Neighborhood Playhouse closed its doors in the face of crowds and set aside the successful Grand Street Follies in order to carry out its repertory plans. And this renunciation of prosperity was no small thing to do in a world of hard finance and theatrical adventure. But the producers of *The Little Clay Cart* must have felt last night when the last curtain fell that they had come off with all their plumage intact. This Hindu comedy as it is done in the Neighborhood is as delightful as the Grand Street Follies were and has a fine poetry and wit of its own. The performance is too long perhaps by 20 minutes, otherwise it is remarkably assisted throughout. Mrs. Aline Bernstein's settings, especially the first scene with the two houses and the beautiful balustrade at the back, are admirable, and the costumes as well. Arthur William Ryder's translation is a fine, free poetic rendering, often in rhyme, and it is good theatrically, fresh and ready in the ear. The acting was now and then a trifle labored, very little so when we consider the remoteness of the piece, but in general on an excellent level. The verses were well read, especially the august lines that fell to Mr. Ian Maclaren in the leading rôle. Miss Kyra Alanova and Miss Dorothy Sands played the courtesan and the maid servant with a loving, flowing delicacy. Mr. Albert Carroll played well the shampooer who turns monk, and Mr. Junius Matthews in the rôle of the scientific and aesthetic thief had the right humor and droll inflection.

In the production you were forced to admire the manner in which mere archaism and foreign convention, with the quaintness and humor attendant on it, were given their proper place. There was no Yellow Jacketing about, no undue playing up of people pretending to walk a long way when they merely crossed the stage to another house or when they heaped imaginary leaves over the dead or stepped over a wall built wholly out of fancy. And, finally, there was most of all something that our stage, our serious stage at least, rarely exhibits, the pervading sense that the occasion was done *con amore,* always with love and pleasure, by everyone concerned in it.

From this quite as much as from the drama itself the lasting charm of the performance arose.

The comedy of *The Little Clay Cart* was written by King Shudraka somewhere between the fifth and tenth centuries A.D. The range of this play extends from poetical comedy to farce, satire, melodrama and a fine, highly formal tradition of the ancient classic. The story of it turns on the love of a courtesan, Vasantasena, for the good merchant Charudatta, who is now fallen to poverty; the love of his little son, Rohasena, who is peevish because his father is so poor now that he can buy him only a toy cart made of clay; Vasantasena gives the boy her jewels to buy a toy cart of gold. Sasthnaka, the king's brother-in-law, whose insulting offers Vasantasena has spurned, meets her in the park, and being again repulsed, strangles her and leaves her for dead. A Buddhist monk revives her and leads her off to a monastery. Sasthanaka accuses Charudatta of robbing Vasantasena of her jewels and murdering her. On the way to his execution Vasantasena returns, and is thus able to save Charudatta's life. Arayaka, the herdsman, having escaped from prison, kills the king and takes the throne. Charudatta is to be rewarded, and Vasantasena, by royal edict, is to be freed from the bonds of having to live as a courtesan.

The characters in *The Little Clay Cart* are varied and unforgettable. The quality of the play cannot be conveyed in any brief account. Everywhere the sentiment and the action is gracious, noble and delicate at the same time. The flavor is one of grace and lyricism and wit. It has the quality of poetry, common sense, proverbs and ballads. And all these qualities, together with the action and words, whether romantic, satirical or droll, seem to move in one crystal medium, unbrokenly. *The Little Clay Cart* is an example of art that expresses a popular life imbued with the poetic. In India everywhere it still survives in that spirit. At the Neighborhood Playhouse it makes one of the most admirable entertainments in town.

Every now and then, Charles Lamb said, a member of the royal family publishes a book just to show that he could write if only he had the mind. Brahms said that it was never safe to criticize a royal composition because you could never be sure who might have written it. By all accounts King Shudraka actually wrote *The Little Clay Cart*. He lived somewhere between the fifth century and the tenth A.D.—in India time and epochs in themselves are of no importance. We know from what was sung of him that he had the lordy grace of elephants and eyes like the bird that feeds in moonlight; that he had a face like the full moon and virtue of a depth unfathomed and alone; and we know nothing more, if that should not suffice. In Hindu tradition *The Little Clay Cart* belong not to the "heroic drama" but to the "drama of invention," among whose rules lay the necessity that the play should be laid in India; that the hero should appear in every act; that the heroine be either a lady or a courtesan, or that the honors be divided between them, on the express condition that in no scene do they meet face to face; that the play advisedly be "full of rascals": that the erotic sentiment, above all other sentiments, take the lead in interest, and that the ending be never tragic but always happy.

Thinking over the attraction and delight of this performance in Grand Street, we may look about for reasons. And the long age of *The Little Clay Cart* appears as one of the sources of its glamour. This play has on it ten centuries and something more of life. During all that time it has been given in India and after every fashion. Sometimes it has been conventional, sometimes popularized in dialects, sometimes in modern clothes and Victorian settings. But all the while it has belonged to the people; it has been theirs in their own terms. In a performance of the old piece we see what ideas emerge as having that in them which can hold the human race so long a time. Life old and new, ancient and modern, has been capable of living itself in the region of the play. For us *The Little Clay Cart* is Indian, it is ancient—far off, indeed, in two senses; but it discovers an ideal region in which space and time are a dream. In this pure realm the play moves. What happens, the loves, the robberies, the villainies of parasites, the gambling, the just and unjust deeds, all move in an untouched and pristine world of idea, feeling, racial tradition; and all are seen in a mutual radiance and charm.

And in and out of this crystal whole run the details of the natural world of our daily life and seem as lasting and as dear as the more abstract elements. There are gifts, games, bullock carts, fear, hate and hunger; the moon shines in those streets, the darkness closes on all eyes; the flowers and jewels, the houses where people live, are scattered through the speeches; the priest washes a yellow garment in the stream; the monkeys will steal the garment if he leaves it in the garden. And in and out run the patterns of the characters. They are characters capable of many epochs and incessant applications: they can be fitted to any generation. This portrait of the droll, esthetic thief debating there in the shadow of night the design for the breach that he shall make in the wall of the house that he will rob, stealing the while that he may buy his beloved maid from her mistress—how inexhaustible he is! And those are portraits indeed of the women, the courtesan, the wife and the maid, and the courtesan's mother, their proprieties and their passions, each in their several veins, their crass and determinate desires, their adventures in danger and romance and lightly drawn squalor.

The scene of the gamblers and the lure of dice and chance that draws the fugitive back into danger: the portrait of the shampooer turned from the vanities of the world into a priest of Buddha, wandering simply and kindly through the garden, over the stream, along the streets, is one of the most charming in drama. The portrait of Charudatta, summing up, strengthening reverence, gentleness, culture and romantic desire, embodied in the hero of a play, is the most lucid and gracious minded that I know.

The production of *The Little Clay Cart* is an interesting case of *bona fide* treatment when we come to foreign or classic plays. Obviously, any drama, Greek, Indian, French or Elizabethan, is alive for us only in so far as it still expresses life. It was at the beginning a body discovered for some informing idea or soul. The necessity in every case of revival or production is to find a new form which does not violate the play but restates it under the conditions that are to be met. To give *The Little Clay Cart* exactly as it was given in its first performance, even if that were possible, could not any longer convey the truth of the play to us. The interest in such a performance would tend too much to the antiquarian or academic. On the other hand, to give *The Little Clay Cart* in a manner always conscious that this is an old, quaint, foreign piece, to rub in its naive oddities, would be to make something out of it which it is not.

The producers at the Neighborhood Playhouse hit a happy medium in this problem. They allow the play its strangeness, its age, its convention, but always in a wise proportion to the real substance in it. They do not ask us to be overtickled at such conventions as throwing leaves where there are no leaves to throw, or riding a horse that does not exist; they merely flavor the scene with these foreign stage conventions. They do not guy the piece. They play with it happily, but they give every chance to the poetry and ideas behind it.

CAESAR AND CLEOPATRA

Caesar and Cleopatra, by George Bernard Shaw. Guild Theatre. April 13, 1925

BYRON in *Don Juan* took as his theme the vindication of the natural man. In this body of Don Juan, as Byron created his idea, is the lure of the primary elements of human life: he is like Dionysos in Euripides' play of *The Bacchae*, strong to persuade all men to follow his beauty and to be drawn to the forces of life in him. The course of his Don Juan through the world illustrated Byron's theme. This hero's function was to break down the resistances that we have built up around ourselves, to strip off the veneer of civilization and bring into play the primary faculties of those on whom he became a power. The lies and hypocrisies and unrealities of humanity were thus to be exposed and revealed and our basic nature vindicated. Byron's theme is simpler and less complex than Shaw's, though conveyed with more power and vitality.

Shaw in his Julius Caesar is creating an idea that has some kinship to Byron's, though it is carried further. The theme of this Caesar of Shaw's is natural greatness. Shaw is not giving us a picture of what the actual Julius Caesar may have been, he is not silly and idle enough to think of startling us with a picture of our hero eating onions or paring his nails, of giving us the shock of the great man as seen by his valet. He is trying to strip the figure of greatness free of all nonsense, of false and confusing pieties and labels. He is trying to scrape the figure and cleanse it of our pet ideas and standard goodnesses. He bases greatness on something like biology.

Imagine some lower form of animal life. It is successful or important in so far as it is complete in itself and in so far as all its functioning contributes to its own unity and own perfection. Say that it clutches some substance in its tentacles, it absorbs what of this substance may contribute to its own rightness in itself. The rest of the substance it lets go. Imagine some other animal that messes up itself, takes on what is not related to its own need and perfection, imitates, confuses its own nature, muddles itself into confusion among other animal forms.

The great human quality in Shaw's Caesar is like the first of these animals. Its concern is with its growth and rightness within its own needs and its own nature. It is supremely selfish. It functions rightly among things, it knows what are its values among the endless choices of its existence. It has the necessity and power of its own vast vitality. Shaw's Caesar is not generous, clement, just, idealistic or any other of the goodnesses that we might ascribe to him. What he does is to take the course that perfects and maintains his own nature. He is, in sum, intelligent in the deepest natural sense, and therefore full of virtue. He gives money freely as an animal might exchange his own energy for something that exercises him or rewards him with something of more value to his nature. He is not so stupid as to wish for vengeance, which would only interrupt his nature. He responds to the beauty and mystery of the night and of time and space. He appropriates to himself the fire and light of love and beauty. But everything takes its place within his existence because of the profound rightness of his sense of what he lives by. In sum, he is an organism that functions greatly.

Meanwhile the humanity around him are fools one way or another, according to their special follies. They desire overwhelmingly what will work their own ruin. They are full of borrowed or reflected ideas, motives, traditions and impulses that are not deeply related to their own needs and natures. (There are people, La Rochefoucauld says, who would never have been in love if they had never heard of love.) They are like some fool animal organism that is strayed and lost among the things that lie around it, that tries to absorb a comb and brush, an ink bottle or anything that is thrown to it out of the cosmos, and that blurs its own individual existence and loses its wholeness among the confusions and enticements of the life around.

If we see a horse stop eating when he hits something that would make him sick, we say that his instinct prevents him from eating it; we take the horse's act for granted. If we see man, however, refrain from an act that would poison his soul, we admire him for it, we speak of his nobility or control. On the other hand, we might see a sow work herself to exhaustion getting food for her young, after she has endured the pain of giving them birth. We may get up a great palaver about mother love even among brutes. The next minute the sow may bite off the heads of her children and eat them up—what shall we say then?

Shaw has arranged his Caesar on such lines. This Caesar is original because of the purity and strength of his organism, its freedom from characteristics and actions not its own. He appears to illustrate qualities that we label as generosity, cynicism, clemency, poetic idealism, practical shrewdness; but as qualities these are only instances of the inevitable functioning of his nature, and we may resent them as much as we like so long as we recognize them for their natural rightness. They are forms of biological intelligence. It is to secure this end that Shaw has arranged Caesar's speeches and actions in a sequence so baffling. One minute Caesar is what we call elevated, poetic, generous, the next he is what we call hard, civil, prosaic. You sit and watch this man and wonder what to think of him; just as you thought him good and great he is something else, just as you said he was a lover, a poet, you find him a cynic and a politician and the next moment an orator.

The purpose of this method is to keep you from sticking sweet labels over Caesar and making him a goody hero in your own evasive style. Shaw wants to keep him straight in his own nature, free of cant, of crystallized definiteness; he wants to force us to watch life freely and strongly expressing itself, to watch greatness as it derives from complete self-exercise, vitality and power.

The difference between the Theatre Guild and some of the producers on Broadway can now be measured by noting what they go on and do with *Caesar and Cleopatra*. They were wise to give it, to take the risk of so vast and difficult a drama. The production so far is barely passable. It can end in a profound achievement for the Guild. But that will depend on their constant study of the performance to guide it toward perfection.

The tempo can be speeded up. The reading can be labored at in order to convey the sense with more ease as well as more speed. The marking that Shaw brings out of the cosmos to the drama of the human lives there on his stage can be more strongly underscored. There is that supper scene, for example, where the passions and ambitions, the petulances and jealousies and hot, passing beauty and splendor and meanness of the characters' lines are seen against the great forms that their race has evolved architectually, and against their racial immortality expressed in sculptured stone, and in the midst of the Egypt where the world seems to reveal itself so splendidly. There is the daylight fading and coming to purple, the purple deepening intensely, the pale orange then, and then at last, when all are gone but Cleopatra, frightened and cowed and in the great colonnade, and the curtain so drawn as to show the dead body of her fierce serving-woman before the image of the god, there is the Egyptian memory and stars of the eternal harmony of the world. All these are dramatic elements as much as the action is.

The moon in the sphinx scene at the Guild can rise as Shaw meant it to do, revealing the huge form as it sits looking for ever across the sands; the music of Memnon can be made to count more overwhelmingly as the voice of the night, of time and of the world—these are as much the drama as the characters speaking there. The ugly green curtain can be taken out of the banquet scene, the doors at the back of some of the scenes can have thickness added to their walls, and so on. And most of all the Theatre Guild has a chance now to give Anglo-Saxons an instance of a point on which they are sadly muddled as a race, which is the difference between levity and gayety. The whole performance can be more joyous and inclusive, more alive with the indescribable and mysterious brightness of life and art.

THE GREAT GOD BROWN

The Great God Brown, by Eugene O'Neill. Greenwich Village Theatre. January 23, 1926.

I HAD the curious experience with *The Great God Brown* of being moved with something that I felt behind the play, but almost always untouched by the play itself. It may be that such an observation makes no sense, that the only way in which such an impression could be received would be through the play; where else should we get it? Let it go at that, then, and say at any rate that I felt a torment of spirit, a groping love of life, a bitter pity and goodness, a warm and courageous desire, that make me, like so many other people in America, wish Eugene O'Neill well, wish that it may be granted to him to fulfil his talent and devotion. I admired the passion for fresh and powerful dramatic form in Eugene O'Neill, and I felt like lining myself up in defense of the audacious integrity of his mood. But by the play itself as it went on I was entertained only now and then, during the first half perhaps, and afterward only interested in what was being undertaken.

The writing in *The Great God Brown* is unequal, sometimes beautiful and keen, often well chastened toward the dramatic point to be expressed, often obvious, sometimes flat, poor poetry, third-rate taste. Now and again the idea is poignant and carrying, now and again commonplace or worse. Sometimes a beautiful speech like that of the intolerable chalice of life fails to stop and runs off into mediocrity. I confess to embarrassment sometimes, even, as for instance when the officer standing over the dead Brown-Dion asks what his name is and the all-wise prostitute says MAN—that seems only second-rate Andreyev in his symbolic vein, and Andreyev can be bad enough.

The part of this new play that has the most immediate interest, of course, is the use of masks. Each of the leading characters is shown with two faces, his own, which represents what he is, and the mask that expresses only the distortion of himself that some may see. The surety with which this device has been employed and has been made necessary to the play's meaning and very existence indeed, the direct economy of the mask's application, appear when we try to tell in words the story. Any such account of it must be a mere travesty.

There are two sets of parents in business together. One of them has a son who is poetic and gifted. The son of the other is matter-of-fact, honest, persistent and practical. Both youths are close friends, both love the same girl, Margaret. The girl loves Dion, though she knows nothing of his real self. She marries him. They sell his share of the business to Brown, and go abroad. There are three children born. Brown, still loving Margaret, has never married. Dion has squandered his estate, has been a painter, a failure, an uncertain husband. Through Margaret's intercessions he is employed in Brown's office, his designs convert the architecture of the firm into imagination and art. There is a prostitute who gives to Dion an understanding that he has never had from his wife, however devoted she may be to him. Brown takes over the prostitute and supports her richly, in order to keep Dion faithful to his wife. Time passes, Dion under the strain of life and the pain of hard reality against his sensitive dreams, degenerates further and further. He has, nevertheless, what Brown never can have, the gift of life. He dies, his mask is put on by Brown, who, unknown to her, takes Dion's place with Margaret and gives her back the old happiness of the first days with Dion. Meanwhile Dion is supposed to be secluding himself by day at Brown's office, working at the designs. Margaret comes for him. In this crisis Brown declares that Dion has suddenly died. There is a cry of murder, the officers pursue, Brown is shot, he and Dion, now merged into one, die. In the epilogue Margaret, an old woman, masked to her three sons, speaks to them of their father.

The settings by Mr. Robert Edmond Jones are as courageous as the play. With extraordinary insight they achieve the dramatic point of the scenes they translate into stage décor. The high, overwhelming panel of the filing cabinet in Brown's profitable and laborious office, the walls of the prostitute's room bursting into red blossoms when Brown has set her up in luxury, these scenes are theatrical in the deepest sense. Mr. Jones' directing is equally close to the play's method. He cannot put acting into the players—he has, for that matter, a variable sense of acting, sometimes inspired and sometimes merely arbitrary—and their performance remains only adequate and never compelling. But the lay-out of the stage movement, of the positions, of the emphasis of individuals and groups is distinct and telling. Miss Leona Hogarth as Margaret and Mr. Robert Keith as Dion have at least a sympathetic relation to their rôles. Miss Anne Shoemaker's prostitute, sure to be admired in many quarters, seemed to me an unctuous and rather tiresome performance, full of important missions to perform, not translucent in spirit, but conscious of meanings, and subtly lacking somehow in taste. The conception or version of prostitutes in the O'Neill plays generally is apt to verge on the adolescent and somewhat tasteless. Mr. William Harrigan, with the fat rôle of Brown, was never tragic, ironical or poignant, though he has naturally perhaps a certain soldier-boy pathos in a small way. But he gave the sense of a good professional security, a kind of inherited dispatch and competency, of a sincere mind and a fine obligation to the play, and he never missed a point.

Of such a technical device as this use of masks, which is kept up all through *The Great God Brown* from the first line to the last curtain, two points are to be made. The first is that the unfamiliarity or rarity of such a device, the more or less innovative side of it, that is to say in our own theatre, will make the play more admirable and exciting to some people and to others will be a hindrance, an annoyance or a confusion that hurts the play's effect. This condition is a matter of time only and acquaintance; a further use of masks in plays would more or less dispose of it. The second point is that when once a device is adopted in a drama and the expressive meaning of it has become clear, the continued significance or suggestiveness of its use will depend on the artist's imagination. You could take a knife and fork to represent a man and wife. But to achieve anything important there must then be imagination exercised in the use of these symbols, otherwise you have only the regular story, plus the knife and fork instead of man and wife, and have achieved nothing beyond the first device, the initial metaphor.

In *The Great God Brown* the masks are used well. Coming on

and off the faces as they do when these human beings confront one another, they say quickly and clearly certain things that need to be said. They are made immensely economical; they are made to justify themselves by being made expressive; they say what nothing else in the play says or could quite say. On the whole, too, they manage not to be confusing or even very difficult, unless it be toward the last, when Brown puts on Dion's mask. By this time the masks are used not only to express the real character and the character sometimes shown the world, but also to express the transfer of one man's personality to another, to carry perhaps one soul into another body. In this part of the play the idea is harder to state, though it is more or less felt. As to a profoundly imaginative use of the masks, points at which their use became a radiant necessity and a great leaping image full of creative life, I should have less to say. For me there were only two such places, though they were extraordinary. The moment when the prostitute, out of her understanding and love, hands the wretched Dion his mask to put on, like a shelter that her heart knows, startles and moves you. At the last when we see Dion's wife talking to the mask of the dead man whom she has loved but never known as he was, folding him now like a child in the bosom of her love, when we see that and realize that it is still only his mask that she kneels to there, the motive becomes suddenly luminous and revealing.

When I met Eugene O'Neill, some fifteen years ago, I saw at once a vivid and shy gentleness; though the emotions could be strong, the inward mood black, and the nervous arousal violent. In the course of these years since I first began to know him I have seen him in varying circumstances, some of them deeply personal, some enraging, or difficult, as only the theatre can be. But the sense I most felt then and have felt since was almost wholly inner.

It was at this time that I began to hear of Eugene O'Neill as "Poor Gene." He was not poor, he had cars, two houses and so forth, not to speak of an inheritance, he drank only occasionally, his theatre fame was growing; but friends were bent on keeping him penniless, inebriate and unhappy. They also, however, had the protective impulse toward him. By this impulse, using their genuine admiration for his talent, their delight in his supposed wildness, his social revolt and his starvation, they spread a great aura of defensive pathos around his name. Pleasuring themselves in his strong moods and his fierce borderings on a rash life, they felt in general only a small part of his moral and poetic continuity. They consciously and unconsciously created a half-false, half-true legend about him of great publicity value in the theatre. As always, every legend has its price and its reward.

Steadily, meanwhile, the idea grew that Mr. O'Neill was a dramatist of social revolution, a bold new thinker and what not. This enlisted a further support of him and a still wider defense of him, none of which lessened the theatrical spread of his name. I think that even then there were a good many who knew that his most intense qualities and appeal and effect on us did not arise from any subject matter, any supposed revolutionary impact, any strong dramatic expertness. They knew that what moved us was the cost to the dramatist of what he handled. They knew that by his capacity for concern, his quivering nerves and passionate involvement, far more than by any dramatic process, he was touching their inmost hearts; and that, whatever the dramatic motive, the real appeal of his play was poetic and personal. To speak of Eugene O'Neill as a realist was once, no doubt, useful to him—realism being the reigning jabber and confusion of that particular moment. But much of his so-called realism was only a lyric use of realistic brutal detail, present most of all in words and phrases. To think, for example, of *The Hairy Ape* as a realistic sociological workingman's problem play is absurd. It is a surface shape of verisimilitude and of vernacular dirt in the eyes; it is essentially surface reality. It offers us one of the most complete and magnificent fables in the modern theatre. This implies all the narrative abstraction and final pattern of fable, which here is so fine that to outline it is but to deceive your hearer into thinking the actual play is much better than proves to be really the case.

Eugene O'Neill has used neither situation nor individual to express the problem of masses or of a social system. His characters are not, like Ibsen's very often and especially Shaw's, almost passive victims of inheritance or of a convention or of a mass point of view. With O'Neill the problem of the individual, a soul in exercise or torment, has been the central interest; and it has often, in one character after another, been poignantly realized within the dramatist himself. The individual as *representing* the mass counts not so much as the individual *in revolt against* or *surrender* to the mass. From this very fact, partly, comes that frequent impression that the O'Neill plays have less of intellect and theory and more of dramatic instinct and personal upheaval.

Whatever may have been said of the morality and immorality of O'Neill's plays, the important issue is not the morality but the moral, since in the moral we find the key to the author's own feelings toward the character and situation involved. This concern of O'Neill's with evil and good is what combines wtih his drama's necessary American roots to give it an appeal so much wider than America. This is one of the main causes of his vogue in divers foreign countries. And for this reason the quality of the moral in his individual plays as they arrive is the measure of his intense growth as a poet.

HABIMA AND SOREL

La Dame aux Camelias, by Dumas Fils. Cosmopolitan Theatre. December 15, 1926.

The Dybbuk, by S. Ansky. Mansfield Theatre. December 13, 1926.

GOING to see Madame Cecile Sorel in *La Dame aux Camelias* after seeing the Habima Players in *The Dybbuk* is an experience that shows with a vengeance what spring life can have, how it can rebound and ease itself and dress itself up brightly; and can forget the far stars and the infinite memories that are stored in the human body. It is like coming from the Arabian desert to the boulevards of Paris.

Perhaps it was because I am worn somewhat thin on middle-class seriousness without much endowment to be serious on, and on sincerity without much to be sincere about—and if it has anything, without technique to carry it into the art of the theatre. Perhaps I am tired, too, of bad dressing among actresses—plenty of money is spent on their clothes, but all over town you see nothing but clothes that might have come from almost any mob shop on Fifth or Madison Avenue, with now and then an expensive cross-street thrown in. At any rate Madame Sorel seemed to me a rest, a change and a good lesson in half a dozen ways. She knows at least how to walk, how to get up and sit down, how to calculate her stage distances and how to wear her extraordinary gowns, creations in themselves; she has diction, voice control and a glorious and shameless exhibitionism, all valuable things in the theatre. To despise such elements only shows that you do not see their point nor the difficulty and labor and watchfulness with which they are acquired, nor their place in the theatre art.

Otherwise Madame Sorel is the most delightful example I have ever known of empty competence. I have never seen so much expression that expressed nothing. Nothing gets through that perfect enameled skin. The heart within that handsome bosom beats with the pulse of the Rue de la Paix. I enjoy this Sorel performance, for a change now and again, because it is so divinely callous. It rests us from the sting of life. It is such pure theatre without any content to carry from life except the burden of the chic; it relieves all throes of immortality because it has no soul. It is as near to pure substance or material, sheer sight, sound and texture, as the human agent in art can attain.

There is the figure, like one of those fine women that Julio Romano and Vasari modeled up out of Raphael and Michelangelo and our Victorians admired. There is the voice going on and on, one method of production, one inflection, one tone after another, saying nothing, but dispatching the business in hand. There is all this Parisian perfection, so intelligent, skilful, hard and fluent. There are the fine, large feet, beautifully shod and reshod as the play proceeds, and never, in the maddest moments of the drama, dismayed from their admirable positions. This is the classic tradition; it has something exacting, aristocratic and secure about it. All it needs is the soul of a great artist to give it life and significance. As it is, the emptiness of content leaves the method all the more clearly exposed to study. And finally we come to the death in the last act; Marguerite Gauthier, after her sacrifice for her lover's sake, faced with death. Or perhaps to Madame Sorel it only sounded like death. At any rate there is the beautiful setting, the chamber pale yellow, the superb bed that once belonged, it seems, to the Bourbons, the lace, silk, maribou, ermine and smart flowing lines of the heroine's draperies. Everything glistens and glows and knows its business in the world. Putting this lady, this Marguerite Gauthier that we are watching there, in her grave will only be like shutting her pearls into their case; they will be none the worse for it.

It seems almost inevitable that we should say that the performance of *The Dybbuk* by the Habima Theatre of Moscow cannot be thought of as theatre; that it is religious ritual and that these people are priests and priestesses. Such intensity and such absorption might seem to belong to a sect or to the religious passion of a race. The theatre might almost seem to be no home for it.

But nothing could be more mistaken. To say so is to be blind to the essence of the theatre as an art and to make the worst possible objections to this Habima Theatre.

Its performance is the most complete work of art that I have seen on the stage since the performance of *The Cherry Orchard* by the Moscow Art Theatre three years ago. When we see *Boris Gudunoff* at the Metropolitan, Chaliapin's Boris is magnificently whole and is superb throughout, but the rest of the production is wore than stale. We see now and again in the theatre great décor, great acting, great drama, but only two or three times in our lives do we see a quality expressed down to the last element in the theatre art, a perfect unity in idea, plot, and every other medium of theatrical expression, the music, the setting, make-ups, costumes, voice, gesture and group movement. Such completeness, such unity in essence and form, is the living principle in every work of art, the supreme soul and test of it, first and last.

As a critic I have an obligation to convey here what this production is like, but could not if I tried. I can only say that the play itself is the well-known dramatic legend of Ansky's, done by Yiddish theatres over the world, given a remarkable production in English at the Neighborhood Playhouse last season and revived this, and now with the Habima Players in the original classical Hebrew. The story, as more or less the world knows, is of the young student, the genius, who loves a girl and who in his exhaustion through penance and study and the fire of his love, calls on the powers of magic to make her his. He dies, and his soul passes into her body. The father of the student has been the friend of the girl's father, the two children have been betrothed to each other before they were born. One of the friends died, the other became rich, and he did not keep the pact; his daughter is to be married to another suitor. When the girl's father has given half his goods to the poor and the dybbuk by the force of excommunication from Israel has been driven from her body, she is left alone in a magic ring. The voice comes again; she dies and her soul joins her lover's. That is the bare outline of the myth; the possibilities of its theme are marvelous, the theme of a love so strong that after death it can drive itself into the body of the beloved. But with the story Ansky has inwoven the ecstasy of a race, all the shadowy origin of its passion, its faith, its primitive mysticism and confusion and strength.

This deep racial element takes *The Dybbuk* far away from me. I feel the presence of a terrific force and fire and tenderness, but much of it is foreign to me; it seems to draw from remote ages and from places far away in the deserts of Asia. In our western culture, in Greece, or in Italy—the Campo Santo at Pisa for example—men strove to create an outer form whose beauty would embody or represent the beauty of the idea within; a result that to their minds made for health and balance, in content and external fact, in impulse and release. But these expressive forms in the sacred objects, dances and rites, that I see in *The Dybbuk*, take their power from what they mean to their worshipers. They are pure symbols, all idea, rapture, fanaticism, fear, strength; pure symbols have no outer claim to representative beauty or expressiveness in themselves. Their beauty is inward, they live in men's minds. This passionate inwardness fulfils all parts of the Habima production of *The Dybbuk* and leads it to its summit.

The décor for *The Dybbuk* has also much that is not close to my visual impulse. But the dim, clay-colored walls, the naked, drab architectural shapes, and above all the extraordinary use of light are completely one with the whole idea. The very stylized make-ups, carried to the point of violent mask patterns at times—noses painted white on one side, black on the other, triangles in blue or green or black on the foreheads and so on—are of a piece, as a whole, with this effect of a dream dreamed by a race for a thousand years and fiercely and tenderly kept. The acting is throughout admirable, every rôle and every ensemble and dance movement is served with devotion. Madame Anna Rovina has the heroine's part, the girl Leah; spiritually and technically her performance is magnificent.

It remains to be seen, of course, how long this group and its art will be intact and capable of such unity and rightness, and just when time and circumstance will lessen its excellence. But at the moment, in this twenty-sixth year of our century it cannot be too highly praised.

I have seen various stylized performances and have seen the designs for many more. As a rule the stylization—the elimination or rearrangement to which the realistic is subjected for purposes of expressiveness—is only partially convincing. Too often it breaks down into mere device, entertaining in itself perhaps, but not profoundly imaginative. To be thus imaginative would mean that what it says could not have been said in the image of any other form. This Habima production is the only instance of extreme stylization that I have ever encountered in which the whole of it seemed inevitable. Here in it we get both the extreme stylization that ritual can go to and at the same time the truth that worshipers bring to ritual.

AN AMERICAN TRAGEDY

An American Tragedy, by Patrick Kearney, from the novel by Theodore Dreiser. Longacre Theatre. October 11, 1926.

THE characters in Mr. Dreiser's books and the incidents that are taking place never seem to me real. As I am reading the book they never seem to be present, never created before me, never given a body of imagination. And yet at the same time they appear to have been real persons, to have happened. They seem absolutely true, understood, but I never believe them real; I feel that someone is telling me about characters that have been and events that have occurred. In the end, of course, this comes to the same thing, since it is all eventually creation; but this double impression, nevertheless, of creation and mere recounting, is a strong one. It does not, however, diminish the impression of greatness. Through all this maze of unequal diction, flatness, this talk about "rearranging chemisms," "nervously searing impressions," this muddle made up out of formal, old-fashioned phrasing, cant terms from popular journalism and modes in popular psychology, side by side with impressionistic effects, scientific and naturalistic effects and effects of ingenious suspense in phrasing and details, through all this the conviction emerges of Dreiser's observation and deep knowledge of his people and of life, and of patience, warmth and a kind of vast and cumulative intensity. The impression that lasts in your mind and life after finishing the book is of a work of art that is large and grave, tedious, profound and free.

The nature of the theatre and the special talent of Mr. Patrick Kearney, who made this drama from *An American Tragedy,* have worked toward an effect that contrasts significantly with the book. The characters and events seem much more real when you see the actors walking before you and when you hear the speeches coming from lips that are alive. And Mr. Kearney has an excellent ear for dialogue, far more fluent than Mr. Dreiser's, though it may be less biting at times because it is less stubbornly maintained and is livelier and brisker with the snap of the footlights. This fluency of the playwright's and born stage ear constantly heighten the sense of actuality in the Dreiser material.

In his use of the two volumes with their almost nine hundred pages and copious range, the playwright has chosen the theme of Clyde Griffith's affair with the two girls, Sondra and Roberta, the death of Roberta when her pregnancy threatens her love's fortunes, the murder charge, the trial and execution. Only the incidents bearing on this are shown. The mass of life around these characters, the families and communities involved in the panorama of the book have been either omitted or sketched into the scenes with a few sharp strokes. The significant epilogue in which we see again the family of Clyde exhorting and praying in the street as they were seen to do in the prologue, is left out. Some ingenious manipulations appear, as when the gift from Roberta to Clyde after he has grown cold to her is shifted from Christmas to his birthday and made to follow a gift from the other and richer girl, and when Roberta's jealousy of Clyde's social life and of the riches and advantages that she has never had, shrills through the speech in which she turns on the doctor when he refuses to perform an abortion for her and tells him insultingly that if she had money he would not act as he does. The trial scene is contrived with great skill and at the same time reproduces very well the interminable account in the book.

The characters for the most part keep their outlines well enough as Mr. Kearney has transcribed them. Without the time that the author allows them and the elaboration of his analysis and comment, they seem necessarily simpler than in the book and the terms of their portrayal seem more elemental. We in turn are led to see them more simply and to feel more glowingly about them than we do as we read them in Mr. Dreiser's pages. Mr. Liveright, too, in casting his production, has hit on three much more than average players for the chief rôles. At their hands these characters become more appealing and their reactions more moving than they are in the novel, where our feelings are concerned with these characters as parts of life, and our vision of them is suffused and trembling with our sense of something larger and more inevitable that surrounds them. One character, Clyde's mother, so fully studied in the book, is used in the play only as a stage element in the latter scenes; and another, the prison chaplain, so subtly conveyed by Dreiser, becomes something almost ironic as Mr. Philip Wood delivers his lines about the saving mercy of God to those who believe in Him and confess.

The sum of all this amounts to a drama in eleven scenes that has good dialogue and some good moving climaxes, but that is on the whole a murder play of the general family of murder plays—*On Trial,* for example—enacted by characters who are clearly drawn but trimmed of most of their complexity and vital implication. This, however, is true and not true, for the fact remains that over the whole play lies the shadow of its deeper source and the sting of the book's large and poignant reality.

This serious and grave approach extends to the production that Mr. Horace Liveright has given to *An American Tragedy,* which shows both dignity and skill, and to the directing of Mr. Edward Goodman.

Watching Miss Miriam Hopkins' affable Sondra you find it hard to believe that she is anything but a charming and lovely young person, with a style, impulse and sweetness, too, rather than that very mixed young lady, human, good, bad and variable, in the midst of the American life around her, that we read of in *An American Tragedy*. Miss Katherine Wilson's Roberta comes truer to the book perhaps, but Roberta is a part that is more easily put into stage terms; hers is a blunter, grimmer and more readily conveyed tragedy. But these are both good performances.

Mr. Morgan Farley does not give us the Clyde Griffiths of the novel; he is less fluent and sensuous and confused, less common and plausible, less heedlessly brutal and tender and inhibited. It is easy to believe that his Clyde would have been liked by the people he met and loved by the two girls, but that would be because of his fineness and the delicacy of his response to experience, rather than because of a versatile and facile responsiveness. But if **Mr.** Farley does **not** duplicate the character, he brings to the stage rôle what is much more important: an intensity of reaction that convinces us of the tragedy and human living involved. It is easy to believe that this Clyde would have killed the girl through intensity and confusion and infatuation for another girl, though not from an emptier, commoner weakness, or sick nerves and lying fibre.

AN AMERICAN TRAGEDY

No play could give us the Dreiser book. There would be two ways of making a play out of it. One would be to take a single incident and a group of characters and explore and comment, warm up, neutralize, lay out detail after detail, till the drab, naive, muddled innocent, eager scene of our American life had been created and brought to bear on the persons presented. For such a play Mr. Farley would be wrong. For this sort of prose realism and close resemblance he would not be suited. A less imaginative actor, with more of a direct talent for simple realistic playing, would be needed. The other way of making a play from *An American Tragedy* is to do what Mr. Kearney has done, dramatize not the mood and atmosphere and social comment so much as the long line of the main story, which is the other essential in this interpretation of our common scene. For so swift a statement you need in the actor a somewhat higher accent, a readier conveyance of the pain, blindness and beauty of what is alive, and this Mr. Farley brings to it.

THE SILVER CORD

The Silver Cord, by Sidney Howard. John Golden Theatre. December 27, 1926.

MISS LAURA HOPE CREWS shows sound discernment in giving the note that she does to her portrayal of this mother in Mr. Howard's play. There are those in the audience, no doubt, who think she exaggerates, makes the character much too extreme; and there are those, very likely, who resent the touch of wit or absurdity that she gives to her characterization. But if you have the faculty of hearing the lines in themselves, of making a division between the rôle and the performance, a distinction between what you see on the stage and the written text of the part, you will appreciate the intelligence and the technical security with which Miss Crews establishes the personage on whom the entire play hangs and the discussion centres.

In *The Silver Cord* you see first an engaged couple waiting for the arrival of the other brother and his wife. They appear; the two young women like each other. Mrs. Phelps comes in to greet her returning son. She is all absorbed in him. The rest of the play concerns this devotion, this all-consuming mother-love that has taken such a part in the two boys' lives. One has been in love from time to time, engaged, involved in a scandal that cost his mother twelve thousand dollars. The other, only after a long absence from his mother's side, has seen a woman that he desired and has married her.

The jealousy theme begins at once and develops throughout the play. Mrs. Phelps persuades the weaker son to break off his engagement. She stops at no arguments, no insinuations, no lies and no threats of dying herself, in order to gain her ends. The girl, when she learns her lover's state of mind, has hysterics; the new daughter-in-law sides with her. The mother has now the task of winning back the other son. She has put him and his wife in separate rooms, she pays one of her old-time visits to her son's bedside and goes into the old appeals, the pride, affection, weak heart, sacrifice themes, and gradually her son comes toward her again. The wife enters, talks the case over with her husband, and, being a biologist, makes matters clearer than most young women could do. The act ends with the two boys running out to prevent the hysterical girl from drowning in the broken ice of the pond and their mother calling out to them from the window to get their coats, they will have pneumonia. In the third act the struggle between the mother and the son's wife continues; there is a frank modern scene of explanations, followed by maternal faintness and devotion and self-sacrifice and frailty in the old style. The wife leaves with the fiancée, the sons remain with their mother for a moment, after which one of them runs out to join his wife and the other sinks at his mother's knees, while she sits there quoting the passage from the Bible about the love that suffereth long and is kind, that endureth much and so on.

Such an account does the play, which is very fertile in detail, small justice, but it affords an idea of its subject matter and the line that it develops.

To return, then, to Miss Crews and her interpretation, it is clear that this woman with the extremes that are given her in the lines and with those two curtains that she has—one at the window shouting at her sons, who run to prevent a girl's drowning, that they will take cold, and the other quoting those terrible and deep lines about love while her weak son, doomed to degeneracy and decay under her domination, sits almost blubbering at her feet—it is clear that this woman must either be taken as fairly absurd or as a diseased and ominous figure. But for the last to be true and to be taken at the full seriousness of its import, the entire play would have to be deepened and darkened in tone. The dramatic substance would have to be subtly and continuously deeper than it is in *The Silver Cord*. It would, meanwhile, imply a far deeper talent than Mr. Howard possesses.

But such is not the case in this play; and so it remains to some extent slightly farcical. Its extremes in detail and motivation go quite beyond its substance. No little of its terrific matter and of its powerful motives are used incidentally; tremendous forces out of life are invoked and are managed with great boldness, but both these forces and this boldness remain to a considerable extent incidental. They are superficially rendered. To be bold without power and humility about the great forces of life is only to present a showy and second-rate exhibition and advantage. Theatre writers like Mr. Sidney Howard, highly journalistic and dipping, regardless, into the depths, advance with notable facility into regions where only the progressively oblivious could ever be quite at home. Such cases are not necessarily insincere through their intention; they may be so through their lack of depth.

Miss Crews is quite right to put into all this the wit she does, to let you know that she knows her character is somewhat absurd and foolish, a woman gifted with words and persuasion, no doubt, but not in this play at least, certainly not this play as it stands, to be taken at the full weight of the evil she may work in life.

It is an interesting thing to observe about *The Silver Cord* that what makes it effective theatre contrives at the same time to make it less profound as art. What makes it more theatrical makes it less deep. This strong shoveling on of effects, this underscoring of points, drives the matter of this play over the footlights with a bang, and sets the simplest people in the audience to debating: all around you in the theatre people are asking if all this is true or not, and are citing instances very like the one on the stage. The extreme case that Mrs. Phelps presents is in line with this theatrical distinctness, but this very extreme of it narrows the play's applicability and makes less significant the statement in the last act that all over America there are mothers like this, draining the lives of their sons. On a deeper basis Mr. Howard had for a time a fine case, but as the play progressed his instance lost a good deal of its point by being pushed so vivaciously.

This is not saying that theatricality is a bad thing. Granted its present substance, a less theatrical statement of this case of Mrs. Phelps and her sons might have been subtler and truer. But the ideal thing, of course, would be to preserve all this theatricality—using the term in the best sense—and at the same time to fill it with a more profound matter and surround it with a deeper texture of life. Which is to say that behind these bold strokes and violent motives there should be more imagination, agony and knowledge of what they cost.

All this, however, must not obscure the fact that *The Silver Cord* is a notable play, always effective, always going ahead. Its progression is always striking; the characters are well outlined and well varied. The device of making the son's wife a biologist, full of explanations and of informations that put people in their places, is an ingenious one; the dialogue all through the play carries well. *The Silver Cord* represents a steady growth in Mr. Howard's control of his medium, and is easily his best piece of work.

Mr. John Cromwell has directed the play admirably. Most of the acting is highly competent. In the case of Miss Margalo Gillmore it is excellent—a fine example of her remarkable talent for a realistic rôle that is in the nature of an interlude rather than the central pivot of the play. Miss Laura Hope Crews' performance is a masterpiece, full of the right flight and understanding.

THE BROTHERS KARAMAZOV

The Brothers Karamazov, based on Dostoyevsky's novel, by Jacques Copeau and Jean Croue, transcribed by Rosalind Ivan. The Guild Theatre, January 3, 1927.

I HAVE the novel before me, but the play that we see at the Guild Theatre must, of course, stand by itself. It is a long play, five acts, beginning with a scene in the monastery courtyard, where we are given the threads to be woven into the play that follows, and ending with Ivan's going mad. As the story progresses we see the love affairs of Dmitri, his devotion to Agrafena Alexandrovna and his relation to Katerina; we see the four sons with old Karamazov, their father; then the murder of Karamazov by the epileptic bastard; then Dmitri unjustly sentenced for the crime, and his departure for Siberia in an exaltation of sacrifice and atonement, followed by Agrafena and his religious brother, Aliocha.

As a play the Copeau-Croué version of Dostoyevsky's matter has a fair pattern of unity, which amounts, if you like, to saying that it is more or less right in the manly way. The characters are, as theatre at least, effectively drawn. The dialogue will pass, unless, that is, you take it as a rendering of that talk we know among the Russians of Chekhov, Tolstoy or Dostoyevsky himself, with its intimacy, subtlety and outpouring, its simple or passionate intensity; in which case it lacks all feeling, flow and centrifugal truth, lacks the quiver and pulse, the rush and pause, the sense of elusive, compelling life. Some of the dramatic motivation is striking, and some of it, like that of almost the whole of the second act, is confusing and to be understood only in the light of the novel.

When the producers of the Moscow Art Theatre gave *The Brothers Karamazov* they, as everybody knows, presented scenes from the book, with narrative passages at intervals to connect them and to achieve a certain kind of continuity, close to that of the novel itself. This arrangement that M. Copeau presents introduces quite another sort of continuity. It is a continuity that winds up what the unfinished novel leaves unshaped and never would have shaped, and that contrives a definite line of cause and action. The result, I should say, is effective theatre with most of the bottom dropped out of it. Not for a second do I believe any of it; I see a degree of expertness and solidity in the conception, a certain stage logic; but I am never moved by it in any sense that I am moved by great art, and especially by great Russian art. Through stage manipulation and remarkable directing that third act with its stair, its shadows, its old man going out to an assignation and meeting his death, gave me considerable theatre excitement, but I never for an instant felt any of the pity and trembling life in which all Dostoyevsky's terrible and sordid and transcendent events and characters are set. I had only the sense of a plot thinly supported by the life on which it draws, and of a good deal of unnecessary, because it was empty, theatre woe. It is quite possible that in this matter the French authors admire logical technique and the Theatre Guild admire success; but the Russian of Dostoyevsky is another matter.

As an example, take the scene where Dmitri departs into exile, his soul full of a mystical passion of atonement and love, and the other personages beseech him to let them arrange his escape. As I saw it at the Guild Theatre it might almost have been out of Stephen Leacock. All this determination to be tragic or burst, to engage in self-sacrifice, this busy protestation from various stage positions, seemed only foolish; nothing has been created out of which it might arise, and nothing put into it that could make its unreasonableness divine. There are people who are always talking about naturalness on the stage and about the unnatural, by which for the most part they mean the formal. Such people should ponder such a scene as this of Dmitri's departure in *The Brothers Karamazov*. Naturalness in a work of art consists in its being true to its own nature. Unnaturalness derives from two defects: the work of art may wander from its own special nature, like a realistic gesture in *Oedipus King* or a formal gesture in *The Cherry Orchard*; or the work of art as a whole may fail to create for itself any essential quality, or nature, in which its parts may participate and within which they take shape. That latter condition we see in this *Brothers Karamazov* scene at the Guild. In it there is created nothing by which what goes on before our eyes is true, and without this truth no form of the natural is possible to it.

As the case stands now, the only thing that could deepen and save this Copeau-Theatre Guild drama of *The Brothers Karamazov* is the acting. It provides superb rôles for the actors and it depends on their powers and their complexity for its meaning, in so far as it has any meaning—for even in the hands of much finer actors than are now provided, what happens would seem rather cooked up after all. If it is not to be superbly acted, I should prefer this play gaily done as Grand Guignol. It might as well, since, after all, that is often what it amounts to.

The acting in the Theatre Guild production includes that of Mr. Morris Carnovsky, who has no idea of what the mystic Aliocha would be like and turns him into a kind of vapid Servant in the House, all treacle and thumbs; Mr. Dudley Digges, who plays Feodor with a certain sincere concern; and Mr. Alfred Lunt as Dmitri and Miss Lynn Fontanne, for the rôle of Grushenka, so marvellously written by Dostoyevsky, who play with their usual good-housekeeping, though in these high, intense rôles they move in a blind alley of the superficial like poor, bright, silly stage dolls. Mr. Edward G. Robinson, as the epileptic, comes nearer to the play and to the Russian than anyone else; he is often very good, and his is the only playing in the cast that could be called so. But all the players, in fact, within the limits of their thin vitality and skimmed understanding, mean well enough, if that interests you.

The chief credit for the occasion goes to M. Copeau. The elements that make up the sum of it are hollow; the play is obviously one that has been largely contrived. But the general layout of the production is noble and cogent; the method is direct and clean, with no false motives or trite appeal on the director's part.

You would have to nurse very simple requirements indeed to think that at any moment in this production there appears the terrible immediacy of feeling and the wildness of heart and soul to accompany such a life history as that set forth in the plot. It is all good enough mechanics, but would anyone think there was torture or ecstasy or consuming intensity anywhere about it? Even that subtle quality of frankness and meditation and emotion comes out at the actors' hands as largely self-conscious and effective, though its place is in the warm stream of human living, and its centre is barbaric, disordered and quivering.

THE BROTHERS KARAMAZOV 83

For the scenes in Karamazov's house M. Copeau has retained his familiar and very expressive device of the stair at the back and the gallery above, by which now the various sons and their father are seen going to and from their rooms. And Mr. Raymond Sovey, though some of his scenes are not up to par, has included this stair in what is one of the most imaginatively designed and lighted settings of the season. The actors' make-ups are far ahead of those in the usual Theatre Guild productions.

PIRANDELLO'S COMMEDIA

Right You Are If You Think You Are, by Luigi Pirandello, translated by Arthur Livingston. The Guild Theatre. February 21, 1927.

THE production of Pirandello's famous *Così è* (*se vi pare*) by the Theatre Guild players is at least passable, with some muffing and not too much precision or distinction, and with two admirable performances. Mr. Edward G. Robinson plays Ponza, the tortured employe, with fine concentration and unity; Miss Beryl Mercer's Signora Frola is one of the most expert and stirring performances of the year. The whole interpretation of the play, however, is greatly thwarted by Mr. Reginald Mason, to whom is allotted the all-important rôle in which the dramatist himself speaks.

This Lamberto Laudisi is the protagonist, or perhaps the chorus, of the drama. The Pirandello theme—that relation of fiction and reality and the nature of truth that is the hero of most of his plays—supplies the dramatic continuity of *Così è* (*se vi pare*) and is completely intrusted to this ironical and smiling philosopher who sits on the edge of the events and human emotions that we see taking place in the Aggazi drawing-room. The rôle should be played directly, with clear stresses, direct reason, urbanity and sequence. Mr. Mason seems to have the impression that Pirandello was writing to give archness a chance. The most pointed remarks, remarks most necessary to the play's idea and progress, he delivers as if he were the whimsical uncle of an English country house. His hesitancies, sly humors and coquetries, of theory and whim, as when, for example, he speaks Laudisi's lines to his own image or self in the mirror, appear to make some of the audience laugh, but they blur the sting of the thought, shift the intellectual basis of the play, and help to turn into a smiling moment what is not so much comic or personal as it is exhilarating or ideal. Such a performance as Mr. Mason's is a deplorable intrusion into the clarity and precision of Pirandello.

Pirandello's theatre and ideas have been so long famous now and this particular play so long available, either in companies abroad or as a book here, in Mr. Arthur Livingston's capital translations, that we are free to leave accounts of *Così è (se vi pare)* and turn to points almost academic.

First, then, we may speak of the element of characterization in this Latin play. The acting at the Guild Theatre might wisely aim at less relation between many of the speeches and the particular character that speaks them, and more relation to the play's general scheme. This rather undue degree of individualization might be said to appear even in the translation of the title, for *Così è* does not mention you but it, and does not say that you are right but that it is so, if it seems so to you. That, however, is of no importance, obviously. I mention it only for whatever suggestive comment may be involved. In many cases a speech in *Così è (se vi pare)* might be said by any one of half a dozen of the people in the story. It does not proceed from the depths of any particular person, but serves rather to keep the argument up, the analysis alive, the structure building. Indeed, the people in this play are hardly people at all; they are figures in the game that Pirandello is playing. They are human traits, situations, mental aspects. If on the stage it so happens that they are made too personal, too actual, the play becomes more cruel and arch; taken on that ground what could be more cruel that the use it makes of such grief, despair and confusion as possess the three people about whom the town's inquiry and our excitement centre? With less individualization and reality in the characters, less comedy and laughter would be necessary to make the play palatable.

This ought to be a good lesson for us Northern races with our obsession about character in drama. Is Pirandello's play poor because the characters in it are but perfunctorily related to its story and idea, are in themselves as characters not profound creations? Not at all. It would doubtless be a greater play if the character element were deeply creative and deeply related to the plot and the theme. But that does not prevent its being an excellent piece of drama through the excellence of its idea and plot. This play exists most in its outline, to which everything else contributes. In this case we are to judge not too much by the degree of character creation; and it is well to remember that to Pirandello a character often appears to be as definite an entity almost as a figure on a chessboard—*ma non,* he says, *si dà vita invano a un personaggio*—but not idly does one give life to a character.

This outline quality, this exhilarating game of motives and ideas, is one of the traits in *Così è* (*se vi pare*) that tie it to the *commedia dell' arte*. This piece, as much as any that Carlo Gozzi admired in the public squares of Italy, is made up not of people but of stock characters, which are here not Harlequin, Punchinello, Brighella, Colombina, Dottore and the rest, but Mental Habits, Characteristic Human Emotions, Thematic Ideas. This is no less a comedy of intrigue, though the game played and the victory plotted for concern not some hero but ideas: the nature of truth is the hero whose fortunes underlie the story. And over this whole play, as in the *commedia dell' arte,* lies the air of improvisation. However bitter its living material, however tragic the human matter that it engages, it is gay with its own ingenuity and speed, it delights in its invention and ruthless vivacity. At the very end we see Ponza maintaining that his wife is dead and, to comfort the mother-in-law, keeping up the fiction that his second wife is still alive; and the mother-in-law insisting that her daughter is not dead but that her son-in-law's delusion has made it necessary to go through a second wedding ceremony and pretend that there is now a second wife; we see then the woman in question when she is brought in to settle the matter. Which is she, they ask, the daughter who is still alive or the dead woman's successor? She is, she says, whatever you think she is. With such an arbitrary end the plot intrigue resolves itself, and at that we are slapped in the face with the unreality and the pure theatricality of the piece, which thus kicks up its heels with its own high spirits and dark joyous game.

New as he seems, Pirandello through the profound sources behind his origin is old. He was born in Sicily, in Girgenti in the south, the Acragas that Pindar called "the most beautiful city of mortals." It was a part of that Magna Graecia that composed a great section of the Greek world and mind; it was later under the domination of Carthage, then of Rome, and in the ninth century was taken by the Saracens and became a part of that Arabic world that was anything but lacking in violence, philosophy and mathematics. Across the strait this same Southern world was that of Thomas Aquinas and Vico—Hegel's source, we may remember—and today of Volterra, Croce and other great names. His use of subtlety and passion are thus by no means new with Pirandello. He knows that, speaking generally, the passions have their own logic; fiercely and darkly they work, sorting their elements together, squaring them at last in that final conclusion in violence. Only vague, soft and fuddled emotions are without this inner and final logic of their own. The stronger the passion is, the more logical, taken alone in itself, since the more completely it will come to a resolution according to its own nature.

Not only do these type characters—these lively abstractions, traditional, though of a new content, more or less—denote the Latin and classic family of *Così è (se vi pare)*; there are, also, speeches long enough to have come from the Attic dramatists, from Seneca and Plautus, and on down through the course of drama in modern Latin countries. Here again, are these *longueurs,* these tirades, speeches longer in wind than the Homeric Nestor boasted, that we of the North have been taught to dread and fear. It is amusing to sit listening to Miss Mercer's fine reading of those pages and pages that Signora Frola speaks, and to observe how this classic form may carry life as well as any other, when there is really any life to carry, and how the tense life in it now, as Pirandello is using it, covers up the traditional form. Technically, too, we may observe that the point is not so much that the speech is long. The point is that the very length itself of a speech should become dramatic, that there should be also a dramatic progression in the thought, and that, when it is delivered, the stress should fall accurately and with a just degree of that resistant flexibility by which the spoken language becomes expressive and exciting. The length of a speech can be made as dramatic and exciting as anything about it.

IN ABRAHAM'S BOSOM

In Abraham's Bosom, by Paul Green. Garrick Theatre.
February 13, 1927.

THE play now presented at the Garrick Theatre by the Provincetown Playhouse has for its theme a blend of aspiration, suffering, poignant futility and confusion. Its problem concerns the groping and defeated effort toward race freedom, growth and opportunity; and its material is full of pain, deep humanity and inherent drama. The figure who is to carry the main thread of this theme is a man half-white, half-black, troubled by white nerves and impulses, darkened in his soul with superstition, weakness and disease. He is Abraham McCranie, the son of Colonel McCranie and a colored woman, and the plot is a record of his story.

We see three Negroes in a wood where they have been chopping. They talk of Abe, the book-lover. Abe enters; he is apart from them, absorbed in his dream of an education and the salvation of his race. Goldie McAllister, also partly white, loves him, brings him food; and now, when Abe has been impudent to the son of his white father and struck him, and the father has given Abe a whipping, Goldie comforts him. The scene ends with their going to sit beneath the trees and the three other Negroes breaking into an orgy of excitement over this picture of love.

We see Abe then, after he has been married for a few years, the father of two puny children who have died and now of a son that is to be strong and the savior of his race. Fortune has deserted Abe, his crops are ruined, his spirit bitter, his family starving; for he is no farmer, what he wants is to teach a school. The Colonel comes and gives him the title to some land. Abe's bitterness changes; he sees the heavens open, sees himself as blest and on the road to his mission. We find him then in his school, a wretched sight, and then closing the school because of the attack to be made on him for cruelly beating one of his pupils who would not try to learn. He moves from town to town, talking his salvation theme and losing his jobs, hounded, sick, bewildered, brutal, fanatical his weak and trifling son turned from the house, Muh Mack, the aunt who lives with him, scolding and complaining, only his wife faithful and slaving and starving for him, never losing her belief. Colonel McCranie's will has ordered that a place be always given him on the farm if he should wish to return. He goes back, his crop is again neglected, the cotton falls out of the bolls while he writes a speech for the inauguration of a new academy that shall be a light to his people. His son sets a low class of whites on him, he is hounded from the hall where he meant to speak. In the fields he lies, his pursuers outrun. Mr. Lonnie, the Colonel's son, comes to find out what the noise is. He tries to steady Abe, but when he tells him that he has taken his cotton crop and found pickers for it, Abe leaps at him, there is a scuffle, the white man is killed. In the last scene, Abe bursts in on his family, his pursuers arrive, as he opens the door he is shot down, his last cry is freedom, freedom. The curtain falls on his wife sobbing over him.

As I ponder this play it seems moving and profound. Certainly the course of its struggle is full of tragic despair: this poor, confused, violent high-souled creature beating out his life in vain against circumstance. There is, too, a certain wise balance of parts in the dramatic elements; the white people mean to be kind, but they are as lost in the midst of a race situation as the Negro is; they are moved now by human or affectionate impulse and now by a blind racial instinct and an arbitrary, desperate sense of self-preservation. The climaxes in the play are strong and bold. I seem, as I think of it, to have been present at a full, passionate story, told by a poet. Certainly this material that Mr. Green attempts is ambitious of power and devastation and beauty; we are in very deep waters with such subject matter as he employs.

But what I remember last is that for three-fifths of the time I was dissatisfied and often more than bored. The first act, up to that really inventive moment at the very last when the three Negroes dance about at the sight of the love between Abe and Goldie, was very nearly unbearable. With better acting, perhaps, *In Abraham's Bosom* might have been better. Of what acting there was, we may say that for more or less untrained actors, with little sense of technical projection, the company was perhaps passable; Miss Rose McClendon, by virtue of a certain sincerity or something in herself, was nearly always effective and often tragic.

The dialogue of this play, apart from some of the curtain climaxes, is flat and seems hastily written. Considering the bold, O'Neill sort of line that the treatment essays, the speeches are sometimes surprisingly false, borrowed, conventional. One of the best signs of promise in such a play as *In Abraham's Bosom* would lie in the ear; for nowhere in America is there better material for dialogue than in his world of Mr. Green's; nowhere is there a more special rhythm and flavor of speech than in the South, or more warmth and naïveté of words than in Negro speech. That Mr. Green made so little of this living stuff, that his lines have so little care and so little passion for the quivering beat of life that the words might carry, is a discouraging sign in what is obviously a marked theatre talent working with material that is wholly vibrant and freshly taken out of our American life.

The best places in this play of Negro life are those like that orgiastic end of the first act; or the scenes where the loose and worthless grandson with his jazz talent sings for his old aunt and the two of them prove to have one blood in their veins; or Abe's prayer when the land becomes his and he dedicates his baby to God and his race. In these there is an essence that is racial, dramatic and moving. These moments take themselves out of the hands of the actors, the pulse quickens, the glow of strangeness and beauty comes over the scene; and for a little we have the sense of a soul working and of poetic truth.

But it is between these moments that the trouble lies with Mr. Green's play. Between these high moments we cannot ask an equal tension and imagination; but we can ask more pains, more reduction of the play's progress to firm outlines that would go better with its bold technical aim. The tenderness of feeling in this work, the love of the country and soil in which this history occurs, the courage of the character delineation and the range of sentiment, all deserve more care and choice on the author's part. The glow that is in these special passages could appear, though in smaller terms of course, in the speeches that lie between them. This play is of the kind that makes you wish it well; and you resent all the more the fact that the gloom that some of its spreads over you is not the gloom of tragedy, for that might be rich and stirring, but of casual form and bad writing.

DYNAMO

Dynamo, by Eugene O'Neill. Martin Beck Theatre,
February 11, 1928.

I HAVE often thought, seeing his plays, that, despite his great theatrical gifts, Eugene O'Neill's talent has two aspects not strictly theatrical that have contributed as much as anything else to his wide reputation.

One of these is the character of lyric feeling behind all that he writes. *Strange Interlude* in its earlier scenes may be subtle and secure, and in its last scenes banal and something short in taste, and *Dynamo* may be concerned at certain times with profound and eternal human problems and at others with what is adolescent, trite and overfamiliar; but it remains true, nevertheless, that the feeling behind everything is close and genuine and personal. It arises from the author's own turmoil and emotional necessity, and has about it the urgency of his needs. From this cause it happens in *Dynamo*, as it did in *Desire under the Elms*, that we feel the presence of two elements: the play proceeds, with whatever agreement or tedium it arouses in us as we hear it, but meanwhile, alongside this agreement or boredom, there runs this personal lyricism, the sense of some individual poignancy whose stress and pressure has evolved these scenes. This in itself is moving and endearing; it stirs in us the impulse to defend Eugene O'Neill, and to respond to feeling that in himself is moving, even though it turns out to be unequal and half-baked. It happens, therefore, that even when we are not at all touched by the feeling itself or the idea presented, we are stabbed to our depths by the importance of this feeling to him, and we are all his, not because of what he says but because saying it meant so much to him. As a play, *Dynamo* seemed to me to have some fine scenes, like that when the mother betrays the son's confidence, but to be uncertain in its whole result; as a personal document, it is significant.

The other aspect of his gift is that for making myths. There can be no doubt that one of the things that has carried him farthest into people's memories is the capacity that his themes possess for effective recounting. In numbers of his plays the theme or central idea sounds infinitely suggestive and fruitful as one recounts it to others or as a newspaper story hands it on; and upon it the imagination builds and weaves onward to dazzling possibilities and infectious meanings. Whereas the play seen in the theatre is not half so good as we thought it might be; and what we have projected for it promised more than what has been created or accomplished. The play of *The Hairy Ape*, for instance, is only fair; it is effective and for one seeing may come off well enough. But the fable is capital—this Man with the Hoe, reduced to beast, returning to the beast's cage, finding no place even there; a few lines say it, and the theme of it remains unforgettable.

In *Dynamo* there is a fine fable, modern style. A young man departs from the old faith and turns to science for his god, whose incarnation he worships in the dynamo. But in that he finds no resolution of his problem; the old god is dead but science provides no satisfactory new god. Reuben Light, brought up in the house of his father, a strict preacher and old-style Christian, who is in love with his wife as she is with him but who distrusts the ways of the flesh, is himself in love with the daughter of the atheist neighbor. After a difficulty with her and her father and then with his own parents, he leaves home and sees the world, of books, wandering, work and women. He returns and finds his mother dead, her heart broken over him. He gets a place in the atheist's power-house, and begins to discover the presence of his god in the dynamo. In the last scene we are shown his prayers and invocations to this mechanical monster, and the way in which he is torn between this dedication and service on one hand and on the other the earthly love for his sweetheart, who on her part cannot live without him. In the end he yields to the temptation of the flesh, and then suffers a revulsion of feeling; he will give his soul to the dynamo. He shoots the girl, and presently thrusts his hands into the dynamo's current and dies.

But to invent, or discover, a great myth—Prometheus, Faust, Don Juan—is a rare and wonderful thing; and it is just here that *Dynamo* most breaks down. Told in brief form, a few lines, a classic fable's length, this story and this search for the new god and the failure of it—a man turns from the old god and worships the machine, in vain

—is effective and good. But it will not stretch to hold a fuller content. It has not the necessary capacity for extension. When we watch the first acts of *Dynamo* some of it sounds obvious and *vieux jeu,* some of it moving and close; and when we see the last act we feel in it the deep and world-old basis—as in Tristan, Launcelot, Tannhäuser and so on—of the struggle between the world and the salvation of one's soul; we feel the subtlety sometimes of the reactions and the catches of intense emotion; but we cannot take seriously this man kneeling to this dynamo and making prayers to it before our eyes, except on the grounds of his having gone insane, and in that case, what he does lacks significance. In sum, what was a good figure of speech—we all speak these days of worshiping the machine—is not a good frame for a play, not, certainly, as we see it in the Theater Guild production.

The writing of this new play of Eugene O'Neill's is divided between a certain close realism on the one hand, or at least a poetic accuracy—gained partly through the use of lengthy asides—and on the other a typicality by which the characters and the events are not individual but are shown moving on type lines and weaving thereby the pattern of the incident. How far this is confusing is not easy to say from seeing the play only in the present production. The line that the Theatre Guild has taken is that of honest actuality. I should judge that this is really as good as the play itself deserves, so far as its content and significance go; but certainly it confuses the issue still further. It is wholly without spell and without imagination. This begins with the settings. The first two acts of *Dynamo* call for two adjoining houses, with a fence between, and a view into the rooms of each house and the families there. Mr. Lee Simonson has provided two frames of houses, the actual two-by-fours, as if the walls were removed and we saw inside. What we see there on the stage appears, in the midst of the pervading general realism, to be mere stripped beams for houses not yet built; there is no drawing and no dramatic creation except in the sweep of the electric wires above the houses. The result as a whole gets nowhere. In the last act the scene in the hydroelectric plant may be, as the program informs us, like that known to the dramatist near Ridgefield, Connecticut; but, though devised with admirable craft, it merely presents an actuality that makes the worshiping hero seem more obsessed and lacking in significance. Giving up the world and the flesh for that familiar engine that sits there to the left of the stage is a trifle hard to swallow or to be interested in. By what distortion, what drawing, what alteration of reality into emotional meaning, the power-house scene might have been converted into the abyss against which this soul plays out its lost struggle toward God, is not so much a matter for the critic's suggestion as it is for the designer's creation. It is his place to discover in that mechanical scene the one line, the shadow, the light, the mass, the restatement that will express the dramatic moment that evolves within it.

The presence of Mr. Glenn Anders as the actor who shall create this unsteady central figure in the play is also of unequal value. Mr. Anders plays as well in *Dynamo* as anyone could imagine him to do, always intelligently, always with that remarkable gift of his by which he can slip at any moment into the most convincing portrayal of feeling, always with that persuasive time-sense that he has had from the start of his career. If the young man he presents is to be rather dull in the head, whining, belonging to the common run, capable of deep gusts of simple human feeling, Mr. Anders is excellent. If there should be more vagueness, mysticism and lift, something less obsessed and more transcendent, he is a bad choice. I confess, seeing the play, I was unable to tell just how typical and ordinary, or individual and exact, or poetic and removed, this Reuben Light was meant to be. My impression was that he wandered rather uncertainly among these various qualities, and that the dramatist has not placed him securely in any plane.

Mrs. Fife, the girl's mother, left me equally uncertain. She may have been meant by the dramatist for a simple-minded, good creature with dreams, or a *bona fide* mystic, or a being who says something wonderful one minute and absurd the next. This last is the way Miss Catherine Calhoun Doucet played the rôle, and it seemed to me to make sense as realism, since a good mystic often hovers between the divine and the absurd. Miss Claudette Colbert, in clothes too *chic*, played admirably the girl's part, one of those Gee-he-gets-my-goat rôles that our American stage provides so liberally for young ladies, though this time there are genuine moments of feeling for the player to create. Mr. George Gaul played the minister, Reuben's father, quite as admirably. The best performance in *Dynamo,* as well as the best written, is that of the atheist who superintends the power-house, defies God, bullies his wife, runs the machines, taunts the preacher, loves his daughter, and is harsh and kind by turns. The first moments of Act Three trouble Mr. Dudley Digges and leave him still not quite at home, but his performance as a whole is well graded, dramatic and always intelligent, and full of the stresses and emphases that proceed from a real power of study.

MACBETH

Macbeth. Knickerbocker Theatre. November 19, 1928.

THE POINT of departure for this *Macbeth* of Mr. George Tyler's, as a part in his "annual presentation of famous masterpieces," was the design by Mr. Gordon Craig. That fact ten years ago would have made a great stir in our midst, but nowadays it came softly into the public ear, mildly important. This is partly because the name of Gordon Craig is no longer news; he is a source now rather than a sensation, as Darwin has come to be in science. It is partly because there is less interest in the serious discussion of the theatre just now; partly because that aspect of the theatre that décor represents is less to the front than it was; and partly because Mr. Gordon Craig's ideas have spread into the very texture of the theatre and even into the realm of the moving pictures.

And finally, it must be said that no little of this indifference derives from the fact that Mr. Craig himself did not come over to America. What we see at the Knickerbocker is scenery taken from the designs he sent, but not actually created under his eye and hand.

That Mr. Gordon Craig is one of the outstanding geniuses in the history of the world theatre is obvious. He has himself more or less gone through with a handful of productions in Moscow, London, Copenhagen, Florence and elsewhere, none of which I have seen. From all reports they came off with varying degrees of completeness and satisfaction, but certainly with stimulating imagination and prophecy, plus a veritable wellspring of vituperation and violence among the tempers involved. Whether or not he could ever carry his ideas through is a question. Whether or not in his last, subconscious self he really ever quite wanted the theatre—I mean his own theatre, safely bolstered with endowments—that virtuous hearts have wished for him and his experiments is also a question. But that does not in the least affect the point that he has been a seed, an upheaval, a light and power in the art of the theatre, not only on its visual side but with regard to the whole production. His influence is evident in the modern Russians, in Reinhardt, in Granville-Barker and lesser men in England, in Robert Edmond Jones, in Norman Bel Geddes and in other American designers.

Everyone knows, therefore, that Mr. Gordon Craig's aim and scope has not rested with décor, but has extended to the theatrical event as a unit. His conception is that of a one directing mind behind all the elements together—the play, the acting, the décor, the directing—as they contribute to the entire event. It is a noble idea, stimulating and rich, though only partially workable. His share in this *Macbeth*, however, includes nothing of all this except the décor, and in the décor not even the costumes, only the settings.

There are those who say that it was not ethical, or something of the kind, for Mr. Craig to turn over his designs to another man and not come over and see them through for himself, and that he is therefore subject to be judged by the result. But this is nonsense; he has as much right to sell his designs to a producer as the dramatist has to sell his play or as the costume designer to sell his plates—so long, that is, as the production does not claim to be his, which this does not and could scarcely try to do.

It must be said, nevertheless, that to turn over designs like Mr. Gordon Craig's for another man to carry out into stage mass, color, light and surface textures, is about as if El Greco supplied somebody with a sketch and a color card from which to paint one of his pictures. At the hands of Mr. Robert Edmond Jones, for example, who designed so remarkable a *Macbeth* some years ago, these designs might have come to birth either better or worse than what Mr. Craig had imagined. Under the hands that have brought them to us now, they come, with one or two exceptions, to nothing at all. Scenically it is a somewhat hideous evening that is offered us at the Knickerbocker.

The costumes were of the old-style Lohengrin tradition, not bad on Christmas cards in the Victorian manner, but astonishing in front of Craigish settings. They hit bottom in Lady Macbeth, who wore for the murder scene a black afternoon affair, up-to-date in figure and showing beneath it a stretch of light stockings and high-heeled satin shoes, and for the banquet scene a sort of Madame Jeritza Madison Avenue effect that was quite beyond words. Even if the settings had come off, these costumes would have muddled the issue.

As to the designs behind these settings, anyone truly interested may look at a series of them presented in the *Theatre Arts Monthly Magazine* for November, remembering as he looks that much may be drawn in charcoal, where the thumb can rub in such miracles of pregnant nuance, that is a wholly different matter when it comes to a stage execution of it. Most of these designs seem to me not very notable, and not, this late in the day, very significant. The outline of the castle seat I thought striking enough, and the notes for the witches would once have seemed to me suggestive—once but not now, for time, alas, takes off the edge from the motives and devices in all art and sadly dims the flourish set on them. The design for the castle scenes, the king's arrival and afterward the circumstances of his murder, I thought superb. That arrangement of square shapes, with those shadowy approaches and that violent lighted door where blood is to be spilt, was full of deeply dramatic imagination even as it came off at the Knickerbocker, badly painted as that was and inexpertly lit. Parts of the witches' scenes might have pleased such as have a taste for a certain obvious chiaroscuro. Most of the settings were much too near the front of the stage and appallingly lighted.

Mr. Lyn Harding gave a dignified performance of Macbeth, in good taste but lacking in power and force, and much too monotonously a case of neurotic decay like that of his Tsar Paul in *The Patriot* of last season. His reading lacked a great deal in general variety and attack. When Miss Florence Reed, at her first moment on the stage, began to decipher Macbeth's letter I thought that, whatever else might be wanting by way of subtlety or penetration, we might be going to have here a Lady Macbeth with a certain raw and primitive energy and edge that would at least refresh the rôle and rouse the energy so often lost from her scenes. But a mechanical approach to the part was soon apparent, a hopeless rhythm, a meaningless phrase and idle vocalization. The sleep-walking scene was wrong in every way; the stair turned out poorly, the doctor and nurse had costumes suitable for Plymouth Rock, Miles Standish or the music master of melodrama, and Lady Macbeth missed the entire effect of the scene, which ordinarily one would think might carry itself. A certain continuity of movement is, above everything, necessary in this scene, a movement containing the whole trance of it, the life carried on by forces beyond its control, the haunted mind and tragic helplessness, the silver light of dream and sleep. Miss Reed broke up her movement into mere empty starts and stops and did nothing with the lines. During the first part of this scene, as Lady Macbeth came down the steps and across the stage—she took some time doing so—I heard a heavy breathing which I took to be some drunk farther down toward the stage who had fallen asleep. People have told me that it was not so, but a part of the player's portrayal of sleep. I cannot believe that such could be true, but if it is true it must serve forever as the immortal high-water mark of all attempts at misplaced realism ever made in poetic drama. The two murderers of Mr. Bernard Savage and Mr. Harold Thomas seemed to me excellent performances. Their one fault lay in not killing more of the cast.

Macbeth presents many difficulties and problems in production, three or four of which we may note here. It is a primitive and barbaric history done over into seventeenth-century matter. This means that in Shakespeare's time it could be understood partly by that core of barbarism so entrenched in the Anglo-Saxon breast, and partly by that contemporaneity of its mind that gave it its final place with the audience. For us it is different. We see the two elements, primitive and Renaissance, and neither of them is quite ours. We cannot quite receive the play as one harmonious unity in kind; and this not because we are more cultivated or essentially knowing, but merely because we are different.

Macbeth takes advantage of its privilege, as poetic method, to say many things, and in many ways, that realism cannot accommodate. In speaking the lines of such long passages as that of Macbeth's about sleep, for instance, we must discover a method that will convey the effect of the mind's being opened so that we see its contents, which may all be present in one flash. To read the passage with breaks in it, as if these reflections arose as one bit of thought after another, is only to make the character sound rambling or irrelevant to the dramatic moment and truth, and the dramatist more or less talky or false. We must face, too, the Elizabethan intention of continuous flux in the action and scenes, a continuity based on short or no waits between the scenes, and on declamation and vitality in the acting.

None of these problems—not even that of the short waits—was solved in this production at the Knickerbocker. But we may say, at least, that for some occult reason, perhaps, the general level of the

English spoken was better than in most of Broadway's Shakespearean productions.

In conclusion it must be said that this whole occasion is nothing beside the Robert Edmond Jones design for the *Macbeth* that Mr. Arthur Hopkins produced in February of 1921, with Miss Julia Arthur and Mr. Lionel Barrymore. The décor of that was not only far better than this present production: it was the most creative and exciting staging of *Macbeth* or any Shakespeare play that I have ever seen anywhere. There was a stage enclosed with a background of black—it was very likely velvet, for no light was caught there to break the complete darkness of it. Neither photographs nor drawings could give anything but the slightest suggestions of the gold frames, or sharp gold lines, or the forms like Gothic abstractions or however you would describe them, that, standing alone against the black, defined the scenes. Three huge tragic masks hung to the front above the action. Vast daggers of light poured down, crossed, pierced, flooded the scenes of the witches. The banquet hall with its gold and light and figures—above all, Lady Macbeth's robe, in which by a hidden combination of many shades an unheard-of intensity of red was achieved—defied any conveyance in words. Some of the effects were like those of early paintings where more than one incident or scene is visible at the same time. For example, in the sleepwalking scene you could see Lady Macbeth crossing from the left of the stage in her long white gown before you saw her enter through the form that made the doorway. The very intensity of this dramatic use of abstraction in this décor for *Macbeth* makes the effort to describe it merely futile. What an irony, considering its place in our stage annals! If this *Macbeth* could have gone over with more success or been more widely understood, it would very likely have marked for our theatre art a revolution of the highest significance.

THE KINGDOM OF GOD

The Kingdom of God, by G. Martinez Sierra. Translated by Helen and Harley Granville-Barker. Ethel Barrymore Theatre. December 17, 1928.

THE FIRST act of *The Kingdom of God* opens in the garden of the old palace of the Duke of Torre Blanca, now converted into an asylum for old men. We see the two old men with their pride, their boasting and quarreling, their resentments and policies, their greed, their drunkenness when a peseta comes their way; and then the young sisters of St. Vincent de Paul, with their heavy basket of potatoes. One of these is Sister Gracia, the daughter of a Minister, the granddaughter of a Marquis; she has given up her home and the pleasures of society for this work with the maimed and halt of the world, she desires to enter so far as she may in this life into the kingdom of God. We see the Mother Superior, then Sister Gracia's parents, her father and mother and sister; her mother pleads with her to give up this consorting with disgusting creatures and to come home to the career she was born to—this would be possible because of the fact that in the order of St. Vincent de Paul the vow is taken yearly and does not bind for life. Liborio comes shivering in, an old black man from Cuba, and we see the young girl—she is nineteen—how she humors him as if he were a child and invents thoughts to comfort him. Her parents leave Sister Gracia there in this retreat, with the sisters, and with these old men who are the ashes, the end, the comedy and irony and foolish pathos of human life and who are to Sister Gracia like her dolls, like her father, like the play of her gentle, tender heart.

In the second act we are in the patio of a maternity home, for women who "have come to grief." There are the girl at the fountain, washing clothes, mocking, whose child has died; the girl whose betrayal has made her so bitter that her baby is nothing to her; and the dumb young mother who fears everyone but Sister Gracia and the doctor. Then Quica appears, her fourth visit to the institution, which she finds agreeable enough, with people to nurse you and feed you and all that; she has spent four years and six months here free and had a thousand pesetas out of them to boot; lovers and betrayals, babies and nuns, do nothing to her zest for love. The point of this scene, so far as concerns Sister Gracia, is the way in which this agony of life around her is tearing her heart, and the culmination arrives with Enrique, the doctor, who loves her and begs her to renounce this calling and marry him; there would be plenty to do as his wife. But she will not leave this work of God's, to Whom she has given her love. The end of this scene finds her trembling before the renunciation of this human happiness, and entreating the Mother Superior to write and get her transferred. She would like to leave at once, she says; it is a case of conscience.

In the Orphanage, where the third act takes place, there is a shortage of food, the board mismanages, cheats, pulls wires; and in the midst of these difficulties, so wordly and squalid, and among her orphans, with their fighting, clandestine love affairs, riots and bullyings, Sister Gracia, now an old woman of seventy, supporting herself with a stick against her rheumatism, but crafty and wise, sweet, gentle, witty, full of the irritability of her infirmities, full of humor, complete in her own soul, rules. She lives in God, but she and the Saviour have little time to talk to each other now, the paternosters must wait on hungry mouths within her walls, evil-doers without, busy hours, quick, watchful eyes. One of her old boys, Juan de Dios, comes in from his first bullfight, which he has fought for nothing, but has won; next Sunday he will get a thousand pesetas. He brings the bull's ear to her. The crowd is waiting for him at the gate; he begs Sister Gracia to come that far with him, so that they may see them together.

There is a riot then about the bad stew, for which there are no peppers. Felipe, one of the orphans, leads the rebellion. The boys plan to go out and sack, they will break open doors and take what they need. Felipe makes a revolutionary speech, after the manner of firebrands everywhere. The boys rise from their seats and start for the town as Sister Gracia returns to face them. She sends them all back to the table, and speaks to them. Do they think they are the only hungry people in the world? There are those poorer still, without mattresses to lie on, without a crust to eat. Men break God's laws, they devour each other, but God does not smile on the wrongs of the world, he endures them, for how long, who knows? All that we can do is try to make the world good. And that we can do not by hate but by love. What they have suffered here, of hunger and injustice, they can remember afterward and seek to put suffering and wrong out of life, by love, by laws. They must promise her that when they are gone and are among men they will spend their blood to the last drop, in order that children may not be forsaken any more, and no more mothers be wronged and go hungry and be ashamed to carry their children in their arms. The orphans promise, repeating her words after her, and now, with supper over, she sends them off to bed, to sleep in peace.

The boys go slowly out, only Felipe remains, sitting on his bench, his head buried in his hands, crying. Sister Gracia goes to him and puts a hand upon his shoulder; he must not cry, men don't cry; they suffer, but they work and hope.

The very fact that such substance is made into a play at all is a part of the foreignness of *The Kingdom of God*, the soul's foreignness as it were; and it is necessary to give this rather long account, however shallow and unsatisfactory, to make this fact clear, and to show also how the drama in this work of Sierra's comes about. In the kind of modern plays we know best, plays Northern or Nordic in their quality and mind, such a story of a woman as this in *The Kingdom of God* would turn more on her inward state, her changes of mind, her development and growth through her experience. But in this Latin piece it is the background itself that carries the drama along. We see first the young girl working among the shreds of life in these old men; then as a woman confronted with the needs of her own body and soul, and with the problem of how life comes into the world, how it comes through the pain of others, how urgent it is and innocent and unceasing, how it cannot be denied; and finally as an old woman surrounded by the life that lies between birth and age, the promise of life opening in these boys and girls, to whom she gives her wisdom, strong rule, humor and love. The theme of her is not inward, introspective, psychological in our familiar sense, but is set against the whole idea of woman the mother, the bosom of life, the love that mediates between harsh law and human needs, which the world of the Mediterranean understands so easily and has turned into the Madonna, the divine mother. Sister Gracia rests for her significance not on her individuality but on her eternity; and she derives her permanence from the need life has of her, moment by moment.

The play is foreign, too, is Latin, in the way the characters are put in, their strong outlining, the typicality of their self-revelation, and their habit of generalizing and running off into philosophic statement anywhere and everywhere. And most of all it is Latin in a particular respect that is difficult for us to understand and that misleads us constantly with regard to the depth of Latin art. I mean the manner in which the subtlety is achieved by a certain *combination* of single simple things instead of by some single complexity. When this method comes off supremely, as in the scene of the young bullfighter and the old Sister Gracia, we cannot see just what has been done but we feel that the sum of these simple motives that make up the scene is one of the most beautiful and moving moments in all the modern theatre.

The difficulties of such foreign art as this appear, as we might expect, at many points in the production, honest though it is and conceived with genuine devotion to this play that is so full of vitality and variety and meaning. Actors who might be good enough as our native American characters and types find themselves straining at these Spanish parts, which, as they became more American and natural, would become less suited to their Spanish *milieu,* and as they became less American and natural would cease to be anything at all. Mr. Harry Plimmer's old Trajano and Miss Georgia Harvey's capital Quica, the erring, repetitive and canny, are the best of these character performances, and the Felipe, a fine part, of Mr. Elisha Cook, Jr., is very good. Mr. McKay Morris plays Enrique the doctor and Sister Gracia's suitor, a brief but cardinal rôle in the structure of the theme, with easy dignity and intelligence. The sisters and Mother Superiors in this production have our usual trouble in such rôles: their mingling of strength and modesty needs to be more simple and offhand.

The leading figure in *The Kingdom of God* is a hard one for our actors because of its peculiar combination of delicate gradations, strong markings, force and tender, human simplicity, and its exhibition of natural emotions playing so freely within such clear and definite conceptions and patterns of thought. Miss Ethel Barrymore distorts the theme and the portrait of her Sister Gracia by the strenuousness she gets into her last scene, that with the rioting boys. She should not make a sermon out of her lines, reducing the children to tears by such thunderous exhorting and delivery. No, what Sister Gracia says is the flower of her being, the gentle, strong music of her life and work and love; it is not these sentiments—all platitudes in their way—that quiet and bless the souls of the children; it is their truth through her. I knew at once that Miss Barrymore had jumped the track when she railed and preached like that and curiously enough I found upon looking afterward into Sierra's text that the stage directions are "speaking quietly." What persuades actors from doing what the dramatist wants and definitely prescribes is one of the mysteries of the stage art. Miss Barrymore's first act is fair enough, bluntly visualized but with its own goodness and beauty; it exhibits throughout that singular dazzle and luminosity of this extraordinary figure in our theatre. Her second act, where the love motive is secured in the drama, is admirably played.

Mr. Watson Barratt's three settings have not distinction, but they are done at least *con amore* and show a real observation of the Spanish scenes.

The Kingdom of God was first produced in 1915, in Barcelona.

STREET SCENE

Street Scene, by Elmer Rice. The Playhouse Theatre.
January 10, 1929.

IN A DRY SEASON, when so many theatres are closed and not a few managers have given up the game for the nonce and gone off to sunny beaches and Hollywood, Mr. Elmer Rice's *Street Scene* has come to many people as a treat, an excellent play, a worthy entertainment; and there is no need to throw any blight over the flower of their enthusiasm. In the realm of the blind, following the Spanish proverb, let the one-eyed be king; we may cheer *Street Scene* and wish it well.

In a setting by Mr. Jo Mielziner, cleverly realistic without being foolishly so, and photographic without idle intrusions of dusty neighborhood detail from Ninth Avenue, where the play is laid, we see the story unwind itself entertainingly, with an amiable pace and plenty of time for the talk of the apartment house people as they go in and out, with engaging colors drawn from the contact of diverse nationalities—Jews, Germans, Irish, Italians and 100 percent Americans—and with a due complaisance and tidy willingness to please. There is a genuinely expert economy in the way in which the life of the Maurrant family is conveyed to us, and an economy of means that is even more expert in the portrait of the wife's career, this doomed Anna Maurrant, whose husband is brutal and indifferent in his treatment of her, is given to drink, is full of principles and ideas as to what a family should be and what his own has got to be, he'll see to that!

The inmates of the apartment house, then, go in and out, linger about the doorstep in the stifling summer heat, sit at their windows, gossip of their children and each other, of the little husband on the third floor who acts as if he were having the baby instead of his thin bit of a wife, of the Hildebrand family whose head has disappeared and who are about to be dispossessed. And through the whole texture of conversation they weave the thread of this pale woman's tragedy on the second floor, the visits of the milk collector that they have all observed, the spreading scandal about Mrs. Maurrant. Idly and emptily they are doing her to death, but it is all part of the day's chatter and the neighborhood news. We see Rose, her daughter, and the married suitor, who wants to take her from the job in his office and set her up in an apartment and a place on the stage; we see Maurrant himself, a member of the stagehands' union, a drinker, sullen and bullying. Meanwhile, Mrs. Jones has something to say about everything, takes her husband, George, to task, and her dog, Queenie, to walk, and professes complete ease of mind about her children, one of whom is a hulking thug and the other almost a tart.

From that on, the play runs its course, clearly foreseen. The baby is born upstairs, Mrs. Maurrant tends the mother all night, she is even more brutally treated by her suspicious husband; he says he is going out of town with a show, her daughter is at the funeral of a member of the firm she works for, and Mrs. Maurrant asks the milk collector—cleverly portrayed by the author as by no means attractive and thus the more indicative of the woman's despair—to come up to her rooms. The husband returns, kills the lover, and mortally wounds the wife, and after a long search is caught by the police. Rose, his daughter, refuses the attentions of the married suitor, and at the last does not accept the love of the Jewish student; she goes away for her own life, with her own ideas about one's dependence on something within oneself and reflections on the history of her father and mother in the light of that theory, not without some smear of egotism—with its attendant confusion—on her own part.

All this time, as a kind of matrix for the story, people have been passing, an ingenious assemblage of types and interests, curiosities of the town, vignettes of Manhattan, incidents of a day, and so on and so on, rendered with an amiable and accurate diversity that carries matters pleasantly along. And in the apartment house itself the well-edited sayings of the different persons and races accompany this drab pageantry and street genre.

Mr. Rice's directing is good. Among the many players necessary for this *monde* of the West Side, Miss Mary Servoss, as the tragic central figure of the woman who is killed, gives a performance that is always convincing, and that, while she is on the stage, lifts the scenes to something like pathos and point. Miss Erin O'Brien Moore, as her daughter, Rose, has to surmount many platitudinous approaches to the character, and speeches that are without imagination or reality, but plays well; she presents a young image that our eyes easily believe in, and a sincere and simple rendering of the character so far as is possible with the lines written for her to speak. Miss Beulah Bondi's Mrs. Jones is excellent playing.

So much for *Street Scene,* then, which on one plane of consideration is pleasantly entertaining. On another plane, where you take the play seriously and where you ask yourself whether for an instant you have believed in any single bit of it, either as art, with its sting of surprise and creation, or as life, with its reality, *Street Scene* is only rubbish, or very close to rubbish. For me, who was not bored with it as an evening's theatre, it is something less than rubbish; it is theatrical rubbish, in that curious, baffling, embodied and persuasive way that the stage provides. The presence of living beings in the rôles engages us, and gives a certain plausibility to whatever takes place and a certain actuality to any character whatever. But is it possible that anyone who could understand the values in the first act of *Anna Christie,* for example, or a play of Chekhov's, could fail to see that the last act in *Street Scene*—to take the most conspicuous let-down in the play—is empty and made up? The girl has found her mother shot, has seen blood, at the hospital she has seen her mother die without speaking, she has seen her father caught and torn and bleeding; the Jewish boy, who loves her so much, offers to leave everything and go away with her, and she stands there making a sententious little speech about dependence on oneself and so on and so on, while nurses with perambulators appear and various persons come prowling around the scene of a murder, and the obvious life goes on, with amusing remarks from odd characters, and the rest of it—obliging journalism in sum. It must be a very elementary principle that the essential idea of a work of art goes through it, and that the themes and conceptions to be expressed must lie inherently in the substance of it, and that they are to be expressed in creation, not in superimposed sentiments. And so it follows that this pseudo-significant patter that the playwright has put into the mouth of his heroine at this point is a bad omen for the play's significance.

Must we gloomily conclude that what most human beings like in the theatre is a farrago of living matter with the sting taken out of it?

If this Anna Maurrant's life and death really bit into us, cost us something, instead of providing a mere thrill and the comfort of pseudo-thought afterward, would we not wreck the stage for rage when we see how little this matter has stung the dramatist? One of the ways we know a work of art is by what its unity in kind has cost, precisely in the same way that the soul within him, determining his form as he comes into the world, prevents a man's having the bulk, strength and peace of an elephant. One of the ways we can tell an artist is by the extent to which reality puts the fear of God into him. A painter, for example, of no worth will paint you anything from Napoleon crossing the Alps to an old mill in Vermont, but a real painter trembles before the mere character of human hands and the problem of their conversion into the unity that is his style.

On a milder level of discourse, we may say that the acting in *Street Scene* furnishes a good instance of one of the problems in the art. For the most part the company at the Playhouse is made up of people who fit the characters ready-made. An Italian plays an Italian, a Jewess a Jewess, and so on. In the hurry and pressure of things there is little time to discover or train actors, perhaps, and perhaps the need for actuality in this particular piece led the casting toward these ready-made types. The result is that in *Street Scene* there is a good deal of entertainment that comes from watching these actual people as we might see them on Ninth Avenue, but very little interest in watching them as actors. They are mostly neither bad nor good. Their resemblances are better than their acting, and they themselves seem more convincing than what they say. As a minor by-product of the perplexity induced by such a situation, I have no idea whether the player written down as Mrs. James M. Qualen, whose janitor, Olsen, seems to me the best performance of the evening, is only a Nordic of that ilk, chosen for his type, or is a capital actor.

JOURNEY'S END

Journey's End, by R. C. Sherriff. Henry Miller Theatre.
March 22, 1929.

WHEN a play has so moving and complete an effect on audiences as the English war play now at the Henry Miller Theatre, and is received with so lively a response and reverence, its news spreads fast. Many people have already heard that *Journey's End* was written by an author not familiar to the profession, that it was first given under more or less amateur circumstances, and afterward produced at the Savoy Theatre by Mr. Maurice Brown, and that it has become one of the events of the London season. And many people, under the sting and emotion of such a play, are sure to say that it is the English answer to *What Price Glory?*, and very much better; and that it is one of the greatest plays ever written—I have already heard both these remarks several times.

The story of *Journey's End* is a unique and poignant one, and turns on hero-worship, nervous degeneration under the strain of the war, force of character, youth, love and kind death. The play has essentially something of the quality of a novel, so single and inward is the thread of its story, a novel with the sounds and lights of a supplementary atmosphere and with divisions for profoundly effective curtains. We see the transfer of one company to take another's place behind the lines. A good deal is told us of Stanhope, who is now in command—he is a fine officer, he has been in continuous service without leave of absence for more than a year, and under the strain of it has become a heavy drinker; his drinking, his bursts of temper, his devotion and tireless labor are bywords among his men. Young Raleigh comes. To the second officer he tells more of Stanhope, how Stanhope's father and his father were friends, how Stanhope had been his hero and was three years ahead of him in school, had visited his home, become engaged to his sister, how he had asked his uncle, the general, to be put into Stanhope's company, had been rebuked but next day found himself listed for it. Then Stanhope appears.

JOURNEY'S END

He resents Raleigh's coming into his company, he is maddened at the thought of the boy's letters home and of his hero-worship, considering what his hero has grown to be. He proposes to censor these letters, and wrests the first one of them from Raleigh's hand. It contains only loyal praise. We have dug-out scenes scattered along, comic matters of food, slackers, and so on, and so on, and finally the colonel proposes a raid, in order to get a German prisoner with possibilities of information. Osborne, the second in command, the wise schoolmaster, Stanhope's best friend, his Horatio and guardian, is chosen, and with him Raleigh, ten men under him. The raid is made. Four men and Raleigh come back alive. All Stanhope can say is to order Raleigh off Osborne's bed. In the next scene Raleigh does not come to the champagne and chicken supper served by way of celebration, there is a row between him and Stanhope which ends by Stanhope's breaking down and crying; he can hold up no longer. Then finally the expected attack begins. Stanhope has had the position wired in an all sides, no one can escape or surrender. Raleigh is brought in wounded. Stanhope is alone with him; Raleigh dies. Stanhope joins the fight outside, as a shell crashes the entrance to the dug-out.

It is necessary to set down at such length the story of *Journey's End* because so much of the play's credit and effect lies in the story.

Taking *Journey's End* as drama you could not say that the actual writing—the lines, words, rhythm of speech—is notable in any way; it is merely average, in fact, though it is never cheap or false in intention. The play would gain in content by the presence of at least one person more profound, if you like—or more profoundly written—than any shown to us; Osborne, the schoolmaster, may be intended as the intellectual element, but he is only a mild study out of a mild novel, as it were; Stanhope, with his high-strung nervous system, has the only brain in the lot. And a number of the scenes, though their purpose is right and their place in the plot right, are not yet quite written and if we heard the play for the second time would come off pretty flat—the scene, for instance, where Raleigh learns that the schoolmaster has been a football celebrity, or, and more so, the scene at dinner after the raid, when the rotter in the company, expanding under the balm of his liquor, is letting us see into his mind. In such scenes the writing lacks all pungency and point, and is not even promising as theatre talent.

It is in this respect, that of writing, of words, of bite and pungency, flash and sting and bravura and gusto, that *Journey's End* compares least well with *What Price Glory? What Price Glory?* is more cerebral, too, and more vibrant than this new play; the whole rhythm and pulse is higher, the texture far richer. The picture of the War is lustier and truer, with more virility and irony, and is more substantial. Indeed, the picture of dug-out life that you get in *Journey's End* has at best the sentimental value of certain sorts of fiction; it is obvious on the face of it that if all that group of men we see there were no more intelligent than they are, there would be more brutality in judging their mutual states of mind and more stupidity and cruel lack of imagination; their shadows and lights would be blacker and whiter and their savors stronger. The gallery of characters in *Journey's End* is more familiar, as types go, in fiction, and more predictable than those in *What Price Glory?*, who represent a more surprising creation and solid talent. On the other hand, this English writer does not rely so much on edge and point, punching things in and smarting them up, as our American writers did, and in the production of his effects he avoids all the benefits of obscenity, profanity, and burly irreverence, on which the other war play drew so heavily. In all these matters, vigor, frankness, gusto and solidity, you could say that *What Price Glory?* tends—and quite consciously, if you remember Falstaff and the Henry plays—to hark back to the Elizabethan, where *Journey's End* savors of modern British fiction and its concern with sentiment. Both the virtues and the faults of this play are more English than American.

Its mediocrities, then, are apparent, but the strong points of *Journey's End* more than balance them. There is, first, the unescapable story, this record of a fine, high-strung young man, mastering his fright and fighting his exhaustion with drink, and the boy whose hero he is, their distance apart, their affection and silences, and at last the boy's death, with a whimper like a hurt child, and the other sitting by him a moment and then going out where death is waiting for him also. The scenes between these two are the best moments in the play; they are, in fact, stirring and convincing, wholly and deeply dramatic, and by being so deeply English take on a certain universality.

There is the study of Stanhope, the leading figure, which is the most subtle and sustained creation that we have had in the theatre for a long time. It is fresh and close, and it profits by the author's lack of a professional craft that might have led him to ladle things out more obviously. This rôle profits also by the acting of Mr. Colin Keith-Johnston, who plays it with fine intensity and understanding. As for the company in general, if you mean acting like that of the Moscow Art Theatre in Gorki's *Lower Depths,* with all the infinite pains, shading, poignancy and color that we saw there, the acting of this British company is one thing; but if you mean the average standards of our theatre it is consistently fair, well directed and adequate. There are instances, such as Mr. Evelyn Roberts' Captain Hardy, or Mr. Leon Quartermaine's Lieutenant Osborne, of a special kind of English self-consciousness, but for the most part the performances, sometimes dignified, sometimes coy, are good enough. The best of them are Private Mason, who serves the mess, and the fat Trotter, good English character-acting by Mr. S. Victor Stanley and Mr. Henry Wenman.

There is the story, then; there is the study of Captain Stanhope; and there is, finally, the dominant quality of *Journey's End*: its lyricism. The most striking thing about this English play is this underlying poetic feeling, not a poetry of the imagination so much, but rather a poetry of human concern. The noise of the front outside, the darkness and danger, the problem of war, really come to very little in the sum of our impression; what we follow is that still small voice, most hidden and inner, of what these beings feel within themselves and about each other. The best things in *Journey's End* are not so much written there as they are felt by the author. It is a voice old in English poetry and daily interest, but, though we seem to feel its appeal, less remembered by us. It flowers in such legends as Sir Philip Sydney, in Shakespeare and in common writing—a tenderness toward all life, a concern about the individual's details and state of mind and his relation to other men, a sense of our human life as complete and absorbed in itself, romantic and subjective. Through this innate lyricism *Journey's End* finds the basis on which it rests, and becomes true in its own way, and, is, with its sentiment, shyness and passion, a moving play.

MEI LAN-FANG

Mei Lan-fang and his Company, in Repertory. Forty-ninth Street Theatre. February 17, 1930.

WE KNOW how much, ordinarily, is seen in the arts—very little indeed by the average eye; and how much rubbish is talked, rubbish that is somewhat insincere, faddish, imitative, or else fetched up from sentiments within the speaker and not from any perception of the work of art. How much more chance, then, a review of Mei Lan-fang has of being oblique, bluffing or fatuous! In his case more than in most, a criticism is apt to be mere autobiography on the critic's part.

In an art that belongs within the tradition of an old race, and in the presence of an artist considered by them a great artist, a good part of our attendance must be taken up with humility. I spent a fair part of my time, during this performance of the Chinese company, trying merely to learn, as one learns a language. We see what we can, and must be thankful for what perception is granted us. In this performance of Mei Lan-fang I saw enough to see that for me it was the highest point in the season's theatre and in any season since Duse's visit and the Moscow Art Theatre's production of Chekhov's plays.

As to the Chinese theatre, we perceive in the first place that it is an art based on music, or at least musically seen, and is a complete art consisting of music, speech and dancing in the full sense, which includes dance movement, gymnastics, pantomime and gesture. Most of the music was lost on me, of course, with its foreign scale and intention, but I was surprised to find how much of it takes on meaning for an outsider and how often the themes are easily distinguishable. But most of all I was struck by the mingling of music and action that I saw on the stage, the admirable accentuation of gesture by music, the way in which the music gave the tempo to the acting; and by the security of an effect achieved through such delicate means. I could tell, however foreign the music, or rather his tone, by a curious brightness and metal, that Mei Lan-fang's voice was highly unusual, and that the poetic wholeness of his art arose from an astonishing unity of time, tone, emotional rhythm and bodily control.

This Chinese art is, in the second place, stiffened and syllabled with conventions; some of which are familiar to us and thought of largely with naïve, indulgent humor, but many of which, not known at all, underlie, like an alphabet, the entire theatrical occasion. The masks of these faces, painted with black predominating where fierceness is to be symbolized, with blue for cruelty, red for the heroic, and so on; the stage properties, where moving a chair may imply another apartment, through whose imaginary door you bend to pass; the duster of horse hair, denoting the divine, the heroic, the holy; the whip standing for the horse; the elaborate usages for the sleeve; the use of the eyes and hands; the prologue on the actor's entrance, the couplet following; there are these and numberless other conventional symbols. Foreigners seize on them for harmless discussions—the easiest way out of so far-off an art—and we can read of them in the voluminous notes supplied by George Kin Leung for the brochure of information that is given out with the programs. We cannot dwell upon them here, but it is interesting to consider their relation to us. There is one element to them, the visual, that we can take for the aesthetic qualities obviously present. The other element in them—whether we know the implications or not—is the symbolistic. When purely symbolistic, these conventions represent—without reproducing—ideas, actions, things, exactly as words do, which in themselves are nothing but sound. There is this difference, however, between these symbols and words: a movement or object symbolizing a beautiful idea, personage, place, tends to be created into something in itself more beautiful and worthy of the association, whereas a word remains the same, plus perhaps our efforts to put beauty into its employment. These Chinese conventions in themselves have doubtless, therefore, taken on a greater and greater perfection.

It is interesting, also, to note the Greek and Elizabethan parallels in this Chinese theatre, the obvious and slighter Elizabethan ones, mostly theatre mechanics, and the more profound Greek characteristics. One of these Greek similarities consists of the scenes, developed over and over again and falling into types, the Parting Scenes, Recognition Scenes, Ironic Scenes, and so on. The other is the method, practised always by the Greeks—a method that is based on our physical nature, for we rise to song with an access of vitality, and that has always seemed to me inevitable in the highest development of the theatre—I mean the rising into music where the pitch of the dramatic idea and emotion seems to require it.

It is interesting to note the antiquity of this Chinese theatre, going back almost thirty centuries perhaps; to note the continuity and innovations in its history, its deep relation to the Chinese soul, the innovations and inventions that are credited to Mei Lan-fang; and to note the fact that the Chinese see these plays from time to time throughout their lives, which means listening to and learning a perfection—something like great music heard many times, always different, always the same—which is one of the signs of excellence in any work of art, and of sophistication rather than semi-barbarism in a theatre public.

Of Mei Lan-fang himself, such facts as that he is the greatest actor in China, a public idol, with the highest honors, "The Foremost of the Pear Orchard" and the head of the Ching-Chung Monastery, that he was an accomplished musician at seven, a success in feminine roles at twelve, and that his house, collections and position in Chinese culture today are known over China—these things we can read in a hundred places and in more than one language.

Taking him—in the way an actor as a draamtic medium must be taken—as we take a musical instrument or the pigment for a painter, we see that Mei Lan-fang is of medium height, slender, with sure, close-knit muscles, small, supple wrists, superb support in the waist—from which the fine movements and gestures of the torso proceed—a remarkable control of the neck, and perfect poise and suspension in the ankles. His face is the classic Chinese oval, with highly expressive eyes. His make-up, that overlay of carmines and darker tones, is the most beautiful I have ever seen in the theatre. The diction is sharp and always pointed. The famous hands are curiously like those in Botticelli, Simone Martini and other painters of the fifteenth century. They are rather tense in form, with long fingers, squarish-tipped; not so much our ideal of the hand, which is based on the seventeenth century of Rubens and Van Dyke, but incredibly trained in the conventions and dance of the Chinese actor's art. And even with no knowledge of that art, you can see with what perfection Mei Lan-fang begins his speech, prolongs the word that gives the musicians the cue to begin, retards the words by which the music is warned to stop.

For our purposes, however, it seems to me that all this is unimportant compared to one point that bears on all art basically. I mean the relation of the art of Mei Lan-fang—the greatest in his field—to reality. That question of the relation of art to reality is the greatest of all questions with regard to art. It parallels—to employ the terms closest to us humanly—the relation of the spirit to the body, or, to go the other way round, the relation of the passing to the permanent, of the casual in the moment to the flower of it.

On this subject much has been written about Chinese art and about this actor that is misleading. We will stick to Mei Lan-fang. About this actor we are told to note his impersonation of women and his impersonation of various emotions. Words are weak and dependent things, and nothing could be more confusing than these are likely to be. In the first place, there is no attempt to impersonate a woman. The female rôles are the most important in the Chinese theatre; and he, in the kind of female rôle that he presents, strives only to convey the essence of the female quality, with all its grace, depth of feeling, its rhythm of tenderness and force. This distillation that he employs of the material into its inherent and ideal qualities, Mei Lan-fang does with an economy both brilliant and certain, a studious care, delicacy and inner music. The impression is one of a perfection, at once fragile and secure, that is astonishing.

But even more important—for the Chinese critics have already often warned us not to go astray with regard to these female rôles—even more important for us is the matter of his realism in general. I found myself most impressed in this regard during the piece from the Ming Dynasty, where the princess stabs the general who had destroyed her family, and then kills herself with his sword. This seemed to me more satisfying than the play about the husband's return, for in the last it was easy to see the movement away from the older, high style. What we must say about the realism and abstraction and stylization of Mei Lan-fang's art is that, exactly as is the case in the classic Chinese art, we are astonished at the precision of its realistic notations and renderings, and are dazzled by the place these take in the highly stylized and removed whole that the work of art becomes. These movements of Mei Lan-fang, that way he has of keeping the whole body alive, even in the stillest moments of the action, of putting that continuous movement or vibration into the head as it springs from the neck; that voice that in its sheer tone moves away from actuality; that sophisticated, poetic use of the eyes, those expressions of fear, pity, murderous resolution, despair, and so on, that come over his face; none of these is impersonation or reality in the usual sense. They are real only in the sense that great sculptures or paintings are real, through their motion in repose, their impression of shock, brief duration and beautiful finality. Every now and then—very rarely—in acting we see this happen; I mean a final creation, free from merely incidental matter, of an essential quality in some emotion, the presentation of that truth which confirms and enlarges our sense of reality. But I have never seen it so securely and repeatedly achieved as in Mei Lan-fang.

THE GREEN PASTURES

The Green Pastures, by Marc Connelly. Based on "Ol' Man Adam and his Chillun" by Roark Bradford. Mansfield Theatre. February 26, 1930.

WE MUST try at the outset to guage the credit that goes to Mr. Marc Connelly, who wrote this stage piece of *The Green Pastures*, and to Mr. Roark Bradford, who wrote the stories from which the play arose.

On one hand Mr. Bradford is the originator, the source and the creative element in almost everything about the play that is profoundly worthwhile or rich with any true intensity and color of life. The basic interpretation of the Negro mind and spirit—the conception of God as a kind, all-clever, good-humored and indulgent father who likes to have his people happy about him; the easy and casual business of the universe, the naïve vision of things in general—is Mr. Bradford's. Mr. Connelly has genuinely felt the character of the book, and at times has kept it and given it a place in the theatre. He has found an effective dramatic sequence for the whole. The device of starting off the mood and plausibility of the play by a Sunday School scene in which the children are hearing the lessons of sacred history; and the theme of the progress of God's career—from that first shiny heaven, full of his angels, all sinless, happy and hungry for fish-fries, songs and innocent pleasure, through the creation of man, who gives him a heap of trouble, and on, after the sight of man's suffering, to the thought that he must save the world by some suffering of his own —belong to Mr. Connelly.

Leading the play thus through numerous scenes and incidents that may sometimes appear merely casual and relaxed, on to a final summit, makes for the inclusion of many conceptions familiar to us in religious art—that, for instance, of God needing man as man needs God—and by ending on the note of God's sacrifice through his own son, achieves a genuine and mystical level. And this is accomplished with no violation of the material of the book. I was brought up very near to Mr. Bradford's own country. The model for his central figure was a preacher on my cousin's plantation, in fact, and Negroes, as I know them at least, have Jesus as the center of their religion and close to their warm hearts. There are God, the Devil and Blessed Jesus; the need for the saints and a Virgin to intervene between them and a stern judge and magical Satan is not felt. Their idea of a Father in Heaven makes such unnecessary. In Mr. Connelly's play, in Mr. Bradford's book and in Mr. Richard Harrison's portrayal of the Lawd, this figure of God, with his kindness, his tricks, his patience, pleasures and human troubles and ups and downs, is a remarkable interpretation of the whole soul of the people in the play. It is, in a fine sense, a creation of an idea in dramatic terms. The fact remains, nevertheless, that most of this, certainly the major part of it with any value, comes from Mr. Bradford's book. *Ol' Man Adam and his Chillun* is a work of full, easy-going, deep and lovely talent. "Based on" is not a very exact or very fair term to describe the relation between *The Green Pastures* and the book: "partly borrowed from, partly based on, partly barnacled on to" would be a somewhat better, at least, way of putting it.

To the whole occasion the designs of Mr. Robert Edmond Jones for the many charming scenes have contributed a large share. None of the settings is callous, mechanical or bad; all are at least conceived with some imagination and done *con amore* and with a notable variety of touch and invention. One scene is especially beautiful: the setting and the whole design for the death of Moses, with that barren world of dust around him, the children of Israel marching past, all dust-colored too; Moses in the centre of the stage; the passing farewell hands laid on his shoulder; his superb make-up and costume; the whole effect like an austere, magnificent Tintoretto. All this, together with the words, the picture of the children of Israel vanishing toward that Promise Land, which Moses has seen but cannot enter, the coming of God to lead his servant to that other eternal Promise Land, Moses' hand in the Lawd's, his head on the Lawd's breast, was one of the most impressive and beautiful scenes that have come out of the American theatre.

There are defects in *The Green Pastures* which the very excellence of so much of it makes more important. It is one of those instances of the theatre art in which the dramatist must find it worthwhile to go on working at it, for the sake of a greater degree of perfection, no matter what public applause and box-office rewards are whizzing round his head. Mr. Connelly has taken these writings of Mr. Roark Bradford's, already on their way to a long life, and added to them his own taste and at times, as in the scene of Harlem life, for example, a very considerable lack of taste. He has brought to it all his theatrical ingenuity and sympathetic fancy. Of the scenes in which the writing is bad, we may cite as the worst that where Cain, fleeing into a strange land of Nod, meets the gal who is to be his wife. As it is written now, with the detail of the kiss—which is not, as I have observed Negroes, a characteristic impulse or theme—with the dialogue stretched out into such a variety of more or less effective and often quite cheap stage motives, with the dialect itself not convincing, the scene is a failure indeed. In this case the story in the original Bradford is far sounder and better Negro psychology and imagination.

As to the singing that separates the scenes all through *The Green Pastures,* some of it needs shortening. As it went when I saw the play there was a good deal of talking in the audience during many of the songs—and all of it, if it is to be true for the ears that have heard all their lives the real thing in the South, needs the addition of some heavy voices: Negro basses and men's voices singing second. We do not now get the full, moving, unforgettable effect that the spirituals can give. That applies to the truth of the singing taken as a fact racially. Taking the spirituals as part of the work of theatre art that is now at the Mansfield, I should say that they are sometimes much too apropos. At the last moment, for example, when the Lawd sits in his chair surrounded by the heavenly hosts, and the idea springs into his mind of his own necessity for suffering, the spiritual sung is, quite rightly, about Jesus, but sounds too much like a choir, in the first place—which is true of most of the singing throughout the evening and in the second place, it bursts out with all the appropriate comment of an oratorio, and worse luck, with the enthusiasm of an oratorio finale. There are many spirituals with Jesus as the theme, and a simple effect of these Negroes bursting into one of them, childlike, apropos only by the roundabout course of the heart, emotionally appropriate but not so obviously so, would be far truer to the racial material and much more disarming and moving.

A most regrettable fact about this production of *The Green Pastures*, however, is the employment of a cast made up almost wholly of mulattoes, many of them close to white. This might do for the angels, perhaps, since they might be dreamt of as a cloud-pale celestial people. But a pale, straight-haired Eve or a pale wife for Cain, all this lessens the characteristic racial quality, throws away something very pathetic and right and necessary. More than half the company have a more or less Southern Negro voice and accent, but little that is of the same warmth and sincerity; and most of their movements, like their voices, are sharpened, and this, too, is a sad blight on the occasion. Most Negroes are good acting mediums—as a musical instrument may be a good medium—but they are often hardly actors at all. The company in *The Green Pastures,* however, acted better than the usual serious Negro players. Mr. Tut Whitney's Noah was fair enough, Mr. Wesley Hill's Gabriel was capital. As the Lawd Mr. Richard B. Harrison gave a performance that was always right, intelligent, simple and fine.

I must say, finally, that we can thank Mr. Connelly and Mr. Bradford for what they have done about the Negro. We have had too many of those portrayals of the Negro for his primitive color and impulses, his sexual powers, his alluring animality—too often writings that only insult the subject and, what's more, reflect the repressions and complexes of the author. It is high time we heard more of their fancy, humor and patience, their devotion, easy temper and rich sensuous gifts, their easy and imaginative love of life and their simple natural goodness.

THE PHILADELPHIA LYSISTRATA

Aristophanes' Lysistrata, English Version by Gilbert Seldes. Walnut Street Theatre, Philadelphia. April 28, 1930.

THE Philadelphia Theatre Association has for its immediate aim the production of a series of dramas that, beginning with the Greek drama, will represent "step by step the various courses in dramatic history, by their masterpieces." The immediate scheme and financial support come from the late Horace Howard Furness, Jr.

At the start, I may say that to begin with a Greek comedy seems to me wise. Nobody knows just how the tragedies were done. We know even less, perhaps, of how the comedies were done; but the situation is at least eased by the ease of comedy itself. If the high spirits, the extravagance, the sound human comment is there, the precise forms of production may be looser and more freely adapted; there is less of Zion than in Aeschylus or Sophocles or Euripides, and we may accordingly be more at home. Tragedy calls for the grand style and for a severity of training in the actors and dancers that is outside our tradition and possibility, but comedy is more obliging and adaptable.

The *Lysistrata* was a good choice. There is no great amount of the literary allusions often found in Aristophanes and no historical and political foundation that we must necessarily know. The comedy turns, as freely as ever, on the question of the male egotism and the female relation to it, on men in war and heroics, on women in war, on women and men in love. The story everyone knows: that plan of Lysistrata's to bring the men to their senses by denying them the conjugal rights of love and so to end the war between Athens and Sparta. The women, old and young, seize the Acropolis, repel the siege of the old men and the amorous advances of the young, and at length bring about the treaty of peace and friendship between the two countries. You listen to this play and are reminded of Congreve's observation about women's great heat and natural coldness. You see how women, loving men for their brave bodies, their courage and strong arms, and for the silly heroism that leads them on, are yet able, when they choose, to see from a barnyard level the capers of these lusty eagles and how absurd they can be made to seem, the captain with his shining armor carrying off a little soup in his helmet, the big talk, the vanity, wind and bombast, the Homeric whistling to keep one's valor up. You see how fully women know what chains and ties, what hungers and disruptions, exist in men and lead to women. They know their own power. They know, also, their own need for men, and the biological difference in the timing of this need; they can wait. In the comedy they wait with a vengeance and the men do as Lysistrata wills.

This curiously sound, universal and penetrating comedy, so healthy, accurate and exuberant, is, then, a good choice. There remains only to report on Mr. Norman Bel Geddes' achievement in the direction and décor, Mr. Seldes' version, and the company's acting.

Miss Fay Bainter, in the rôle of Lysistrata, actually gained by not being a strapping goddess; there was something of pure will in her command of her weaker sisters that made a more amusing comment on the female influence in human society; she gave an intelligent performance, not very magnetic, but fair enough. Miss Hortense Alden, in the part of Myrrhina, who enacts the famous scene with the mattress, pillow, unguents and other agencies by which the husband's flame is baffled and delayed, played with real comedy and a good speed; and Miss Miriam Hopkins, as a much weaker sister spirit, played delightfully. Mr. Sydney Greenstreet, as the fat president of the male senators, operatic and crooked, and Mr. Ernest Truex, as Myrrhina's husband, gave hearty and gay performances. Miss Mary Blair took the rôle of the First Old Woman, largely contrived—with a genuine dramatic gain for a modern version of the play—by Mr. Seldes to carry some of the burden of the original chorus in Aristophanes. That strange and distinct talent of Miss Blair's gave the part no little splendor and acrid point, it was a fine performance. Some of the players, Miss Hope Emerson, for example, who did the Spartan Amazon, Lampito, could not act at all, but we may let that pass. There might well have been a more extensive conviction of Greek physique and temptation when the husbands return to these sighing but rebellious ladies. Which is to say, a few more beautiful male presences—achieved by make-up and art, if not actually beautiful. This is needed to point the comic meaning; Aristophanes intends that not only these longing males but these wives themselves, however resolute, should do a bit of suffering.

Mr. Gilbert Seldes rearranged, with the chorus of old women, the opening of the play for an ensemble effect where Aristophanes begins more singly with Lysistrata. This device ties the play more to the décor side of the occasion, perhaps, and in that sense is a gain; but the original beginning is more dramatic. The new version strikes happily on the ear, it has a real theatrical beat; and it is full of turns and quips that are for the most part akin to the original gayeties in the dramatist's Athenian heart. The tone of Mr. Seldes' writing is admirable; and, where there is need, the fuller sound that denotes the more serious implication comes readily into his style. You have only to look into the usual translation from classic comedy to see how fluent and alive this new rendering always is. Meantime it is nothing against Mr. Seldes or Mr. Geddes to say that in all honesty Aristophanes is untranslatable, which is practically a truism in any discussion of Greek drama. He has an elusive, full, flying quality, something of glow and shimmer and lyric brightness, both brutal and fanciful, that wings its way beyond the mere words. We should keep reminding ourselves to call this *Lysistrata* not a translation but an adaptation.

The setting that Mr. Norman Bel Geddes has designed for *Lysistrata* consists of two plinths with a double gate between, denoting the entrance to the Acropolis, various walls, a descent of steps whose sides are sheer planes, varying constantly in their different lines, and a forestage that carries well out into the auditorium of the theatre and ends in steps. To the steps on one side, behind hangings where the boxes should be, leads an entrance to the stage. The colors are in varying reds, with gradations into grays, browns, blues, yellows, and so on, set against the changing sky beyond. It is a superb design, active and alive in every part, and highly dramatic. Most of all it is dramatic by means of the subtle levels, the play of elevations and upward and downward rhythms. The animation given to the players through this one means constantly reminded me of Shakespeare. Presences that flutter and fly and engage us in their contagious feelings and actions by means of Shakespeare's poetic style do something of the same thing in *Lysistrata* by means of their places in the scene; a flutter and stream of life appears to pour from the stage.

Some of the costumes are excellent, some flat or mussy or worse. The make-ups are far too casual. Most of the headdresses are bad, and the arrangment and style of the hair in nearly every case is inexcusable.

There are two things, certainly, that Mr. Geddes should do with his production. In numerous places, it should be cut; things are dwelt on long after their comedy and dramatic value are exhausted. In the first scene of the old men, for instance, two-thirds could be spared, and the meaning remain all the more striking. The other need is for a greater economy and simplification now and then. A longer moment is needed here and there in which there is less commotion and multiplicity. Such an economy would rest and enliven the total effect of the evening; and, what is even more important, it would afford a relief or contrast against which the extraordinary vitality in action and design would appear more distinctly. A more distinct rhythm of reserve and abundance would reveal even further the fine teeming quality behind the whole.

In a sense, however, this last point is only a way of indicating what is the most promising and rich characteristic of Mr. Geddes' genius, its abundance. He throws off enough in a production like this of *Lysistrata* to nourish a score of small designers through as many seasons, and when all is said and done, you feel that he could go right into another creation with powers as full. In this respect of abundance and excess, he resembles the Renaissance, and is, as well, very happily adapted to Aristophanes, who poured into the comedy such inexhaustible powers of invention and his own kind of poetry. The theatre gift of Mr. Geddes is in the nature of a source, and, through that, exhibits the harshness, beauty, surprise and prolific creation that is proper to it.

These notes on his *Lysistrata,* however good or bad they may be, constitute an important record in the American theatre.

THE SHADOW OF WINGS

The House of Connelly, by Paul Green. Martin Beck Theatre. September 28, 1931.

WE ALL in our youth must have wondered as to how it was that sinners and side-steppers by the hundreds escape the world's censure of notice, while such as Guenevere, Héloise, Francesca or Macbeth or Othello go on forever, remembered and weighed, loved, hated, wept over and punished. We see later that it is because they are worth the trouble, include some scope of human nature, that those who forget are forgotten, that, in sum, wings cast shadows. For this reason it is a high compliment to say that the Group Theatre, with their production of Paul Green's play, invite of us all real criticism and concern.

The simple information about the Group Theatre is that for some years its organization, or dream at least, has been under way; that in it are a number of players who might prosper in the obvious commercial sense; that part of its present state is due to the assistance of the Theatre Guild, from whom come some of the members, some financial support, the play, which was the Guild's property, and the sponsoring of this first production, after the close of which the connection between the Theatre Guild and the Group Theatre stops. The Group Theatre announces a plan for other plays, in something of a repertory system, and expresses the hope of developing, through a variety of rôles and casting and through working together, a company of actors.

In this first production by the Group Theatre we have a play that the dramatist could not quite write and that, written or not, the players could not quite act—not by a long sight, to be quite honest, could they act it. The choice, nevertheless, is a good one. The *House of Connelly* provides a sincere vehicle, full of well-defined acting parts; it has less mere facility, a more profound source, more richness in texture and scope in emotion, than most plays that could have been available. This honesty and serious intention in the choice of a play was prophetic of the general character of the whole event. There was not an instance of stage cheating for effect, or of hollowness; there was no forcing, no individual grabbing of the scene; you felt the play free of tampering or intrusion. The promise that lies in such an attitude is obvious; the very genuine welcome given on the part of the daily newspaper reviews to the Group's first venture rested basically on that.

The story of *The House of Connelly* happens in 1905, and turns on the fortunes of an old place where for a hundred and fifty years the Connelly family has lived, in all its pride, its dwindling fortunes, its fading blood. One of the tenants has a daughter, Patsy, who is ambitious for land. She entangles the weak young head of the house, he falls in love with her, she finally is in love with him. The household consists of the old mother, two unmarried sisters and an uncle. The uncle, whose broken-down lusts and knowledge of where the family is drifting teach him some degree of common wisdom, advises the young heir to marry this girl and let her help him get the plantation on its feet. The three women of the family oppose the whole idea of marriage with poor whites. There is a young lady visitor from Charleston, but the match with Will does not come off. In the end the uncle shoots himself, the mother dies, Will and Patsy marry, and, before the return of the wedding party, the two sisters, the younger compelled to it by the older, leave the old house forever. New blood has come into the Connelly stock, the land will live again.

This short outline is necessarily a mere travesty on a play whose best virtues lie not in the story but in the characters and the lines they are given to speak. The characters in Mr. Green's play are clearly defined; their words—all but the heroine's—are profoundly Southern and have been well heard by the dramatist out of his own life in the South. Sometimes a detail though tiny is so startlingly Southern that none but a Southerner could savor its exactness. I will take but one instance, that where the older sister, speaking of how they had tried to do their part by their brother and of their many efforts, says, "We talked to him." You must be born in the midst of the Southern training, where young ladies are taught what is their duty toward the men in the family, and the habit of "entertaining" someone is to be early acquired, if you are to know how perfect that touch remains.

The weakness of *The House of Connelly* lies in the girl motive. There is tied up in this tenant's daughter the theme of the new life blending with the old, the new conditions, the strengthened blood turning back to the land, and so on. But this, though it is so large a motive in the drama, never gets quite expressed. Throughout the play, time is lost in other talk and other scenes when what we need is to get the main theme established. What has seemed to us the old love story of a beggar maid and prince turns out eventually to be the deep-laid scheme of a young woman who, with her eye on possessing the land, has seduced a weak, intense young man, and at last grown to love him. All this crucial matter is poured out in an explanatory speech, delivered at the very crisis of their emotional relations, and written like some college girl's explanation, arid and without the engaging passion or reality that so many of the other characters' lines have had. And the upshot is that thereupon the play's back is broken. On the whole, obviously, the trouble is that at bottom no dramatic image is ever discovered, no action or moment that would create for us the girl's meaning and point in the play.

The uncle's rôle, rather too long for the sting and pathos intended by it, runs somewhat too far toward the Russian flavor; and his suicide seems to me unconvincing, as well as being both untrue to this Southern type or temperament and harmful to the play's total impression on the memory. *The House of Connelly* remains, notwithstanding, well worth a dozen more facile works. Uncle, girl, problem or not, it is at its source poetic, by which I mean the richness, quiver and dilation that it often gives to the material presented.

Of the settings that Mr. Cleon Throckmorton has done, the first is no better and no worse than the usual mess we get when an outdoor scene must be realistic: one way to put it is to say that this setting is on the plane where we actually resent the girl's picking pokeberries off dried oak bushes—a trivial state of mind indeed. The garden scene will do well enough. The third scene, that of the dining room in the old house, is beautiful and is right in its blend of reality and unreality. Of all this season's designs that I have seen, this one setting is the one most genuinely dramatic to the play it serves.

The directing of the play by Harold Clurman, Cheryl Crawford and Lee Strasberg, is, in the earlier scenes especially and sometimes elsewhere, too slow. In its management of the actors as persons, individuals, and in the scenes where the action moves forward and the interest tightens, it is on the whole admirable.

This brings us to a problem very pressing and delicate when a play with Southern characters is to be produced: the extent to which the actors shall attempt the Southern accent. In the first place there is no one Southern accent any more than there is one British accent, but scores, depending on the section, the social class, the individual person speaking, and so forth. In the second place few actors not Southern can catch the right effect. It was to some extent a good decision, then, that led the Group players away from this attempt in their speech (though Mr. Tone in his first scene, however he may have reverted afterward, caught the right placement in the throat, the right voice and rhythm, very well indeed, without travesty and to the furtherance of his effect). Clearly the general intention of the directors was to present the play on its universal side, the story as it might happen anywhere; and this, in so far as concerns the main themes and straight movements of the scenes, was also a wise decision. It is also true that where the acting can really search out the depths of the emotions and character portrayed by a dramatist, mere surface qualities are easily dispensed with and forgotten. The old problem of the relation between exact surface and inner content is obviously involved. And meanwhile it is clear that it might be easier to be cosmic than to be local, in the same sense that prophecy may come more readily than baking bread, and that those who cannot be Southern can at least be universal.

There remains the fact, however, that much of Mr. Green's play is very Southern indeed, double-dyed Southern; and in the light of this the problem of its production is more difficult. Disregarding the matter of the speech, we have left the vividness, animation, responsiveness, whatever you please to call it, that is Southern and that must underlie these characters; who may in turn, once that is achieved, be as universal as you like. In the later scenes, where more action and plot appears, I felt less the lack of both surface and vividness; but in the earlier scenes, where an atmosphere was to be established (not necessarily a Southern atmosphere but the dramatic atmosphere intended by the author) the whole impression seemed to me very poor. In the Christmas-supper scene, most of all, I felt as a theatre critic that the scene was moving and right for the first moment, when the sisters in silence were setting the table; from that point on I felt no flow among the people present; only Mr. Tone and Miss Adler seemed to me to get anything beyond the obvious. As a Southerner, since the flow and poignance in the scene failed me, so that it did not breathe with universal human life, I felt myself unbelievably exasperated at the lack of all Southern quality externally and emotionally. There was also, to be quite honest, about a good deal of the whole event a lack of any personal elegance or distinction, however threadbare; as seen here on the Group Theatre stage the Connellys were not the kind, or if you like, the class, of people whose Chekhovian dramatic débâcle we were supposed to tremble at.

Among the players the sincere intention and right spirit were easily apparent. Mr. Morris Carnovsky as the uncle gave a performance that was technically very careful and sincere, but was neither pathetic nor aristocratic, both essential to his drama. I can only say that the better it got the worse it was, the more tedious, platitudinous and maddeningly deliberate. This reflective cud-chewing in the supposed Stanislavsky method is anything but Southern; it lacks the right self-respect, declamation and proper pride. For violent inner confusion it substitutes only what is external; and it presents what is essentially only relaxed mediocrity where what is needed is a certain lyric vagueness and defeatism. I have seen in my time this Southern type, where there was in the whole failure a dim, sweet echo of bright lances broken, if you like foolishly, in some tragic combination of chivalry and exhaustion.

This is not to pick on Mr. Carnovsky; the dramatist himself does not fully understand the character. Many of Mr. Carnovsky's audience have never seen aristocrats of this type, and so his performance is good enough for them—as Pausanias says of the relic of the monster in the temple, those who have not seen a dragon have at least seen a great pine cone.

Mr. Franchot Tone as the young Connelly achieved the whole pathos and range of a finely written part, with all its immature moods, its tortured, confused loyalties and its power to feel. The depth of such a performance as this of Mr. Tone's must not blind us to its remarkable accuracy also, at every point. He has no great externality of talent, such as the mimetic; but he has what seems to be the finest understanding and the most delicate discernment of values among the members of the Group Theatre.

That the whole event of the Group Theatre's initial venture of *The House of Connelly* should remain ambitious and praiseworthy but not really distinguished as theatre is a thing to be sorry for.

EUGENE O'NEILL'S NEW PLAY

Mourning Becomes Electra, a trilogy: Homecoming, The Hunted, The Haunted, by Eugene O'Neill. Guild Theatre. October 26, 1931.

TO HEAR the bare story, shortly told, of this new O'Neill play, with all its crimes and murders, may easily bring a flouting smile or recall Mrs. Malaprop's announcement of Sir Lucius' and Bob Acres' duel: "So, so, here's fine work, here's fine suicide, parricide, and simulation going on in the fields!" The same thing could be said of *Hamlet* or *King Lear* or *Oedipus King,* of course, but this is sure to be the line the jibes will take from such of the play's critics as are unfriendly or impatient or incapable. As to the length of the event, the actual performance at the Guild could be considerably shortened by going faster in many places, though, take it for all in all, the length of the play itself is for the most part organic with both its meaning and its effect. As to its depressing effects, we will come to that later.

The title, as we see, intends to dispose at the start of the relation of *Mourning Becomes Electra* to the Greek drama. The story of the house of Atreus was set down by Homer, Pindar, Aeschylus, Sophocles, Euripides and divers other Greek writers whose works are not extant. From this house shadowed by an ancient curse, Agamemnon, brother of Menelaus, goes forth to the war at Troy. His wife Clytaemnestra, the sister of Helen, during her husband's absence takes for her paramour Aegisthos and shares the government of Argos with him. In due time Agamemnon, having at the god's behest sacrificed his daughter Iphigenia and bringing with him Cassandra, Priam's daughter, returns, and is murdered by Clytaemnestra and her lover. Electra, his daughter, is shamed and degraded and prays for the return of her brother Orestes, long ago sent out of the country by his mother and now become a man. Orestes returns, kills Clytaemnestra and Aegisthos. He is pursued by the Erinnyes, and only after wandering and agony and a vindication of himself before the tribunal of Athena's Areopagos is he cleansed of his sin.

Mourning Becomes Electra begins with the mother and daughter, Christine and Lavinia, waiting, there in this house of the Mannons, the return of Ezra Mannon from the war, which with Lee's surrender is about over. A thread of romance is introduced between Lavinia and Peter, and between Lavinia's brother, Orin, and Hazel, Peter's sister. Meanwhile Captain Brant comes to call; he pays a certain court to Lavinia, and she, acting on a cue from the hired man, who has been on the place these sixty years, traps him into admitting that he is the son of one of the Mannons who had seduced a Canadian maidservant and been driven from home by his father, Lavinia's grandfather. She has all her data straight now. She has suspected her mother, followed her to New York, where Christine has pretended to go because of her own father's illness, but has in fact been meeting Adam Brant. Lavinia has written her father and her brother, hinting at the town gossip about her mother. We learn that Captain Brant had returned to avenge his mother but instead had fallen passionately in love with Christine, who loves him as passionately as she hates her husband. From this point the play moves on, with the father's hatred of the son, who returns it, the son's adoration of his mother, the daughter's and the mother's antagonism, the daughter's and father's devotion, to Christine's murder of her husband with the poison sent by Brant and substituted for the medicine prescribed against his heart trouble. Part One of the play ends here. Orin returns, after an illness from a wound in the head. Christine tries to protect herself in her son's mind against the plots of Lavinia. Lavinia, in the room where her father's body lies, convinces him with the facts; they trail Christine to Brant's ship, where she has gone to warn him against Orin. Orin shoots Brant. Christine next day kills herself. Brother and sister take a long voyage to China, stop at the southern isles, come home again. Substitutions have taken place, Lavinia has grown like her mother, Orin more like his father. Meanwhile his old affair with Hazel, encouraged at last by Lavinia, who now wants to marry Peter, is canceled; he finds himself making an incestuous proposal to Lavinia and is repulsed by her. He shoots himself. In the end Lavinia, speaking words of love to Peter, finds Adam's name on her lips. She breaks with Peter, orders the blinds of her house nailed shut, and goes into the house, to live there till her death. Justice has been done, the Mannon dead will be there and she will be there.

So bare an account serves the plot a little, but can give scant indication of the direct speeches and actions heavily charged with the burden and meaning of the scenes; nor does it convey the power and direct arrangement of some of them, that, for example, of the brother and sister at Brant's cabin, where the mere visual elements convey as much as the words. The chanty with which this scene opens, the song and the singer's drunkenness, the lonely ship in the dusk, establishing as it does the mood of longing, futility, land-chains and the sea's invitation and memory, is a fine idea and greatly enriches the texture of the play.

It will be obvious that the American dramatist, as the Greek did, used a well known outline which he could fill in to his purpose. Obviously, too, Ezra Mannon is Agamemnon, Captain Brant Aegisthos, Christine Clytaemnestra, Lavinia Electra, and Orin Orestes. But to dismiss the matter by saying that Mr. O'Neill has merely repeated the classic story in modern terms is off the track. Let it go at that and you will miss even the really classic elements in the play and get only the Greek side of it that is self-evident and that would be easy for any dramatist to imitate.

The story itself follows the Greeks up to the middle of the third division of the play, and here the incest motive, the death of Orin and the transference of the whole situation and dramatic conclusion from the mother to the sister depart from Aeschylus, Sophocles and Euripides. Adam Brant's relation to the family adds to the rôle of the lover the motif of a blood relationship. The old hired man, the confidant, parallels to some extent a Greek device, familiar to us in countless plays. The townspeople and workmen are now and again a kind of chorus. Many of the shadings and themes are from the older plays; for a good example, the servant's line in Aeschylus about the dead killing one who lives, which underlies one of the new play's main themes. The death of the lover, as in Aeschylus and Euripides, not as in Sophocles, comes before that of the mother, with throws the stress where the O'Neill play needs it. The division of the play into three parts is, of course, like the trilogy of the Greek dramatists. On the other hand, the dividing line is much less distinct in *Mourning Becomes Electra;* the final curtain of the first part, for example, falls, it is true, on Mannon's death, as in Aeschylus it does on Agamemnon's, but there is not the same effect of totality because of the stress put on Lavinia; in *Agamemnon* Electra does not even appear.

The magnificent theme that there is something in the dead that we cannot placate falsely is in the Greek plays and in the O'Neill play. The end of the play is by imaginative insight Greek in spirit: Lavinia goes into the house, the blinds are closed forever, the stage is silent, the door shut, the exaltation is there, the completion, the tragic certainty. Finally, the peculiar kind of suspense employed in the play is Greek. The playwright has learned the adult suspense of the classics as compared with the adolescent concept of suspense, hit off happily enough at times, that reigns in the romantic drama of the North. Classic suspense does not depend on a mere crude strain, wondering how things will turn out, however entertaining and often dramatic that effect may be. The classic suspense has even a biological defense: you know that in life you will come to death, but just how the course of all your living will shade and fulfill itself you do not know, and you are borne up by an animal will to survive, a passionate participation, an absorbed contemplation of the course to be run, till the last moment completes itself. In the classic form, where the outcome is already known, lies the highest order of suspense. Knowing how things will end, you are left free to watch what qualities and what light will appear in their progression toward their due and necessary finish. You hang on what development, what procession exactly of logic, ecstasy or fate, will ensue with them, what threads of beautiful or dark will come into their human fabric. Suspense proves thus to be not necessarily a contrivance, effective as that may be; it is an inner quality.

It is interesting in our confused and feministic epoch that this new employment of the theme gives the play to Electra. Nowhere in Greek does this happen. From Sophocles there survives what must be only a section of a trilogy, the *Electra;* and though so much of the torment and waiting has been hers, Electra is at the end let off with a betrothal to Orestes' faithful Horatio, Pylades, and the forebodings and remorse rise in Orestes only, who has struck the death blow on his mother. In Euripides' *Electra* the conclusion is the forebodings of Orestes and the marriage of Electra to Pylades; in his *Orestes*

Electra cleaves to her brother, who is in a violent neurotic sickness, quite modernly indicated; they are both in danger from the State for their action, and the whole situation is solved with a trivial and silly dénouement, gods from the machine, killings and abductions, wholly undramatic and redeemed, in so far as it is redeemed, only by Euripides' dialectic and poetic glamor. In Aeschylus, Electra appears only in the middle of the trilogy; the central hero is the royal line, represented by Agamemnon and Orestes.

Along with these more accessible and manifest likes and dislikes, there are numerous points about Mr. O'Neill's play that are additions to or changes from the original Greek and that are yet both high creative invention and, in modern terms and material, re-creations in the most profound sense of Greek equivalents. The most brilliant of these is the incest motive, coming toward the last of the play. (We must recall Shelley's remark that of all tragic motives incest is the most powerful, since it brings the passions most violently into play.) For Orestes the gray forms at the back, invisible at first to all but himself, are the Erinyes, the Furies who will avenge the crime he has committed within his own blood. They are the daughters of night, and when they have been appeased, their other selves, the Eumenides, the Gentle Ones, will pass by and leave him peace. For Orin Mannon there comes the sudden form of his desire; Incest: the realization and admission of what it has all been about all along, his feelings toward his father, toward his mother, toward Brant, toward Lavinia. This recognition of his obsession is his avenging Erinyes. In this detail alone might rest the argument that Eugene O'Neill, placing a Greek theme in the middle of the last century, has written the most modern of all his plays.

The motive of the resemblance among the three men, Mannon, Orin and Brant, is a great dramatic image: it provides a parallel to the Greek motive of a cursed house, and at the same time remains modern and fresh. The Greek husband returned from the war with his paramour and after sacrificing his daughter; Mannon's return will bring the son also home again, to a more subtle and complex situation than the other. The Islands of the Blest, everywhere in Greek dreams, the southern islands that are the symbol of so much modern meaning in *Mourning Becomes Electra,* make a fine motif. The mother in *Mourning Becomes Electra* is not killed by her son but takes her own life; his essential murder, nevertheless, of his mother turns in his mind with a terror more modern but no less destroying; his mind storms with the Furies—"thoughts that accuse each other," as Cicero, writing in the sophistication of four centuries after Sophocles, defined them.

It is not the Guild's fault if there is no overwhelming performance in *Mourning Becomes Electra*. The casting of such a play is very difficult, and doubly so in the absence of any training in our theatre that would prepare actors for the requirements of such parts. The best performances came in the scenes between the mother and son, where Mme. Nazimova's sense of theatre and her fluid response combined with Mr. Earle Larimore's simple and right attack on his rôle, were truly convincing, and in the scene between husband and wife, where Mr. Lee Baker gave a wholly right impersonation and the exact dramatic value for the play. Mr. Erskine Sanford turns out admirably in two character parts, the village doctor and the old workman who takes a bet on braving the ghost in the house. Miss Alice Brady had the rôle of all rôles in the play most difficult. Her performance of this modern Electra was sincere, and was sustained at times not only by a sort of *tour-de-force* achievement, but with real physical power, voice and all. In a few scenes she was pathetic as well, clear and moving, and her beauty most impressive. No doubt there was some instruction from the author himself as to keeping the face like a mask, rigid and motionless, as if fate itself were living there in this passionate and resolute being. As for the Greek of that intention, we must recall that in the Attic theatre the mask for Electra was very likely one of tortured lines, that the Greek theatre changed masks if need be from one scene to another, and that the Greek actor in the part could avail himself of gesture, dance movement, and a thorough training in voice, metre, speech and singing. Realistically, which is to say, in life, such rigidity never occurs except as a sign of disease. Aesthetically it belong only in the midst of a general stylistic whole, as in the Greek drama or the Chinese theatre that Mei Lan-fang brought to us. Technically it is immensely difficult, and derives not from an actual rigidity at all. Rigidity, masklike to the utmost, if you will, is a form of rhythm, as silence, when perceptible, exists within a rhythm. It is unfair to bring so great an artist as Mei Lan-fang into the argument, but he gave us the whole model for such a problem in acting—the eyes constantly moving, the head imperceptibly in motion, supported by a complete and often almost invisible rhythm of the body, the emotions precise and compelling because of their very abstraction. Miss Brady's performance had several unforgettable moments. On the whole it moved gravely and in a manner remarkably well sustained just below the surface of the motives set for her by the dramatist; but her performance, by failing both the darkness and the exaltation of the part, often made only oppressive and unvaried what should have been burning and unconquerably alive and dominating. When we come right down to it, however, the best acting in the play is Mr. Earle Larimore's. In all his scenes up to the very last part, where he mouths too much and makes faces instead of a more intense concentration on his effects, he is excellent. In the scenes with his mother especially, he contrived by a certain emotional humility before the moment in which he shared to come out securely right.

Out of Mr. Robert Edmond Jones' curtain and four settings, the rooms and the ship seem to me adequate without any haunting of the imagination, the front of the house dramatically right save for the lighting toward the rear, unnecessarily cruel to the actors. Mr. Philip Moeller's directing was admirable all through for its taste and evenness, its clear movement and fine placing of the scene. Its one fault was its tempo. There can be no doubt that Mr. O'Neill's play suffers greatly and will be accused of pretentiousness where it is wholly sincere and direct, because of the slowness with which the speeches are said. Very often the effect is only that of a bourgeois respect for something to be taken as important. If it is the Greek spirit that is sought, the answer is that the Greek reading of lines was certainly formal but not necessarily slow; the chances are, in fact, that in the Greek theatre the cues were taken closely in order to keep the music going. And the Greeks had the advantage of music, dancing and a great declamatory style, the lack of which will have to be balanced by anything rather than this obvious spacing and pausing and frequent monotone that we encounter at the Guild.

In *Mourning Becomes Electra* Mr. O'Neill comes now into the full stretch of clear narrative design. He discovers that in expressive pattern lies the possibility of all that parallels life, a form on which fall infinite shadings and details, as the light with its inexhaustible nuances and elements appears on a wall. He has come to what is so rare in Northern art, an understanding of the depth and subtlety that lie in repetition and variation on the same design.

As to the depressing element of *Mourning Becomes Electra,* I have only to say that it seems to me above anything else exhilarating. There is a line of Leopardi's where he speaks of poetry as "my delight and my Erinyes"; and once, thinking of the eternal silence, he hears the wind among the trees and goes comparing the infinite silence to that voice, and remembers the eternal, and the dead seasons, and the present and living, and the sound of it, *e il suon di lei.* In this immensity his thought drowns, and shipwreck is sweet to him in such a sea. When the play ended, and the last Mannon was gone into the house, the door shut, I felt in a full, lovely sense that the Erinyes were appeased, and that the Eumenides, the Gentle Ones, passed over the stage.

KING JAMES IN CHINATOWN

The Good Earth, dramatized by Owen Davis and Donald Davis from the novel by Pearl S. Buck. Guild Theatre. October 17, 1932.

THE NOVEL of *The Good Earth* has a certain fable quality: it begins and ends with the life of Wang Lung and his family in their relation to the land, the land that gives, the land that takes you back to rest when you close your eyes for the last time. The story opens with the young farmer and his old father under the same roof, and brings to them O-lan, the slave that is to be the wife; it traces the family history on through the sons and daughters, the famine and prosperity, the young and lovely second wife, the splendid house of the old lord's that has become Wang Lung's, and then, at last old age and his going back, with the gentle Pear Blossom and the idiot daughter, to the farmhouse and dying there, as the sons, treating him with reverence the while, promising to hold his blood together by holding on to the land, smile over his shoulder at one another with an understanding that the land will now be sold. The play stops short of this; it concludes with the death of O-lan and Wang Lung's going back to the land. Such an arrangement has quite as much of a fable form as the novel has. But the form only; there is little stamp of fable or impression of any one, single, unified theme. Only imaginative theatre creation can achieve that. It cannot be done by mere stage repetition of a motif—in this case the land, the land, the land.

The dramatization of *The Good Earth* lacks also much of the fullness of the novel. But that is inevitable and not the theatre's fault. The play cannot be the novel, and that fact is nothing against its being a good enough play. *The Good Earth* drags partly because the scenes suffer by the brevity of their dramatic motivation and the long-drawn-out performance given to them at the Guild; some of them, in fact, seem endless. It suffers even more through not persuading us to any sort of reality. There are all kinds of reality, just as there is one glory of the sun and another glory of the moon and another glory of the stars, for one star differeth from another star in glory. But unless a work of art can discover what kind of reality it is to possess and can then achieve that reality, it can never be satisfactory to us.

This is not the place to discuss the qualities of Mrs. Buck's much praised novel. As a matter of thrust, bowels and power, by which I mean, of course, the lack of them, it is one thing; as a gentle idyll, based on gentle and sympathetic acquaintance with China, it may be quite another. Whatever else, *The Good Earth* may certainly be said to have a genuine purity of intention. Along with this there is a certain use of biblical prose, a point that has been much stressed by reviewers and admirers of the book. It is more than evident to any reader and suits very well the simplicity of the author's plan. This style largely consists of such as, "And it came to pass," "wheaten bread," "smote," "Now when Wang Lung and his son heard this," "a moon of days had passed and the thing was not yet complete," and so on. It is fair enough in its way, and more so if we know very little of the prose it is being compared to. *The Good Earth* has little, however, of what that Jacobean prose truly exists by, little of the inmost heart of the English language, of the homely, the immense, the final poetry of image, the bite, the life. On every page of the Bible we have something of this—"mine enemy sharpeneth his eyes upon me"; "hiss him out of place"; "devour the strength of his skin"; "pour out my gall upon the ground"; "feed sweetly"; "garnish the heavens"; "the balancings of the clouds"; "the flakes of his flesh"; the horse "swalloweth the ground with fierceness and rage"; "I have seen the foolish taking root"; "my brothers have dealt deceitfully as a brook"; "Moab is my washpot"; "rottenness in his bones"; "stripes for the back of a fool"; "confidence in an unfaithful man in time of trouble is like a broken tooth and a foot out of joint"; "destroyed all those that go a-whoring from thee"; "seal up the stars"; "make the weight for the winds."

Of that other quality of Jacobean prose there is none in *The Good Earth*: English language that carries the full rhythm implicit in it, and the plainness and sonority in the combination of which it surpasses every other—"Behold, I shew you a mystery; We shall not all sleep, but we shall all be changed. In a moment, in the twinkling of an eye, at the last trump: for the trumpet shall sound, and the dead shall be raised incorruptible, and we shall be changed."

The reference to Jacobean is, of course, not scholarly, since more than eighty per cent of the King James version of the New Testament comes straight out of Tyndale, nearly a hundred years before. But the point here is the same.

All this quotation of what is high and basic word or image and what is final and essential rhythm, in Jacobean English, would be foolish, of course, except to say: first, that we find in *The Good Earth* only a mild and surface pleasance of the biblical style; and, second, that this style from the novel is carried into the play with some success, thereby making the problem of its production all the more difficult. In addition to the biblical, there is also the constantly recurring imitation of the Chinese-classic and folk-tale effects; which, in their turn, add also to the problem. This leads us to our main question. But we will come later to the ultimate reason—which in art is always an æsthetic one—why the production of *The Good Earth* was a failure.

Mr. Lee Simonson's settings for *The Good Earth* were, despite the marvels of Chinese design so easily to be found, without distinction. They were sadly cursed by that notion of stone color so prevalent in our theater when we are going to be ingenious about using the same wall or shift for more than one scene. By this I do not mean the real color of stone or of the thinly whitewashed gray bricks prevalent in the humble Chinese houses; I mean that sickening stippled effect that no designer in our theatre seems, sooner or later, to have avoided. In *The Good Earth* it ends by being a sloppy messed-up surface that has none of the right austerity and, when lighted, looks merely soft and foolish. Except for the rich, red-lighted bed on which poor O-lan died, the settings contributed nothing to the dramatic needs of the play. The make-ups varied; some of them are entirely independent of China; some, like that of Mr. Claude Rains, needed only a candle inside them to be ready for Halloween; some, like Madame Nazimova's, were good enough. The costumes had the excuse of the character poverty in most cases, but where rich luxury was implied they were nothing. I am, of course, not asking for bright satins, or embroidered wistarias, dragons or flying cranes, which musical comedies and restaurants have so often favored. I am only saying that a certain dramatic truth, namely, the hero's passage from poverty to riches, should be registered, as theatre in the costumes. Without going into a discussion at this point, I could add, too that beauty, even magnificence, in clothes is not necessarily a question of their cost but is an essential quality. The most magnificent costumes I have ever seen are the coronation robes of Japan, which would have in their essential quality a great magnificence, so far as theatre goes, if they were cut from burlap. The Chinese tidiness about the head and the Chinese carriage, even sometimes among the poor, were shamelessly absent from this Guild production.

There were signs of honest effort among the actors. None of them came to anything except Madame Nazimova as O-lan and Miss Helen Hoy as the fool child. Madame Nazimova as the plain, slave wife, though her pace was much too slow in most scenes, did convey the goodness, the homely love and the kind of mute pain or pleasure that O-lan should have: which is to say that to a significant extent the qualities implied in the character were created. Meantime the chic that is natural to this actress appeared, however drab the woman she was playing. In the doorway, for example, when O-lan enters just before her death, the figure seen there had style and beauty, and this without doing any harm, for it elevated and simplified the scene. Madame Nazimova alone in the company achieves any style at all.

Mr. Philip Moeller in his directing did two very hampering things. He left the movement of the scenes too slow. He either prevented or did not insist upon the right rhythm for much of the speech. To have that more or less biblical prose on hand and to speak it more or less off-hand or, as they say, naturally, which the actors did, as if it were everyday among us, mixed matters completely up.

To come to the ultimate grounds for the failure of this attempt at a play like *The Good Earth,* set in China and with Chinese characters, we may note that the whole trouble goes back to style. It can be simply stated, though it may be almost hopeless to overcome just now in our theatre. What our acting has arrived at is a realistic method, the attempt to portray people and actions more or less as we actually see them in the life around us, which amounts in most cases to the actors acting very little but themselves or letting the play act them. It is immediately clear, then, that such a production as this must have for its object being Chinese, as we know the Chinese.

It is quite as clear how this may bring disaster. If the actor does not seem Chinese to us, we resent it, which takes away from the play's effect. If the actor seems Chinese, we are struck with the resemblance, and the more apt is his performance to run into mere impersonation. The more he resembles and the better he impersonates (merely) a Chinaman, the more he distracts us from the play or the scene in hand. In that case the better he is the worse he gets. If the whole company of actors were indistinguishable from Chinamen—which would never happen—the artistic plane of the event would be very low; for we must know to a due and artistic extent that they are actors acting Chinamen. Thus it is, as we can see at the Guild, that realism can bring us to an impasse.

In the theatre of Louis XIV these Chinese characters would wear plumes and heels, with a few characteristic or symbolic ornaments or properties—something of the famous *chinoiserie* of that epoch—exactly as that stage and its décor would deal with Red Indians from America. We should then have at least a work of art with totality of style and conviction. The alternative to this would be something like the Moscow Art Theatre, which, after many years of training and of experiment, might have found a way of translating the Chinese elements of *The Good Earth* into the terms of the Russian theatre art. That would mean finding a style for it. We might then accept it for what it is, meaning theatre art, and not resent it for what it is not, meaning China.

Whether or not *The Good Earth* is worth the trouble is not involved in the aesthetic problem of the Theatre Guild's failure.

SORROW'S SHARP SUSTAINING

Lucrece, by André Obey, translated by Thornton Wilder.
Belasco Theatre. December 20, 1932.

MISS KATHARINE CORNELL, despite the fact that her play will have closed before a month's run, may wisely tell herself that it is better at least than doing *The Green Hat* or Mr. Somerset Maugham's *The Letter,* with their vulgar plausibility, or Mrs. Margaret Ayer Barnes' appalling *Dishonored Lady,* any one of which was not to her credit as either a choice or a performance. If *Lucrece* is a failure as theatrical enterprise, there is, at least, much to be said for having compassed, as Miss Cornell has done, some of the great tragic pathos, some stylistic removal, something of openness and splendor in beauty. There is also that lovely scene where we see her sitting with her serving-women as they spin, pantomime in which Lucrece herself could not have been more perfect. Miss Cornell's venture has, also, been the means of presenting to a famished theatre some very fine costume designs and a theatrical piece that, for all its shortcomings, offers moments of technical experiment, or, at least, variation. She has plenty of reason to be proud of herself for her venture, and the mere embarkation upon it has enlarged her place in the theatre.

The play tells the Roman story known to everyone. In the opening scene of *Lucrece* two serving-men stand and listen to their Roman lords at supper. We learn that there has been a wager: returning suddenly, each lord was to find out how his wife had honored him. Among all the wives only Lucrece was found properly at home, chaste, seated among her women; of the others the less said the better. We see Tarquin depart, fired with base designs. In the next scene Lucrece must welcome her royal guest and give him a room in her husband's house. Later that night the crime occurs, and the rest of the play deals with the sorrow of Lucrece and her agony, her message to her husband, a resolution that she must die. In the last scene the mob is at the gate, calling out against the king, Lucrece tells her story and dies by her own hand and vengeance moves toward Tarquin.

I have not read Obey's *Le Viol de Lucrece*; though I should guess there is in it a certain Paris chic and rhodomontade to be found and not rarely. And I am certain that the French recitation, the command of stage eloquence that both the language and the training imply, forward a certain unity in the play's total effect and tie it all more together. In its present form, as we see it in Mr. Wilder's translation at the Belasco, the play might, with vast powers of acting spent upon it, go much better than it does now. This, however, is no particular compliment to it, since, as Dryden said of music, what passions cannot acting raise and quell! As it stands, *Lucrece* is neither rich nor simple. You have a sense of complex implications that are constantly defeated by a thin simplicity in literary manner. The dramatic moment is perpetually being dropped by this tone of extra-pellucid style-writing. There is too often some banality in the figure (hands cupped behind the ears—"cupped" hands are in every story where streams flow or pity is asked—or "the vast sea of humanity"). There are, also, too many banal contrasts in phrase, though the worst banalities lie in the too obvious simplifications at many points in the writing. Meanwhile it should be noted, in plain justice to Mr. Wilder, that translating from any Latin language into English has its special and often insurmountable difficulties.

So far as the chief character of the play is concerned, the climax is reached in the long speech setting forth the agony and resolve of Lucrece, a speech on which the curtain descends. This is also the climax in the defects of the writing. Nobody could say this speech. What we should have here is either to speak in rich images, a sensuous and austere movement in ideas and ornament, a compelling texture in the style, or else to speak directly and purely, the statement bared to its bones. The speech falls between these two qualities and remains only feeble, uncertain and unglamorous. All that vagueness of direction, that uncertain, self-conscious rhythm, the figures of speech lapsing into patently simple cadences, bits, for example, like that about dying calmly and serenely, or the final simile of Minerva at the bottom of the sea, such passages need abrupt poignancy or else the magnetism and magic of the high golden style of the Renaissance. As it turned out, even Miss Cornell, even with her almost infallible theatricality of stage presence, got nowhere with the passage. The more intensity (realistic) she put into it, the more vacant the speech seemed, and the more vacant the speech, the more evident her struggle with it. Watching the scene, I understood the rape, the shame, despair and resolve to die, and that this was the heroine's reaction, but at most pretty much all I got out of it was that she was trying matters over to write them into a pretty book.

The result when it comes to acting such a play as *Lucrece,* certainly the English form of it at the Belasco, affords an interesting problem.

These are the two sides of the situation:

To get formal delivery and movement we must go to actors more or less trained to it. Most of our better actors are trained in the realistic school and get nowhere in a formal style. Most actors capable of the formal, or poetic, style require words, speeches, fine sound rhythms, to carry them along; few of them are capable of any intense projection from within. But in this play of *Lucrece* such actors often find themselves suddenly deprived of anything to say or have to say little things very simple or tame or pseudo-modest and merely literary. In the last act, for instance, when Brutus and Collatine return, Lucrece tells her lord of her woes and presently falls dead, Mr. Pedro de Cordoba, who can get about with considerable sonority and pose when the dramatist treats him to the chance for it, finds himself faced with things that might have been possible to him, perhaps—and even endurable for us—by sheer eloquence and spendid posture, but that are now obliged to be done by intensity alone, by that inner pressing intensity of realism, of which he is incapable and for want of which he is left looking only foolish, racked with gallery-god sobs, rolling his eyes, as Alcibiades said of Socrates in the battle, like a pelican. Brutus fares likewise. The chivalry of Rome, indeed, appears very much dressed but not invited. The scene becomes, therefore, Miss Cornell's, whose more or less automatic conveyance of tragic theatre is such as can survive the impotence and thwarted stylization of the whole last scene of the play, not to speak of surviving that black mourning dress of hers, which takes its motive from Shakespeare but which looks as if it had been made for some figure in Pirandello.

The continuity of Miss Cornell's performance was broken only in the scene of the long speech. This arose partly from the impossibility of the speech itself, plus the prose look of her négligée and her short hair, and partly from her lack of determination as to the style into which she would fix the rôle—and that is a very serious accusation indeed. Mr. Brian Aherne discovered a certain slender Renaissance exoticism for the part of the young Tarquin, which was a possible substitute for a more realistic brutality and lust. He showed also a certain awareness of the sensitive values in movement and pose, all of which was a good thing, since the lines he had to speak were of little help to him. Mr. Aherne's make-up was admirably heightened in color; his wig, drawn low on the brow and down on the neck like the hair in the busts of Lucius Verus or the head of Trajan as a youth, with something about the brow heavy and Asiatic like the Bithynian Antinous, was a lesson in style. This particular excellence is rare on our stage.

The progress and scheme of the play require two narrators who sometimes accompany with words the pantomime of the characters, sometimes serve as commentary on words and actions, and now and again take on the functions of the chorus in a Greek play. Mr. Robert Loraine read the part of the Second Narrator, sometimes with robust privacy, sometimes with almost comic domestic inquiry and confidential ease. Miss Blanche Yurka as the First Narrator, superb as a Sybilline figure from the Sistine frescoes, wandered at times into a kind of melodious absentia, but to a fair extent achieved both the sense and the feeling. The problem of this use of the two narrators was an interesting one, as to tone, timing, accentuation and dramatic continuity.

Mr. Robert Edmond Jones' décor for the play drew not so much on classic Rome as on the Renaissance in devious styles and epochs for its motifs. The costumes of the serving-women, with the extreme fairness of their make-up, contributed to the lovely effect. The men's costumes—Tiepolo frescoes, Henri Quatre, Rubens' tapestries—very fresh in their stage note as historical costuming and very superb as design, were among the finest things our stage has seen for a long time. The scheme for the main setting consists of two curved rows of columns with their entablature and, in the space between them, at the back, a stretched cord, from which a hanging completes the background for the scenes. I thought that the whole arrangement, fine as it was, might well have been heightened in effect, the porphyry columns, especially, which needed either more polish or more color, and the baldachino, which was a trifle tight in line and not high enough up.

For this occasion Mr. Deems Taylor has written the music. It came off mildly. I should have imagined a great chance here for the offices of music, opportunities for following the voice, for dilating the meanings, and for preparing the lustre and prophecy of the scenes as they came and followed one another.

FOUR SAINTS IN THREE ACTS

Four Saints in Three Acts, by Gertrude Stein and Virgil Thomson. Fourty-fourth Street Theatre. February 20, 1934.

IN MY opinion the production of this opera is the most important event of the theatre season, and it is already the end of February. It is the first free, pure theatre that I have seen so far.

Four Saints in Three Acts has been described, reviewed and broadcast; and Miss Gertrude Stein's method of writing, with its word tricks, rhythms, buttons, anapæsts and so on, its meanings submerging and emerging like a dolphin, has been well known for twenty years. The general news of *Four Saints in Three Acts* has called it the Stein opera. In view of the acclaim that went to her latest book, *The Autobiography of Alice B. Toklas,* this makes better publicity, but it is, also, just. The spring and melodic fantasy of the music, the scenario, the choreography and the décor arise quite profoundly and organically from the piece Miss Stein has written. The alternations of rococo frolic and sensuous intensity are paralleled in her text. Once that is said, we must hasten to add that the actual words themselves in this opera production are a very secondary part of it. They are adapted to singing, but numbers and alphabets would not infrequently serve quite as well. They do give Mr. Virgil Thomson a happy libretto verbally and, in an elusive manner, emotionally.

But it is true of Mr. Thomson that his gifts include the uncommon one of the marriage of singing and word, and that his phrases flutter, and descend into the stage scene very much as the phrases of the Stein text also do. Now and then a provocative word or phrase or a sudden bloc of emotional drama draws outward to engage the ear and to elicit inquiry. But in the main the words go their way regardless. This should not trouble people who are accustomed to endless operas, with arias, quartettes or dramatic dialogues of which they understand not one word of the Italian, German and often little of the English, where it is English—I heard Caruso once when he struck a pin at Miss Farrar's waist, sing a whole air, O Spilla Crudele—O Cruel Pin—with exactly the same applause from the audience. Nor should it trouble people who have always known by instinct or cultivation that Mother Goose, with, for example, "Hickory, dickory, dock," which at least lives in the ear, is better poetry than Longfellow's "Be not like dumb, driven cattle," which was born dead. And finally it can be said that, whereas often in singing you hope to be spared hearing the words, Mr. Thomson's line and phrase often make you anxious to know what the word was. And among lesser details and motifs devised, he has added the brilliant invention, not in Miss Stein's text, of having St. Theresa two selves instead of one, sung by two voices, a soprano and a contralto, by two singers dressed the same. The fruits of that device are fresh and happy and dramatic to a degree, both as music and as drama.

The character of the music is neither "modern" nor traditional; it releases us from any decision beyond fantasy and freedom or delight in itself. This music is melodic, though always briefly; it flits lightly, flutters, or dwells for a moment poignantly, and it is capable of many flying lyricisms. It has in it elements of jazz, pre-war melody, the ballet and, among others, something that suggests the Gregorian trimmed down shall we say to Lulli, somewhat as Titian to Watteau —at any rate there seems often present a certain finality out of France. The text itself must have left most of what we now see on the stage to be created by stage artists. Mr. John Houseman in the directing and, especially, Mr. Frederick Ashton in the choreography worked admirably. Indeed, Mr. Ashton's contribution might easily be undervalued, though almost anyone should see how the brief formal ballet of the three couples, with its kind of Galatea, sea-nymph theme, is enchanting. The décor of Miss Florine Stettheimer, in the second act a trifle monotonous, seemed perfect to the whole production. It was witty, delicious and iridescent, based on cellophane and modern painting; a sort of whimsical Victorian coquetry with the baroque that is a fresh step in stage décor. Miss Kate Lawson's costumes, not always as well executed as might be, were equally absorbing. The choice of Negro performers was very shrewd. Their relaxation, absence of prosaic, obvious analysis, and technical intuition without trained technical brittleness, were half the battle in such a venture as this. Only Miss Altonell Hines as the *commère* appeared at times to have her tongue in her cheek, otherwise everything was to all appearances *bona fide*. The phrase "baroque fantasy" passed out by the producer as a hint to the wise is a good one for this piece of theatre art. Not the great baroque with its solemn magnificence or intellectual variation on the theme, but baroque in its unbroken air of spontaneity, its charming and capricious flights, within the key and hidden unity of the whole.

I wish I knew some way to make sure of being taken seriously when I say that *Four Saints in Three Acts* is as essential theatre the most important event of our season. Bullying clichés and fad talk might help to cram that fact down people's throats for the moment at least. Such an approach is not needed at all. This piece of theatre art is the most important, because, for one reason, it is the most delightful and joyous—and delight is the fundamental in all art great or small—what a joke on the hard-working, hard-punching, expensive and self-evident aspect of the average musical show this whole event is! It is important because it is theatre and flies off the ground. (The only thing comparable to it in this respect is the flying wildness behind the mind of Mr. Henry Hull's Jeeter Lester in *Tobacco Road*.) It creates instead of talking about. After all, we can imagine writing a play about a professor's home, a boy's troubles, capitalists, et cetera, good matter enough, just as our legs, our blood, our hats and problems are good. But only now and then in the theatre can we hope for something of the quality of a thing in nature (a tree, a melon, a sheet of water, a flight of birds). The point in such a case is not that it is beautiful or not beautiful, but that it lives in itself, and is in essence a constant surprise, the surprise that comes with living things, where we do not know what exactly will be until it has happened, and where it neither was expected nor is unexpected. It is from such works as this, truly alive, that we can best make our conclusions and our applications, deep or trivial, to art and to delight.

It is horrible to think, if *Four Saints in Three Acts* turns out to be the success, or the vogue, more or less promised by the first night's reception from both the audience and the press in New York, what imitations of it will follow. However they may miss fire, they may some of them have the prosperity with which second-hand imitations often surpass the original. Whatever happens, *Four Saints in Three Acts* cuts the theatre loose from the predictable and the repeated. The scene about the pigeons, so brief and soon gone, is like some singing of little sea shells, and is a case in point. At the same moment it intrigues and baffles imitation, and in that fact precisely lies its theatre life.

MOLIERE KINDERGARTEN

The School for Husbands, Molière's comedy in an adaptation in rhyme by Arthur Guiterman and Lawrence Langner. Music composed and arranged by Edmond W. Rickett; lyrics by Arthur Guiterman. Empire Theatre. October 16, 1933.

ST. PAUL says, speaking of all flesh, that the dead is sown in corruption, it is raised in incorruption. Our theatre usually reverses the process with Molière; he is raised in corruption. One way or another he manages to survive after a fashion. Even in the Theatre Guild's bright evening, by some flight of fancy presented as an "adaptation" of *The School for Husbands,* the result is lively and worthy entertainment. It would have been more so if something more of the elements that make Molière what he is had been retained.

Since, then, we shall not quite find it in Molière's play, we had best, perhaps, review first what one sees on the Empire stage. The entertainment consists of a story, or "intrigue," mingled with ballet, and takes place within a décor very prettily designed by Mr. Lee Simonson. It is one of those permanent perspectives common in the Louis XIV theatre and centuries before. In this case we see a kind of city square, with a curtain rising on either side to show the interiors of two houses. There are two brothers, Sganarelle and Ariste. They have each in charge a ward, the sisters, Léonor and Isabelle, whom each in turn hopes to marry as well as educate. Ariste, dressed as the fashion prescribes, fine and costly, favors the theory of freedom, of letting his ward and afterward his wife have perfect freedom whenever she chooses. Sganarelle, the other brother, keeps his ward shut up like a nun in glittering array. A young man named Valère loves Sganarelle's ward, Isabelle. There is to be a fête. There is then an interlude which the program says comes from Molière's *Le Mariage Forcé.*

We then have soliloquies by Sganarelle, about the problem of his age, can he cope with marriage? and so on, and some amusing versions of philosophers and gypsies and so on, from whom he asks advice, also a dance of youth and love—in which Mr. Charles Weidman is most agreeable. Finally Sganarelle awakes from his dream, and is still set on marrying Isabelle, who finally thwarts him by pretending that it is her sister and not she that he sees going into Valère's house. Just as her sister returns from the fête, Isabelle emerges, safely married. The liberal brother is plighted to Léonor; and thus is Sganarelle, the narrow, suspicious and old, justly rewarded. Besides the dances and interludes there have been also various pleasing interpolations of songs.

In the production Mr. Osgood Perkins gives a performance that is to his credit, though the play often forces him to be what Molière never meant at all. I would suggest only one thing: he might study his cues so that the fundamental meter of the rhyme form that Mr. Guiterman has written might be better preserved, and thus increase the wit and pleasure. In the Guild company there is also Miss June Walker's voice and use of it, very witty and disarming.

Miss Walker, Mr. Michael Bartlett, as Valère, Miss Joan Carr, as Léonor, should study their make-ups. They belong to an enameled world, these Molière young people, and should look it. The actors' hands especially needed attention. The wrists and hands should be like porcelain for such rôles, the palms and between the fingers rouged the color of sea-shells. Such items accord with the surface unreality of the play.

The whole scene of the carnival crowd needs a complete restudying, for make-ups, masks, ensemble and pretty much everything. We should note the smoothness of Mr. Langner's directing, in all but the ensembles (good ensembles at the Guild are rare). Such a gain in pseudo-reality only helps throw out of gear the stage conventions elsewhere in the play. Mr. Simonson with the historical costumes did what he seems usually to do. Some of the ballet clothes were delightful; the colors in general were happy. But the designing does not sufficiently enforce the characteristic of the costume; and thus the costumes lack boldness and style, the emphasis goes soft. On his very first page of the play Molière sets forth exactly the details of the dressy liberal brother, Ariste's, clothes: the blond, full wig, the small hat, the long collar, the short, tight doublet, the long sleeves, the full breeches (eight yards were needed to make a pair of breeches such as Ariste wore), the shoes trimmed all over with ribbons, and at the knees the canions, those rolls of starched linen adorned with lace, fastened below the knee, often so large that you had to spread out your legs as you walked. Let this single item of the canions serve for this whole discussion of the costumes at this Theatre Guild Molière. Ariste has two or three plain loops, only of ribbon, at the side of each knee. The designer, of course, knows of the canions, and has chosen the simpler style, which is also to be found in that century. What I mean is something more elusive and subtle; one way of putting it is to say that, though it is historically quite admissible, Mr. Simonson's Ariste design, besides missing the Molière drama, misses a certain style-drama in general for a historical costume.

This, then, is what we have for Molière at the hands of the Theatre Guild and Messrs. Arthur Guiterman and Lawrence Langner; and as I have already indicated, it is certainly an engaging occasion. The audience, and some of the reviewers perhaps, partly enjoy it, partly endure it as a classic, and partly feel toward it more indulgent than delighted. We are entitled, however, to ask why, if we are going to bother with the play at all, change it so much from Molière. Is it our habit of worshipping the hero so long as we do not have to do his will? Of wanting to have the lion but not have him roar? Or how shall we say it? At any rate the fact remains that here in this version of Molière it is what is left out that contains the basic elements by which Molière is Molière.

In the first place the order. In Molière it is the progression of things, what follows what, what leads to what, that is half the point. This is outside our tradition of mind, so to speak, and we shall never comprehend it. From this point of view our theatre, for all its genius, has always been, and always will be, except when it is a second-rate imitation of foreign works, barbaric. This shows in the present version of *L'École des Maris*. For example, the exposition, which has been praised as the first notable exposition in French prose drama, is knocked into a cocked hat by changing the order. Molière began his play with the two brothers talking together. This follows his technique of starting off with a statement of the idea in terms of two contrasting characters. At the Guild we turn this around and start with the pretty ladies and then the brothers with their thematic remarks—which is merely a silly meddling re-arrangement, an ignoring of Molière's order of thought for the play. Much of the dramatic business of the setting and costumes in this play is thrown away. Molière does not present four brightly attired characters, two guardians and two orphan wards. He gives us only two: Ariste, dressed in the height of fashion, and his ward Léonor, to whom he allows the same lustre, and the drab, sour Sganarelle, dressed drably in serge, and obliging his ward, Isabelle, to be as plain as a nun.

The same applies to the scene. Molière prescribes a kind of public square, a *place* in Paris, which follows the *Commedia dell' arte* traditions from which he derives. Why mess things up by showing the interiors of the houses on either side?

There is a final brainless aspect of this adventure into the classics, which is a matter of the thesis. What I see at the Guild may be harmless enough, of course, so long as we know that Molière's thesis has been wrecked.

The thesis for *The School for Husbands* is that a man must make a friend of his wife, and so on, if she is to become a trusted friend and companion. But what we now get is that on to this is grafted the thesis from *Le Mariage Forcé*, which is that an old man cannot hope to be a competent husband to a young wife. Obviously, the two themes neutralize one another. If the husband is old, there is no point to the trusting companionship motif; if the husband is young, there is no point to the youth-and-age motif. Thus it happens that all the sense is taken out of the Sganarelle rôle as Mr. Perkins has to play it. Meanwhile Molière has very carefully disposed of any confusion as to the age-youth motif by making it the generous Ariste who is the older man; he is older than Sganarelle by twenty years in fact.

"Molière is quite rifled, then how shall I write?" asked an English dramatist, exactly twenty years after the presentation of this very play. Etheredge, Wycherley, Durfey, Farquhar, Dryden, Congreve and every comedy writer in Britain borrowed and pillaged from Molière. Congreve gave him the most profound study; Dryden remodeled his comedy method because of Molière. Characters in Molière were not, as in the English tradition, seen in development during a play; his characters were static. This was because, strictly drawn from life and then simplified to a type, they were based essentially on an idea. Our dramatists, hit and miss, went on, nevertheless, with their efforts—Dryden, for example, diligently tried to follow Molière's principle of developing a comic character from a central incongruity.

In many respects one after another of these dramatists got from Molière what seemed handy; none of them, not even Congreve, ever learned, or it may be, even quite perceived, that solid tone and integrity of the whole, as it were, through which Molière's sum and supremacy is most apparent. These British dramatists did, however, after all, have much in common with Molière, through their mere closeness to him in time. Since then we have gone a long way indeed from Molière. This "bagatelle," as it was called by some of our critics, of *The School for Husbands* is due, then, a few notations, if for no other reason, for the sake of certain backwoodsmen scattered over our country who may think, from something or other they read here or there, that they have missed a distinguished Theatre Guild production of a Molière play.

"*Le dénouement de L'Ecole des Maris,*'" the great Voltaire said, after showing how little Molière owed to the *Adelphi* of Terence, "*est meilleur de toutes les pièces de Molière.*" Caesar called Terence a halved Menander, and Voltaire says that Terence' style is pure, sententious, but a little cold, that Molière's diction is almost as pure as that of Terence, and that he leaves Terence far behind "*dans l'intrigue, dans le caractère, dans le dénouement, dans*—the mirth or comedy that envelops and pervades the whole—"*la plaisanterie.*"

Technically it is worth noting that in this play Molière departs from the five-act form, hitherto common to both tragic and comic drama, and uses the three-act form that ever since has seemed most fitting for comedy.

The idea of the education of girls made bold and, for that day especially, very strong, controversial matter for *The School for Husbands*. The basic idea beneath this one of education is far more profound, however, and is as true now as then; its depth and tenderness connect it with Molière's gift for detachment and with his own suffering and the unhappy story of his marriage. Without loss in either mirth or movement and holding on to as much of the older "intrigue" pattern as, considering his public, seemed prudent, Molière, nevertheless, completely expressed his idea.

In *The School for Husbands* we have the first play in which Molière came into his own, with regard both to the expression of himself—it was written the year before he married, at forty, Armande Béjart at sixteen—and to the habit that he followed from then on of studying at first-hand as dramatic material his own self, balanced, within the play that he writes, into the two elements of feeling and contemplation, a poignant revelation of himself seen in the sane scale of human society. Boileau's final word for Molière was *contemplateur*.

It is somewhat obvious that producing Molière in English and today is a huge order. But there can be no harm in pointing out some of the aspects of a dramatist and a play to which the Theatre Guild has, in a vein of indulgence and pleasant liveliness, called its audiences' attention.

LAUREATE BRAINS

The Green Bay Tree, by Mordaunt Shairp.
Cort Theatre. October 20, 1933.

A REVIEW, as such, of *The Green Bay Tree* requires first a brief account, however tedious to those fortunate enough to have seen Mr. Jed Harris' production, of the story. In the studied and exquisite drawing-room—where Mr. Robert Edmond Jones, using about a tenth of his powers, has done beautifully and dramatically what no other of our designers could quite do—Mr. Dulcimer is seen. He is perfectly served by Trump, his man; he arranges, with gloves on, the flowers sent from his place in the country. And he is most concerned about Julian, who has been a good deal absent and preoccupied of late. Julian arrives. Dulcy proposes trips out of town; Julian is not very much interested. He has something to talk over with Dulcy, goes to change and returns for dinner, during which he tells Dulcy that he is in love and wants to marry Leonora Yale; who he explains, is beautiful, self-supporting, a veterinary in fact. She knows that Julian is not Dulcimer's son. Will Dulcy increase his allowance? On the contrary, Dulcimer retorts, he will cut off the present allowance.

Suddenly we hear that Leonora is coming by, they are going to the ballet. The hasty dinner ends, the room is cleared and made more beautiful. She enters. The war between her and Dulcy begins. The curtain falls. In the next scene Julian enters; they have not been to the ballet, but to Julian's father's, above the dairy business. Once, fifteen or so years ago, in Wales, Dulcimer had heard a record of a boy's voice, had sought him out, paid his father five hundred pounds and adopted the boy, whose name is really David Owen. But now Julian has found old Owen, his father, rather better than he had thought. To study for a profession will be impossible in Dulcy's house; he will live at his father's. Dulcy is cynically displeased. There is an abrupt good-night. The curtain falls on Dulcimer, alone, sitting listening to a record of a boy's voice of long ago. Few acts in any plays whatever achieve a curtain so inventive and telling.

The second act is in old Owen's sitting-room. From the moment Dulcimer paid him the five hundred pounds he wholly changed; he now is prosperous in the dairy business and a lay preacher at some chapel. Julian makes uncertain progress cramming for the exams; Leonora, tutoring him, is on his mind; three months have passed. She and his father, respectively, are bent on saving him. A telegram arrives. Dulcy has returned to town. Julian is delighted; his father exhorts, scolds, threatens. On Julian's argument that Dulcy has come around about the allowance, Leonora agrees to dine that evening at Dulcy's. The last act opens with dinner at Dulcy's designed as a café game: notes from table to table are exchanged, et cetera. The money discussion begins. Dulcy still refuses. He tries to show how Julian is trying to force himself into another character, not the real Julian. He proposes a trip in which there will be time to think it all over. The telephone rings, the test has come, Julian cannot take the step. He does not answer, but falls sobbing on the sofa. Dulcy orders Trump to make ready Mr. Julian's room. Breakfast next morning begins another scene, Dulcy all charm. Julian wishes to leave town as soon as possible, but must first see Leonora. She arrives and offers to marry Julian at once, says his father has been up all night; then she understands what Julian's decision really is. While Julian dresses for going out, Dulcimer taunts her; as she swears she will talk with Julian again, his father comes in. Dulcimer is scornful of Owen's pleas; Owen to save his son shoots the corrupter. The short last scene shows Julian as the inheritor of all Dulcy's wealth. Leonora comes, she will marry him provided he gives up the fortune. Test. Futility. She departs. The old life begins. Trump, Dulcimer's man—Julian hopes he will stay till the end of his life—is to bring the flowers for Julian to arrange.

About this play there are so many points to discuss that I am driven almost to summaries.

First, as to the motif of the homosexual element in *The Green Bay Tree,* it seems to me wasting time to ponder the literalness of Dulcy's relationship to the young man he has educated, tinged, colored with the arts, and taught to need him emotionally and culturally, and to supply an enrichment to his life, not to speak of the fascination and nourishment that Dulcy means for Julian, plus, according to capacity, the affection and delight that Julian brings to his feet. What happens here needs no exact detail: only stupid people think that in these matters there is for all instances literally a point at which it must be classed as one thing or the other, for there are few things in this life that are either one thing or the other.

There is a type of person, seeing *The Green Bay Tree,* who, either by sheer lack of sophistication or some subconscious self-indulgence, will not quite divine this theme in the play. There is, also, a type that, enjoying the play, would choose to deny it, in the sense that some races tend in part to maintain themselves by certain lies, as certain lies live by some races. It seems to me an idle obstacle and waste of intelligence and time, sadly bourgeois, trying to make out Dulcimer's and Julian's relationship as only a sort of sybaritic, cultural luxury, dominance and dependence, when all the while the point of the whole thing should be clear to anybody.

Without this point granted, Mr. Jed Harris' remarkable achievement in the directing of this play cannot be perceived or explained. From divers people who saw the London production of *The Green Bay Tree,* one hears that he has toned down the play. Their meaning is obvious. But what I should say, taking it all as intelligent theatre, is that he has toned it up. What Mr. Harris has done should be a lesson to a certain type of Freudian thinker, or, shall we say, wandering disciple. He does not isolate a human phenomenon and set it up as a kind of psychological, single dummy, extracted, or hypothesized, from some supposed life. He creates a life through whose relationships and manifestations the phenomenon, or characteristic, can be made to appear as a living part. To cite great examples in drama— far off, of course, from *The Green Bay Tree*—this is what Sophocles in his *Oedipus Rex* does with the theme of incest; which amid the magnificent conflagration of human passions and characters is only the match, half overlooked as we follow the play, that set the conflagration off. It is, also, what Plato does about love in the *Symposium*; where the particular variety of love soon becomes only a detail in a great immortal theme. In sum *The Green Bay Tree* under Mr. Harris' hands does not present a babyish, social, pseudo-scientific stress or employment of a theme, but its intelligent use.

Second. When the playwright in *The Green Bay Tree* goes so far as to make, in the dramatic grapple traditional for ages, one character a veterinary as pitted against another sensitive, beauty-loving, luxurious and charming, he presents a concocted combination or tangle that is nothing but sheer, raw theatre. It is like what Sudermann does in *Magda,* where bringing the primadonna back from world triumphs for a grapple (limelit) with an aged, provincial, military-minded father is about like tying a cat and dog together by the tail: the evolutions and all are foregone. This is not, accordingly, high substance Mr. Harris is dealing with, and he has shown his intelligence by letting it go for what it is. The crises posited by the dramatist in the situation—such as Dulcy's telegram arriving after Julian has had three months of people trying to improve him, or the father's shooting his son's corrupter—Mr. Harris lets stand as frank theatre, intensifying them meanwhile to their full theatre values. This is not only shrewd stagecraft; is also one way whereby he protects the play from any such false claims to importance as might relegate it to the theatre's merely vulgar or trivial side.

Third. Obviously *The Green Bay Tree,* though excellent theatre and most absorbing to watch, is not great drama. If, dealing with such matter as is involved, any of the characters had assumed for themselves more depth and for the play's subject more ambition, the result would be banal and cheap. If the homosexual theme, with its unaccustomed stage possibilities, had been used crudely, the whole would be merely risqué or raw. If used singly, a great play, which Mr. Harris knows very well this is not, would have been necessary to give it embodiment and point.

What the dramatist intends in these respects I cannot tell exactly; the theatre, in its search for the sure-fire, wades easily into deep waters; and Mr. Shairp is well screened by the objectivity that he adopts, standing apart from the whole affair. Mr. Harris' achievement lies in an equal rounding of the whole. The domination of personality, culture, arts, sexual psychology, crude inner workings, beauty, grubbiness, et cetera, are all, in his production of this play, seen in scale. He keeps the characters' emotions and motivations in a certain blend of pressure. To an amazing extent he thus destroys all pretense in the play; he allows the theatrical its plain and frank exhibition, and assigns to the whole event its due, but not specious, plane of intellectual or spiritual significance—to be distinguished from its remarkable emotional effects. The tone and taste arrived at in dealing with this play seemed to be unique in our theatre, which with its energy, its willingness like a prostitute to oblige by the moment, and its lack of any general meaning, needs above everything (and understands least) this landscaping and subordination within a decision and perspective.

Not to be too solemn, and remembering always that this play is what the French would class only as good *theatre,* I may say that all the five rôles making up *The Green Bay Tree* are very fine parts to create. I am not sure—recalling how Mr. Noel Coward, as willing to be deep as to be trashy, tossed off in *The Vortex* subject matter that would have cracked the brains of Ibsen—as to the extent to which the dramatist himself knew this, beyond mere stage chiaroscuro; but I am sure that Mr. Harris does, however much he may have left these rôles at the pitch capable to the actors and, perhaps, to the play. Mr. Heggie, as often, is good for the minute and bad for the half-hour, much less for the whole play. He has not realized it, apparently, but the rôle is superb. Old Owen is in a way the main destiny in the drama of *The Green Bay Tree*: the others step aside, one way or another, but he stays. In him the circle of life turns from the sale of his son to the atonement in killing the man who will corrupt him. Owen's reform, violent fanaticism of atonement and religious indulgence are the foil to Mr. Dulcimer's self-knowledge, cynical pattern for living and hedonistic clarity. Mr. James Dale should go on lessening his pointless stridency in many places, though Mr. Harris has cleverly employed this actor's capabilities by leading him to dance against the beat as it were. What Mr. Dale needs now is to sort his effects, make each count in a given kind of passage. For example, as things stand he uses the same barking, airy staccato for full moments of reaction to sharp emotion that he does for an idyllic description of the pretty days at his country house. At present, nevertheless, his performance helps greatly by keeping the situation away from the morbid and from any depths not guaranteed by the play as written. Miss Jill Esmond has been well placed on the stage and well set off during all her scenes; but she has not explored her rôle; her scenes with old Owen are a great chance for any discerning actress. And, as Miss Esmond does her scenes, you cannot tell whether the actress herself has decided on how much the character she plays is talking like a fool or how much the self-confidence and strength exhibited are only blind and stupid egotism.

As for Mr. Laurence Olivier's Julian, it is a long time since so subtle, fluent and right a performance of a younger rôle has been seen in this town. All the characters in *The Green Bay Tree* are tragic. Old Owen's could supply the "metaphysical comfort" attributed to such tragic rôles as Lear if only Mr. Heggie could compass that. The rôle of Julian, however, is that of a fluent, lovely element—what Dionysus meant in Greek—by which life avenges itself on the three others, with—despite their character and outline—their several kinds of setness or barren denials. They all want Julian, but each wants him not in Julian's but in his or her own pattern. Of them all Julian, because he never comes into any form, is least vulnerable. The moral of this *particular* play, if it were a great play, would be that there is no moral; there is only life, flowing, attracting, responding, destroying, Dionysian and consuming. And, otherwise, these others in the play, Dulcimer, reformed Evangelist Owen, dog doctor, resolute Leonora, since they cannot get life the way they like it, will have to like it the way they get it. To know how delicate moving, securely slight and varied Mr. Olivier's performance of this rôle is, you would have to see it.

VALLEY FORGE

Valley Forge, by Maxwell Anderson.
Guild Theatre. December 10, 1934.

WASHINGTON, in the first place, belongs to an age when a man played a rôle. You set yourself a rôle, or position, in which you would act; and from the nature of this rôle derived the perspective within which you were to be seen. What might seem artificiality, or even hypocrisy, to some callow modern was to the people of that era only the fulfilment of some clear intention or final resolve. And Washington was a gentleman within a definite civilization or society. That there are gentlemen—a term variously conceived and varying with epochs—still among us, most of us would admit or even insist upon. That we live in the midst of a society defined and resting on some recognized basis of theory or social order within which a gentleman is resolved into a pattern, nobody could say.

Trying to express Washington, then, as a whole is an impossible task. Most of the conceptions within which he acted, formulating his character and expressing his mind, would be unfamiliar now to the general public. From this fact partly derive the silly distortions that such a character has endured from such of his historians as wish to make an involved turnabout of their portrayal—since they cannot gauge or convey what lies behind the main sum of Washington they fall back on wooden teeth and sex. I sometimes think that we could illustrate a great deal of the Washington crux by one remark of his, treasured in the Lee family and remembered all his life by General Lee. The saying is on the surface simple, but is not so; you could not have a better example of the personal and the social combined. (Even the word "virtuous" that he uses has a different solidity of meaning from what it might mean now.) "A man," Washington said, "ought not only to be virtuous in reality, but he must always appear so."

Mr. Maxwell Anderson shows his theatrical tact—as well, I may say, as his easy-going habits as a dramatist—by avoiding both these impossible phases of Washington's history. He does not, beyond certain implications, show Washington in his international aspect, nor try to place him in some complete assumption of a rôle however splendid. In *Valley Forge* we have for the most part an aspect of crisis, of character and deed, that anybody in the audience might understand or, at least, respond to. It is a critical moment in the history of the Revolution which we are shown and in the frame of which the entire play is kept. The soldiers are starving, the cold is intense, and desertions are too frequent; surrender threatens. The earlier scenes of the play present these same frontier soldiers, their special kind of humor and their special virtues, in combination with Washington's influence on their minds. In the next act we see the British Headquarters and General Howe. A lady who once fell in love with Washington and loves him still is resolved to make her way to his headquarters. After being refused the opportunity, she is used finally as a means of deceiving Washington with regard to the French alliance. She arrives in a man's uniform, but finds Washington too busy and absorbed to think much about her.

We have then a scene in which one of the soldiers reports rich bins of corn belonging to the British. Together they organize a foraging raid, and there is a good comic invention where one of them who had been up to then barelegged, appears in the red trousers of the adventuring lady. In the last act members of Congress come to interview the commander. The treachery, subversions and self-seeking at the centre of the government are obvious. The drama is thrown back on Washington; on him its development must depend. From then on it moves towards his final decision to sign a peace with the British. The climax is turned from that, finally, through the rough loyalty of those soldiers who have returned from the corn's capture. In this last scene of *Valley Forge* the cumulative mass of motifs is admirable: the young boy who has risen from his sickbed to die in action, the wounded comic soldier, the rags and dying, the rough courage and half-mutinous free spirit, all lead to a good last curtain in which the theme of liberty, through the dramatic and poetic imagination, is suddenly realized, warm and compelling. For drama of this nature, homely and tinged with poetry, this is the right direction. Some sort of psychological realism might doubtless

VALLEY FORGE 167

discover how to demur, analyze, negate or inflate the idea of freedom. Mr. Anderson has left the idea simple and full, as it must have been for those men that we see in the Valley Forge hovel and as it must have been even for Washington himself. He knew that he must create the future, however ideal and destined to be imitated by revolutionary Europe, in terms of the simple and virile present that lay ready to hand. Few final curtains have the emotional ease and force of that in *Valley Forge*.

The settings for this new play would add more to their scenes by looking either more like nature or more like art. And the play provides material for the lesser rôles that could be much further developed. Mr. Erskine Sanford as the congressional visitor, and Mr. Victor Kilian, the soldier comic, are capital. Miss Margalo Gillmore leaves the lady, the only suggestion of a love theme in the play, quite undetermined. She and Lord Howe (Mr. Reginald Mason) play their scene together as if somewhat under the aegis of English social comedy—Sheridan, shall we say? When, therefore, Miss Gillmore appears at Washington's headquarters in her bright uniform, we are not sure how to take it: clearly, Washington is high, resolute and absorbed, but the motif of the lady's visit loses its content. The whole scene in fact is thin and poor, without a relation in tone to what has gone before it and without any content of either significance or wit. It seems merely a rather loose and casual and undeveloped kind of interlude device. The whole motivation of the lady, as it stands, is an unfortunate reflection on the method and the sense of style of the author.

The problem of acting Washington, if he were taken in a longer vista, seen under his remarkable and widely varied aspects, would be enough to stump any actor. But the dramatist here has made the task easier by keeping Washington chiefly within a certain dramatic situation or moment in experience. There are sidelights of character, gradations of feeling, that arise from the man in general; but, for the most part, the dramatic attack is simplified. Mr. Philip Merivale was a very wise choice. In his performance the conception of vigor and force displayed has nothing loud or obvious about it, and this is right, too, since Washington was civilized. The English he speaks is admirable, a great deal closer to Washington's English, very likely, than most of the speech heard nowadays on our stage; in fact, there were moments in the speaking elsewhere among the players at the Guild that suggested why Mrs. Washington always spoke of "dirty democrats." Mr. Merivale's Washington, if lacking in any final sense of great character, has a real degree of elegance, without any of what might seem sheer stuffiness. Washington himself in the rôle would surely be all wrong. It would not be his fault and not too much the play's fault. Such are the ways of history, life and art.

SPANISH PLAYS INDEED

Field of Ermine, by Jacinto Benavente, adapted by John Garrett Underhill. Mansfield Theatre, February 8, 1935. Bitter Oleander, by Federigo Garcia Lorca. Translated by José A. Weissberger. Lyceum Theatre, February 11, 1935. From Lorca's Theatre. Five plays, translated by Richard L. O'Connell and James Graham L. New York. Charles Scribner's Sons. 286 pages. $2.50.

THE ATTEMPT to bring such a play as Benavente's *Field of Ermine,* as it stands, on to the English stage is in its way, I suppose, only another way of saying that you do not know what the stage is about. Or should we say it is an evidence of not sensing how much the soul of a race is manifest in its language? At any rate, you watch the performance of this Spanish play at the Mansfield Theatre and find yourself in a state of wonderment. Miss Frances Starr, who is essentially a player of the sort that rests on the stage—actors will know what that, as distinguished from the projective excitement of real acting, implies—has a method that is enough to kill any scene where there is either drama or changing states of mind. And in a Latin play like Benavente's, Mr. Charles Derwent strikes you as only a means of enunciating final syllables; with him in it the Spanish scene dies. The rest of the company play without mental excitement and without comprehension of the basic language behind these forms supplied by the translator. And Mr. Underhill as a translator would get in any dramatist's or any actor's hair.

In many spots Mr. Underhill's lines could not be spoken by any actors; they sound like a schoolroom version of a passage far removed in every sense from the language that we speak. There are, in fact, constant assortments of *whiches,* verbal structures and hightoned words that, though they may suggest distinction in the translator, compel a despair in the actor; for only by the most violent mental control, sharp stress on the essential units of the sentence, and vivid stream of magnetic emphasis, could these speeches be brought into line at all. Such intuitions of method or powers of enforcement are not at all evident in the company now presented in *Field of Ermine,* they would be a great deal to ask of any company. Everything that they do in the performance is essentially dull—all but the rôle of the brother's widow. The net result is a sort of pity on the part of the audience for the actors who have to struggle with such a play. Imagine! Imagine being pitied for being in a Benavente play—Benavente, a rich and fertile theatre talent, a sharp and often beautiful Spanish mind, and such a contriver of actable matter as we rarely find.

Whether or not that lyric tendency of the latter portion of *Field of Ermine* could be adjusted to prose Broadway taste is a question at best not easily answered. But it is at least clear that the statement, the terms used and the eloquence of passion and imagery would have to be adapted to our way of saying things. To keep Benavente's piece as it stands, to present it literally rendered into English, is only suicidal theatrically; Spanish and English are too far apart for that.

The linguistic is only a small portion of the difference between Benavente's theatric medium and that of the American theatre. When Miss Starr, or instance, feels that on a certain sentiment she must roll her eyes to the gallery, she only shows her innocence of the emotional and moral idiom characteristic of this play. When Mr. Derwent, expressing a certain gloom about himself—he will be missed, it seems, after death by mendicant dogs at the corner near his club—falls into that sugared deliberation and sentimental choplicking, he merely misses *in toto* the philosophical habit, the ironic salt and the traditional declamation of another race, a Latin race. The scenes in this Spanish play often sound wrong because the actors have accumulated nothing for them.

Nevertheless, there are ways of reading Benavente's lines, even in the English of this translation, by which either an impression of cerebral energy is conveyed, or else the emphases and parts of an involved sentence are first identified and then are established, definitely, by intonation and timing.

As for *Bitter Oleander,* the Spanish play at the Lyceum Theatre, celebrating the twentieth anniversary of the Neighborhood Playhouse, the racial removal from us is parallel to that in Benavente's play. *Bitter Oleander* is by a genuine poet, and the piece itself is said to have made some dramatic history in Spain. In the story of Lorca's play the bride runs away with a former lover, now married; there is a stabbing and the mother of the bridegroom is left without any of her men. There are dances and songs, a wedding and so on.

Many passages in the performance that the Neighborhood Playhouse gives are clear and moving. The drawing in various scenes is clean and final. The whole approach is, to a considerable degree, stylized and simplified. The direction indicated is noble and right. The fact remains, nevertheless, that such a direction can achieve fruition only through the traditional and racial.

Racially the play is hopelessly far from us. A country like ours, where the chief part of a wedding is the conference between mothers-in-law, the trousseau, the presents and the going-away gown, can scarcely be expected to feel naturally in terms of wedding songs, grave and passionate motivations, rich in improvisations and earth-born devotions. No amount of dance lessons, chantings and drill can convert this portion of *Bitter Oleander* into what is convincing for us. The whole of it at best is an importation that is against the beat of this country.

Bitter Oleander, in its poetry and in its method, suggests now and again D'Annunzio's *Daughter of Jorio,* one of the most hopelessly inexportable, untranslatable fine dramas of our time. For the seventh century B.C., for Sappho's era, in the Grecian isles, there are many motifs and movements and lyricisms in *Bitter Oleander* that would have been easy. Mr. Lorca's bold and poetic mind expects a flowering toward the splendor and rigor and gravity of the heart. Fundamentally the difficulty of this play for our theatre is that we cannot sufficiently take it for granted, cannot receive it as we receive the ripening seed toward summer or the fruitful autumn. We cannot be natural or at home with all its full choric passion, its glowing simplicity and its basis in a Latin tongue, whose deceiving simplicity mocks all translation.

It may certainly be said that there has been no more beautiful mind than Lorca's. We may say too that it is a mind at the same time passionate, complex and lovable; it is also, as the theatre must be, contagious and friendly. His is a genius, too, that is marked by a seemingly inexhaustible invention. It is hot with the variety and multiplication of images, images that are like new bodies, new and convincing presences, or sudden revelations in light and that are cold with their precision and finality.

In his plays we feel easily the effect of space and energy that belongs to the classical and Mediterranean. Meantime, we are apt to feel quite as well a sense of irregularity, willfulness and violence. And that is partly true of Lorca's particular Spanish genius and practice: and it is the defect of a marvelous excellence in him. It is, as it were, the Spanish in him. Quite possibly for us it may appear to be a greater defect than it actually is, since we are used to a drama that makes small demands on our imagination, that is "processed," you might say, and eased along by expert, if obvious, mechanics or manipulation, and that, moreover, is carried off under cover of a mild realism.

Lorca's theatre, on the other hand, has only its own reality; it is never to be seen as anything but theatre—a work of theatre art—and it uses the theatre medium as frankly and directly as a painter uses paint. Whether or not his plays fit into our notion or theory as to what a drama should be, they have the originality of what is true. They have a splendor of freshness to them and an almost harsh immediacy in sensuous response—which is to say motifs and details that blend and excite, and that convey as few modern poets have been able to do the orgastic or visionary. Very few of Lorca's most seemingly extravagant or complex images are not organic to the scene and characters in which they occur. They are a part of all that blaze of invention and fecundity and perception that his work exhibits. They are close and quick and lovely, daring and unaffected as the vision of a child, and yet wholly sophisticated in the sense that some great music might be, music our last master, which knows all.

This flowering in Lorca's plays is alive; it can announce and convey its colors. To be violent and glowing and at the same time articulate is to exemplify one of art's first requirements, one that is rarely fulfilled, even in the theatre art, where it is so especially needed. It implies with Lorca a necessity for expression, a pouring out, a love that fills up with abundance and knows all sweet device. His tradition belongs to another race than ours, a race apart to some extent as the Spanish is, even from other so-called Latin races; and

SPANISH PLAYS INDEED

his tradition is racial and Catholic, the beautiful and profoundly proved and ancient forms of the Catholic Church are his inheritance and deep benefit. His bold and poetic mind expects full images in the hearts of us—another way of saying that his work may be one of the sources of salvation for the theatre of today, poor and dry, cheaply feasible, plausible, limping and hesitant as it has become, a theatre not even good enough to be bad.

What a special imagination is exhibited, and how outside the run of the general theatre is the passage *Asi Que Pasen Cinco Años* (If Five Years Pass) of the child and the cat, the janitor's dead child in his coffin, smothered in roses, and the cat the children have killed and thrown on the roof—they so want to escape the burial awaiting them, however different for the two. It is a scene unlike all others so far as I know, bizarre, fairy-tale, grotesque and infinitely pitiful. It is a scene that reduces most of its Teutonic parallels to their own just treacle and itch of symbolism; even the Hannele scenes in Hauptmann's *The Sunken Bell,* beautiful as they are, suffer by the comparison.

> io también iba, ay!, gata chata, barata,
> naricillas de jojadelata,
> a comer zarzamoras y manzanas.

I too walked alas, snub-nosed cat, cheap, nostrils like tin,
to eat mulberries and apples

> Señor, que florezca la rosa,
> ne me la dejéis en sombra

Lord, let blossom the rose,
Do not leave it for me in the shade

The performances at the Neighborhood Playhouse were in general sincere and painstaking, though the tempo of the whole was too slow. Of them all Miss Nance O'Neill's seemed to me by far the best. She has a genuine comprehension of the simplification, the meaning expressed by combination of details, the innate discipline that characterize such a rôle as that of the Spanish mother. As words on my part, all this may sound plausible enough; but for all that, the fact remains that for such rôles Miss O'Neill is unique on our stage.

NOCTIS EQUI

The Tragical History of Doctor Faustus, by Christopher
Marlowe. Maxine Elliott's Theatre. January 8, 1936.

"HOW GREATLY it is all planned," Goethe said of Marlowe's play. I quote that for what it is worth; the great Goethe said like things about certain fairly flat Roman versions of Greek sculpture that, all afresh, he saw in Italy. And this tragical history of Doctor Faustus is, as a matter of fact, none too evenly disposed in its planned development. Only a variety of emotional pressures on the part of the actor who plays the leading rôle can register for the audience the stages of Faustus' struggle and his progression toward that climax of damnation. And yet Goethe was right; for this drama, in its length and stretch, is planned with greatness. The ground plan of its conception is dazzling, though doubtless beyond performance quite for any dramatist anywhere and ever. One way of describing a certain aspect of this piece is to say that it is one of these special instances in art which lead you to blame yourself rather than the artist for whatever shortcomings may appear in it, such is the radiance of its ambition and the spell of its audacity.

To me at least this occasion of Marlowe's play with the Federal Theatre was completely absorbing; and I was forced again to wonder, as we have all done before now, what other course, or, rather, separate parallel line our English drama might have taken if Marlowe had lived. There was a brain less shining and flexible than Shakespeare's, with less, too, of good plain sense plus flying after summer merrily, less of the easily universal, less of penetrating inwardly; and yet masculine, agnostic and passionate, learned and bold, indeed reckless, compulsive, crammed. This brain had its own order, as a drama like *Edward II,* coming later, plainly showed. Its sincerity was now naughty, now imperious; and its music was of a violence and splendor that persuade us less than they enforce themselves. Where Shakespeare is complex, Marlowe is intense; it is astonishing, sitting there at *Doctor Faustus* to see how he can hold his own. This verse, sometimes so tortured with its Renaissance image or cerebral pride, sometimes so wide in pomp or daring in aspiration, comes straight out over the footlights—to, I may add, an audience whose attention is such as I have not seen elsewhere in the theatre this year.

Mr. Orson Welles not only acts Faustus, but directs the play. Mr. Paul Bowles has written music that can often float you into the scenes' Elysium, as it were—notably those where Helen's apparition comes. And Feder—a name that, not to speak it profanely, seems one of the attendant spirits or demons of the piece—has done the lighting. On an apron stage, well used and frankly admitted, he has created a body, a dramatic medium, of light, by which the divers scenes are given, the entrances and exits effected and the dramatic moods established. What was sheer sprinkled-in fireworks on Marlowe's stage spreads now from firecrackers to complete revealments or images. The settings appear, through the means of light, to be some chiaroscuro of the cosmic. They seem some concentration in space. It is as if we dealt here with that *Topos-nous* of the Gnostics, "space-mind," the agent between Creator and creation.

One way to say all this is to say that in his own epoch Marlowe's play, though this sort of production in light would have been close to its innermost quality and knowledge, could never, by the sheer lack of science, have been produced thus, exactly as the Greeks knew that the blood was carried to the lungs but, not having the chemistry by which oxygen would be apparent, did not know why the blood was sent there. On the other hand, of course, we have not any more the fires of declamation, that orchestra of recitation and sound poured forth, the wide and mounting scope, of Elizabethan acting that in Marlowe's day went to the creation of this drama. It is plain that Marlowe in this piece did not rely on physical horrors in order to arrive at his effects; as Drayton said, "his raptures were all fire and air"; he relies on poetry alone to bring before our eyes the dramatic vision of a scene. Very likely, then, light rather than material scenery is a happy resolution of his stage needs. And still above that, there is that chief expressive medium of the poetry spoken. And that poetry, mostly given to Faustus, is spoken far above the average by Mr. Orson Welles, who has a beautiful even voice, perfectly placed, and has, too, a remarkable sense of timing.

The approach made to this Marlowe production seems to me one of great tact and imagination, highly to be praised. It is only a further compliment to say that, though the play is not heavily cut, it seems ruthlessly short—*O lente, lente, currite, noctis equi,* you in your turn think, making yet another use of the verse where Ovid in Corinna's arms asks the horses of the night to go slow, go slow—by what ironic dominance did Marlowe make this express a damned soul pleading for more time!

The acting in general is adequate, especially with regard to hearing the lines. Mr. Jack Carter as Mephistophilis brings something to the part that the ordinary actor of the rant school might miss; he needs only to feel like troubling himself to study the vivid meanings written there. Mr. Harry McKee was the best clown I have ever seen in Elizabethan revivals, the brain really seemed to chase about with the lice he talked of. From Mr. Welles' conception of Faustus I differ largely in but one respect: I see no reason why Faustus should be mussed or grimy; on the contrary it seems to me he should be in general very *soigné* and distinguished, so that we may realize how many of the things he asks for are not those of medieval squalor but of choiceness, rarity, depth and fascination, cosmic and chimerical as well as sensuous, and born of that Renaissance that was haunted with so many kinds of beauty. Mr. Welles may also with time become more meticulous as to the verse stresses or patterns here and there, though he has already to his credit some veritable triumphs in reading, not least in those involved passages that hang in the air by almost less than a thread. He possesses also both naturally and by study a notable gift of projection, no mean asset for Marlowe's lines.

Not only in the reading is Mr. Welles good; he is even better at certain spots in his design for the stage movement. The best of these, fortunately, concerns the most marvelous and admired motif in the plays: those that touch Greece and Helen. On the steps to the apron's left Mr. Welles' Faustus sits when he speaks the lines about pleasure conquering his despair:

> Have I not made blind Homer sing to me
> Of Alexander's love and Oenon's death?
> And hath not he that built the walls of Thebes
> With ravishing sound of his melodious harp,
> Made music—

Some scenes later, when Helen comes, just before the play's end, he has Faustus sitting to the apron's right, in an exact balance to that former position. At the back of the stage is Helen, not stupidly classic but looking like Diane de Poitiers on a tapestry in a silver moonlight, the long open bodice, the high breasts, the coif, the stiff folds. Presently Faustus will go to her and she will give him her hand, for we are not to think his enjoyment of her is ghostly or unreal. But for the moment Mr. Welles by a very brilliant invention has Faustus there at the front right, looking out away from Helen when he recites those lines, borrowed from Lucian but forever divinely Marlowe's:

> Was this the face that launched a thousand ships,
> And burnt the topless towers of Ilium?
> Sweet Helen, make me immortal with a kiss.

MISS LORD'S DAY

Ethan Frome, dramatized by Owen Davis and Donald Davis from the novel by Edith Wharton. National Theatre. January 21, 1936.

NO MATTER what the outcome may be, an event in the theatre may differ almost generically from the majority of events, for the mere reason of some presence in it, be that actor, dramatist or what not. When Miss Lord appears in a realistic piece, no matter how inferior the play may be, it should be taken as a theatrical event of the first rank.

In my experience of the American theatre, I should say, after much thought in the matter, that the greatest single moment I ever saw was that first scene in *Mariners,* where the wife, in her white dressing gown, comes down the stair. It was in a silly Clemence Dane play that went to pot long before the last curtain. What Miss Lord did in that first scene seemed to illustrate all life—by what tension, projection, and what technical and mystical combination of excitement, who shall say? I have seen her do this thing in other plays; she did it, too, in the film of Mrs. Wiggs.

As for the book of *Ethan Frome* and the play that Messrs. Owen and Donald Davis have made from it, I, like everybody else, have known Mrs. Wharton's story for a long time. I am sure that it has a certain security within some New England psychology, as they say, and I know that technically—in the obvious technical sense that belongs to art of secondary rank—the story comes off well. Nevertheless, *Ethan Frome* has always struck me as basically genre. Its general sense, despite its urgent subject matter, is period genre. If the term offends, I should as soon take it back. The point is that in the book, and also in the play, one feels rather too definitely the intention. A certain thing in art is being done. I am not such a fool as to mean that we must disapprove of artifice, arrangement, intention in art. I merely mean that, after a certain plane, a work of art transcends all such elements in its nature and creation, takes on its own living mythology and breathing fable and, like all high things in art, becomes again a form of life. I should never say anything like this of Mrs. Wharton's story. I know that many will be against me here, especially those who have not read the story for twenty years; but to me the ultimate word for it would, despite its urgent locale and stern, obvious content, be "clever." Clever, even brilliant, as a tour de force. But we have no sense of pain in it, no impression that, for all its tragic matter, it cost its author much beyond the cerebral labor of its execution. We have no sense that the author is either, on the one hand, stung by its distress and frustration, or, on the other, if you like, exalted by its pity and suffering. The impression of mastery that Mrs. Wharton may give is of technical mastery, not of the mastery of living substance. She is, rather, a kind of literary mistress of all she surveys.

The dramatists for *Ethan Frome* have made an uncommonly good dramatization of a novel. The surface of the dialogue, or of the diction rather, is far above Mr. Owen Davis' average, in accuracy, in sharp, indigenous phrase and in simplicity of line. The result, however, of this whole stage event of *Ethan Frome* is that we have something that may be depressing but is not tragic. I perceived the thematic element in it, I believed in the reactions that it won from the players. Moment by moment I felt a certain emotion; an hour after, it seemed to me only a play after all, an arrangement as we say in painting.

Mr. Jo Mielziner these last two seasons has made an astonishing progress inwardly. In this play his indoor scenes, those two rooms in the farmhouse, are dramatic to a degree, admirable. Any student of décor must long since have realized that outdoor scenes are almost impossible to do, if, that is, we are to take stage décor as serious art. The snow, sky and walls that Mr. Mielziner has created are both real and exalted, they are triumphs.

Mr. Raymond Massey as Ethan Frome played well. Miss Ruth Gordon's method gave the girl a quality too special. In this sense she was miscast. Her performance, as stage performing, was otherwise excellent, from those mute moments of her self-obliteration to her uses of the half-grotesque.

Miss Pauline Lord cleans the whole thing up and tops everything, the story, the play, the scene, the acting. There are things here that Mrs. Wharton, for all her ability and confidence in approach, could not even have imagined. By what process it is in Miss Lord's portrayal that her opening of a door and standing there—or any of that continuous perfection of her playing—can begin our entrance into a region that we cannot explain, nor predict technically, nobody can say. Her performance has a miraculous humility, a subtle variety and gradation and shy power that are indescribable. At her own cost and some decisive selection among the things that are her own and the things that are not, she knows what is right for her and finds the strength within herself to sustain and project it. She must have a rôle that suits her, one in which she feels right. When she does so, there is no other player who can bring into it such tragic elements, such bite, or so sharp a stain of life.

Here is an art which could derive from no tradition and on which no tradition could be built. It is form so entirely related to the particular artist's own meaning and interpretation that, divorced from her, it would only be a mannerism or decadence in straight style. It has an immediacy that prevents its even remaining in the memory as technical moments or outlines; a trick of the voice, of pause, a gesture now and then, we recall; the rest has moved so far inward that it is largely our own response that stings and moves us still. Of this art of Pauline Lord's you know that its small voice haunts your ears and its weakness overpowers you, as you go back to it in your thoughts, thoughts tender and somewhat awed by that of which you seem to have heard only the echo.

THE COUNTRY WIFE

The Country Wife, by William Wycherley.
Henry Miller's Theatre, December 1, 1936.

THE COUNTRY WIFE, as we see it revived, cut and very much toned down, charmingly mounted, carried off by Miss Ruth Gordon in the leading rôle with delightful security, seemed to me entertaining enough, if not quite up to Dryden's line: "For wit the immortal spring of Wycherley."

It could be said, what's more, that the version Mr. Miller uses is at least closer in quality to the Restoration text than that of Garrick, which persisted well into our great-grandfathers' epoch. And the conception of Wycherley as presented here is much more intelligent than was common in the last century, when such distorted rot, for instance, as Macaulay wrote of this dramatist was accepted by many as worth while. Just how far the mind of Wycherley could be presented straight to a modern audience, who could say? He has long been represented in the general mind as the most indecent author of the most indecent play in our literature. It may, for example, come as a surprise to some that in the seventeenth century he was regarded as a moral force; the great Dryden, even speaks of how Wycherley had obliged all honest and virtuous men by his bold, general, useful satire. It might also be a surprise to know that the defect not seldom dreaded by his admirers, then (and now, if you like), was (and is) that Wycherley may at any moment break out into moral indignation, show himself as what they call "a ferocious moralist," exposing "the vices of nature for our disgust," manifesting the unhappy protest against life of a man who has lived "semi-consciously against his grain." You might, they said in Wycherley's own time, conceive from the tartness, severity and spirit of his writings that he was an ill-natured man; when in truth, as Lord Rochester said in another case, he was "the most good-natured man with the worst-natured muse."

It can also be said of Mr. Gilbert Miller's Wycherley that it is far closer to the author than the Theatre Guild's version of *The School for Husbands* was to its Molière original. Wycherley's plays were all produced between 1671 and 1674. By 1671 Thomas Durfey in *Sir Barnaby Whig,* is asking how, with Molière quite rifled, is he going to write? That *The Country Wife* is based partly on *L'Ecole des Femmes* and qualified by *L'Ecole des Maris* is obvious. That Wycherley, with that virile independence of his that has been mentioned so often, should depart from these French plays is to be expected. The difference between the two men is fundamental.

Molière writes for a defined and civilized society, is himself a profound social student, a popular genius, ventilated and just, rational and passionate, a ripe and equable designer in social drama. That Congreve, Ben Jonson, Shakespeare have their respective values in comedy is manifest. It is equally manifest that Molière remains outside our scope. The restlessness felt by many of the audience seeing *The Country Wife,* and a certain general indifference felt by almost everyone as to its outcome, may be partially ascribed to the fact that for us today, at least, the play has little to say as a whole; its pervading tone means very little; the spots, in either the present version or the play itself, at which Wycherley bursts into his moral *terribilità* are, after all, spots, where Molière's work achieves its unity from the light that falls on it from social living, and where the order and tone are the very dialect and sincerity of his nature. *The Country Wife* has been rated as the most perfect of English farces. Compared to Molière, Wycherley's play is footless and sunless. We should do much better to take such a play as fantastic—fantastic farce. Despite the realism of Wycherley's surface, or the shadow of his amusement, or the running brunts of his indignation, it is much better to see his hero, Mr. Horner, as extravaganza, heavy with sarcastic vindication, rich with the precision of some summer madness. The text of impotence which he announces for himself, and which thereupon serves as a focus for all the play's situations, is thus kept free for its essential farcicality. By announcing his impotence Mr. Horner opens the way for the confiding response and contemptuous indifference of the husbands and at the same time vastly enlarges the opportunities of the wives. The famous "china" motif ensues here—Mr. Horner's "china" that the ladies come to see and remain to inspect and so on and so on, with all the scandalous ringing of the changes on that theme.

THE COUNTRY WIFE

The décor of Mr. Oliver Messel was entertaining always, his costumes charming, rich and bright. Nobody in the company was bad, and Mr. Miller has preserved in the whole occasion an easy good taste that would not be enough for Congreve but is quite enough for the Wycherley text that is presented. Not the least of Mr. Miller's effects was an escape from quaintness, the stifling rose fever of the theatre. Mr. Roger Livesey as Horner gave out a strange husky potency and sarcasm, never vulgar, always what-will-you? as it were. Miss Ruth Gordon as the country wife, shams, sins and all—Molière's Agnes yes and no—was a fresh perfection that would no doubt have surprised Wycherley but would have delighted him. Inch by inch this careful player had the rôle explored, witty, sly, outrageously innocent. In the asides, which the play abounds in, Miss Gordon was a marvel; I have never seen passages of this kind in English comedy done so well, with such a draft of the audience into the player's confidence.

It happened that the performance at which I saw *The Country Wife* was the first matinee, and the audience was largely made up of women. As a comment on modern drama, feminism in drama and so on, it seems worth recording that not until well along in the play— when Miss Gordon, not Wycherley, had got under all our skins— did the audience smile every much. This is something to ponder.

As everybody knows, the foundation of Restoration comedy consisted in treating sex comically, with an eye, however, on a social point of view that was more actual and definite than we are apt to think. And we all know Walpole's saying that life is a comedy to those who think, a tragedy to those who feel. When the dramatists of the Restoration deal with sexual incidents, adultery or even rape, there is plenty of innuendo but little sexual emotion to it. When sex gets the bit in its teeth, we have, obviously, either the tragic or the pornographic. But Wycherley was neither, not tragic, though indignant and fierce, not merely for the game of it pornographic.

Watching this audience, I thought of Ibsen and the load of feminism he finally got around his neck, and of Wycherley's own recognition of the problem, as found in *The Plain Dealer*. Two ladies are speaking of the fairly appalling passage in *The Country Wife* about Mr. Horner's "china." After seeing that scene one of them has cast out all china, that pretty furniture of a lady's chamber; though the second lady begs to be excused from thinking the worse of hers "for that of the playhouse." " 'Tis now," says the first lady, "as unfit an ornament for a lady's chamber as the pictures that come from Italy and other hot countries; as appears by their nudities. . . ."

One of Pope's letters speaks of Wycherley's second marriage ten days before his death at seventy-five:

> "He had often told me, as I doubt not he did all his acquaintances, that he would marry as soon as his life was despaired of. Accordingly, a few days before his death, he underwent the ceremony: and joined together those two sacraments, which wise men say, should be the last we receive: for, if you observe, matrimony is placed after extreme unction in our catechism, as a kind of hint of the order of time in which they are to be taken. . . . I saw our friend twice after this was done, less peevish in his sickness than he used to be in his health; neither much afraid of dying, nor (which in him had been more likely) much ashamed of marrying. . . ."

This is an unsatisfactory piece of criticism, but so is the play unsatisfactory. Its criticism of life, once more applicable, violent and admired, is outside many of our values now. But its quality is, nevertheless, alive and actable.

HIGH TOR AND HIGHTY TIGHTY

The Wingless Victory, by Maxwell Anderson.
Empire Theatre. December 23, 1936.

High Tor, by Maxwell Anderson.
Martin Beck Theatre. January 9, 1937.

IN ART, reality and the imagination come out eventually to be the same thing. No matter how far the material may be from the strictly factual, the surface actuality, no matter how near it may be to the actual surface, the prose minutiae, you will see that the full exercise of creative imagination can bring it into a reality. When by the creative process of art, something is there where something was not before; it is in this very something that the reality consists. We may say too that no matter how far flown the imagination may be, the result will have reality in so far as it has completeness and organic unity.

Only the fact that Mr. Maxwell Anderson has done other plays of a different caliber could justify any notice of such a play as *The Wingless Victory*; it has not any reality at all, of any kind. A seaman, having failed with his family and in every Salem respect, has gone away, swearing he would return when he could buy the town. He now comes home, with a cargo rich enough for that and—hail Hergesheimer's novel of *Java Head*—a Malay-princess wife (plus two children). He establishes himself in the ancestral house, lends money, sets up again the family business, all in vain: the wife—whose legal status the town doubts—the dusky brood, and the feeling that he may have been too happy in begetting them, will not go down with these cavilers, solid citizens and sour saints. And so, after a good deal of the vague rhetoric of egoes and moral cross-currents, we arrive at a crisis. The man must either give up the dark lady and send her packing on the ship again to the East, or lose all, even tea with the neighbors. He decides, after some versification, that the wife must go. On the boat again, the Malay maid has preserved a good Eastern poison, which serves for the children, maid and mistress; and the last moment finds the heroine dead in the arms of the hero, who, together with a recalcitrant, worthless brother, is now going to sail around till "his dust lies down with hers."

The ethical interlarding of the story, what with the theme of race prejudice, plus the theme of religious narrowness, comes to nothing. If you sail in from the sea with a dusky lady, uncertainly wedded to you, the town is no rarity that looks you over suspiciously. For Salem to be singled out in this respect may seem hard, but no matter, it has, at least, the house of the seven gables. And almost anybody with a modicum of sense will see that, even in stage Salem, the flashing profundities of this heathen Malay convert remain vaporish: people who have won what standards they may have by hard discipline, ugliness, bitter lines, hot denials, could scarcely be expected to be bowled over by such prayers as this, delivered beside the first-act window (at a crucial moment dramatically):

> Dark oracles of heaven,
> that blaze and burn, swung by an unseen hand,
> forgive me if I give my god no name,
> for men have many. But there is one law only
> over the sun and tides, and He sits alone,
> giver of laws, and I worship Him, and ask,
> under what name is chosen, for those I love
> peace in this house. The terrible sea has been
> my child bed, and my children's cradle. Blood
> and a black treason lie at their beginning,
> and murdered men look down upon our sleep
> and curse, and will not live again, and yet
> these are the ways of men, and a woman bears them,
> forgiving, and a god forgives. What wars
> they make, what pitiful scars they leave, what eyes
> lie staring at your moon, and will not waken,
> this we have seen together, but these men-children
> are children still, and loved, and a woman's heart
> goes out to them, even guilty. Drive us no more
> for the evil we have done, let us eat our bread
> beyond the salt of weeping or the sea,
> these little ones and him I love, and I,
> here on this shore.

HIGH TOR AND HIGHTY TIGHTY

That is a long quotation, but it is necessary, or people who have not seen or read the play would never believe at what tired rhythmic patterns, superfluous images and lyric clichés this writing may arrive. It sounds like a Stephen Phillips version of an Arthur Symons translation of a decadent German versifying of a lax translation of Euripides. To its service, however, Miss Katharine Cornell has brought the instrumental qualities of herself as acting medium. What this may mean, for or against the play, and for or against Miss Cornell, you will have to decide for yourself. She has to deliver some of the worst speeches in recent playwriting, and seemingly does not shirk the onus of delivering them. This may be due to her loyalty to the text and sincerity as an actor or to her mediocrity or lack of distinguished instinct as an artist—the risk of your decision is hers. The play is semi-tosh from start to finish, and the dying, analytical languor and the verse's cadence here and there are little help—all despite a situation potentially dramatic.

"High Tor," on the other hand, is a fantasy of many virtues. The theme of industry messing up things is familiar but not inorganic; the combinations of gnomic fancy, trade, centuries and stubborn lyricism are calculated for a genuine entrance into our hearts and acclamations. On the whole the evening is an engaging one, with talent behind it. Suggestions of *The Tempest* and divers versifications of spirits and escapes, Rip Van Winkles, love, and relative actuality, seem to detract nothing too much from the whole effect—Shakespeare himself did his borrowing—and I should say that there is a certain glitter to this story of the young man who would not sell his Palisades promontory to the trap-rock company, what with those ghostly Dutchmen and that Dutch ghost of love, Lise, wife of Mr. Byron McGrath's Captain Asher, serving as foils to the mingled modern elements and bank robbers, town fiancée and so forth. The general story of *High Tor* is something of spell and fantasy. The mingling of Broadway comedy and other elements, traditional and deathless, is a good sign. The drift and smile of Mr. Anderson's piece are pleasantly moonlit. It has no little reality.

As for the performance, the casting of Mr. Harold Moffet and Mr. Charles D. Brown, as rock buyer and droll ghost, was a stroke of genius. Mr. Burgess Meredith gave an admirable performance of a part that might have been merely bumptious and overevident, since only true feeling on the actor's part could distinguish it from the long since banal. Miss Peggy Ashcroft, imported from London for the rôle of the ghostly young Dutch wife, shows certain delicate qualities convincing for the rôle. But her reading of the yards of verse written for the character seemed to me to turn verse into something unnecessarily tedious. Must verse reading be panted, spit out and subdivided like this? Links of meter strung together on pauses! The frustration that comes from metrical disruption! She should listen to Mr. McGrath reading verse as it ought to be read.

Mr. Meredith broke down only once: after the Dutch ghosts were finally departed he had a few lines to say from a centre-stage knoll of soliloquy. Whether this breaking up that he did into four or five beats, pausing, enunciating, was intended to continue the pulmonations of the Ashcroft ghost, or whether some director order mucked up Mr. Meredith's own method, who knows? In general, however, he read the lines with intuition for the sense.

ETERNAL REINHARDT

The Eternal Road, by Franz Werfel. Play translated by Ludwig Lewisohn and American stage adaptation by William A. Drake. Score by Kurt Weill. Dances arranged by Benjamin Zemach. Manhattan Opera House. January 1, 1937.

IT IS to be expected, as a part of human weakness if nothing else, that when a race sets itself apart, draws a special line as its definition among other people, these people should, intermittently at least, hate and assault it. It is not surprising, therefore, that Hecataeus of Abdera, a Greek living in Egypt, around 300 B.C., should without malevolence say that the Jews under Moses' teaching had "an inhospitable and inhuman manner of life," which in the ancient societies meant something much more serious than the words now may imply. Nor are we surprised when Manetho, thirty years later, settles the whole business of this Jewish population as lepers, outcast Egyptians, half-savage Bedouins, and reasserts their vice of unsociability, following Moses' prohibition of "any dealings with anyone whatsoever except their confederates." Pliny, centuries later, was speaking of them as a race full of insults to the gods, which was merely the repetition of one of the ancient Greek characterizations of the Hebrews.

Though hard things said about the Jews continued, it would be a mistake to take such attacks too much as special; since all around the Mediterranean the divers races, in a manner not wholly ancient, were calling one another names. Nevertheless, there were proscriptions enough against the Jews in classic times, though paralleled now and then, one is relieved to note, by the Jews themselves, whose Palestinian history is not without savagery and slaughter, sometimes of foreigners, sometimes of whole villages of a differing Jewish sect nearby. Later on we shall have the terrific four centuries of Jewish persecution, beginning with the First Crusade. And finally during the last few years comes the series of European events so much to the Jews' disadvantage.

The core of all this, for our present purposes, is to note the fine starting point it affords for this drama of *The Eternal Road*. In a room in the synagogue, at the bottom of that superb stage lay-out that Mr. Norman Bel Geddes has designed for the play's visual body, a company of Jews have assembled, fled thither to escape the mob outside. This is the old story of the persecution and exile and wandering, timeless, a part almost of the race. Any knowledge of that story will show how it is intense, sometimes fanatical, and always of the stuff from which arises passionate legend. Their rabbi reads to this desperate crowd in the synagogue pages from the sacred history; the curtain above rises; a wandering land appears; and then in episode after episode are shown the histories, one story after another, one leader after another. A slight love story emerges from the congregation: a young Gentile woman follows into this danger and isolation the man she loves; and by way of comment and solution we get the story of Ruth—a bit sweetened from some of its broad original folk touches.

For the most part, however, this progression in the upper parts of the stage concerns the great names, those who have led their people out of tribulations, toward God.

The dramatist's idea here has wonderful implications and possibilities, this dream of life as one continuous line, the great dead, the living need of them, their presence. The idea has many classic ramifications. In Athens there were shrines to heroes, as Thucydides records. Aristotle, of the scientific bent, dedicated an altar to Plato; and the blunt Diogenes declared that Plato's soul took rank among the deathless gods. Even as political-philosophic theory this motif had a place. "If," Aristotle says in the *Politics*, there exists in a state an individual so preëminent in virtue that neither the virtue nor political capacity of all the other citizens is comparable with his," he should be regarded as not at all a member of the state. "For he will be wronged if treated as an equal, when he is thus unequal in virtue and political capacity. Such a man should be rated as a god among men." There had been the Greek heroes, there were later the *Manes* of the Romans, and long afterward the saints of the Church. It is these saints that Israel's figures, Moses, Joseph and the rest, are most like. But they are to be seen as more intense, more powerful in their leadership and myth, and as more directly under the very voice of their God, by whom the decisions of their souls are shaken, and in whom their souls' violence finds response. Around these shining figures the Jews in that synagogue can rally through religious and racial sentiment, since they cannot do so through national sentiment.

The idea in Werfel's play, that in the midst of persecution and wandering, this people can turn to its great heroes—almost the friends of God as it were—ends in the beautiful motif of a little boy who has seen those bright forms, those wandering shadows of his race, and hears even the voice of the Messiah speaking to him out of them. His heart is fresh, all the centuries are but one morning in his heart; and then suddenly the mob violence strikes across that; the wandering of his people begins again. And meanwhile we have yet the sense of the dream; it began at the first and is strangely deathless; it is indeed unique in kind in the world. It reminds us of that remark of Varro, Cicero's friend, which St. Augustine refers to: that the Jews were, among others, a people whose imageless cult still maintained what others had abandoned.

Essentially this Werfel story is austere in outline and is burning inwardly. Mr. Geddes' décor provides a variably imaginative sequence of planes, surfaces, lightings. Against the lofty sky, sometimes night, sometimes one or another hour of the day, the figures and groups of the many players are disposed and varied. Distinct accessories are introduced: an Egyptian façade, a desert tent, a well, a field of wheat, and so on. Upon this stage Mr. Max Reinhardt has devised the procedure of the play-spectacle. A good many of the scenes promise well, such, for instance, as that moment when Moses stands far up, with the tablets of the law. Even such scenes, however, are apt to develop into the inconsequent; and the trivial, elaborated and tasteless appears where imagination and dramatic images are required. Say, for example, the scene of the Egyptian bondage, the bondsmen hauling at the obelisk, the overlords above, the more or less chorus below. You cannot take as tragic anything so involved and foolish as a forestage of half-naked young ladies rhythmically handing bricks to one another, while to the side there are maidens with duplicate baskets weaving, while another young person, in a lustrous wig, sings trivially a bit of bondage song, while presently on the levels above all these there will be leapings, or just have been—what difference could it make?

Worst of all, the last curtain, end of the performance, is inexcusable, the whole company setting off on the eternal road via the footlights, the angels out taking bows, and Mr. Geddes' fine synagogue scene garishly exposed like empty chicken crates.

The dances, though created by Mr. Benjamin Zemach, a fine artist, are such, alas, as must be perfect or else are mere plugging about, plus some jiggling, which they mostly were. Mr. Geddes' costumes in the main lacked drama and lacked style, as indeed the whole occasion did. Either more stylization or a more simple and realistic intensity is needed if the enterprise is to be much more than a vapid and profuse spectacle, punctuated by a few top moments and many momentary promises of splendor sadly unfulfilled.

The speech of the synagogue congregation might vary as you please, but for the great figures of time and the world's dream an English more uniform than we hear at the Manhattan would be desirable. Mr. Kurt Weill's score was in itself often dramatically expressive, at times beautiful. All in all we might take, as an example of what was at least possible to this moving drama, that scene where Boaz comes and lies down smiling, singing his lovely song, by the sheaves in his field, under the stars. It is beautiful, with that pure and single effect that in any art the thing has when it is right. To ask such quality of the whole production would be of course to ask imagination, and choiceness, and sincerity. These we have a right to demand rather than expect, though line after line remembered from the great Hebrew poetry of the Bible tells us what we seek, and leaves us astonished at so much confused intention—half vision, half vulgarity—and expert engineering as Mr. Reinhardt's enterprise exhibits.

There can be no doubt that Mr. Reinhardt's ability and power in the theatre in the earlier part of his career made him one of the most important figures in the modern theatre, especially when it came to the encouragement and opporunity he gave to people of talent in all directions. But this later tendency to pile it on, to dazzle and seduce us with excessive quantities, can only be a sign of poverty and decline. This elaboration and pretentious profusion only serve to remind me of what Cicero wrote of Accius and his efforts to gild the classic pill with spectacle:

quid enim delectationis habent sescenti muli in Clytemnestra

—what do I care for six hundred mules in *Clytemnestra?*

CANDIDA, CANDIDA, CANDIDA!

Candida, by Bernard Shaw. Empire Theatre.
March 10, 1937.

IN A SENSE, all drama moves toward a condition of farce. This is because the theatre's very essence consists in the heightening of its material. Heightening that is free, fluent, almost abstract, unless it has the restrictions of character and rational measure, floats off into farce; which is thus closer to poetic drama and serious tragedy than to plain everyday prose realism. The usual condition for farce is the lack of strict connection, or the racing ahead of the plot with regard to the characters. *Candida* is fundamentally a farce, a kind of cerebral farce, as it were. It is not so because the immense heightening given to all the characters is too much detached from their actions; the farce appears in the detachability of the reasons—often put into their own mouths—given for their actions. We often sense thoughts, theories, motives assigned by the author to the characters and not wholly necessary to them in the light of what each is and does. These theories and principles make a pattern among themselves, culminating in Candida's explanation of her decision to stay with her husband and its implications, in the last scene.

This last scene is a good example of the point. If we take the play as a farce of ideas pitched delightfully against each other, Candida's explanation of her choice of husband versus poet is capital entertainment, capable of real emotion but remaining a fairly reckless, or at least free, solution of a built-up pattern of theories, ironies, controversial wagers and attacks. This special brand of explanation for the final solution of the problem of her choice between the two men has been, obviously, predicted all along through the play; it arrives effectively enough. If you choose, however, to overlook the prediction, and to take her explanation as an independent passage in the play, then you must face one of two interpretations. Here we have a woman who, as is usual with Mr. Shaw's characters, is from the ordinary standpoint safely moral, whatever wild words or theories she may let fly. Candida does the conventional thing: she remains with her husband instead of going off with the poet. And, like every other woman in the parish, she loves her husband. She treats him and the poet, nevertheless, to a full dissection of her decision, which she says is a matter of choosing the weaker, who needs her most, etc., etc. If we do refuse to take the play as cerebral farce, then either she is a slightly tedious creature (self-illusioned, all-understanding, given perhaps to a wee sermon now and then) who is now making a perfectly natural choice, but must stir up a lot of semi-tosh about it, true or not true; or else, while staying on with her loved husband (not to speak of her children), she will, from out a wise and gentle heart, dilate on the occasion for the two men's good, especially her husband's, who needs the lecture more than Marchbanks does, who can take it laid on thicker, and who can rather more satisfactorily be punished a bit.

The whole play indeed is made up of clicks, curtains, balances in motifs—such as, for the most obvious example, that of Candida's father finding one by one that the whole house of them is crazy. The single shortcoming in Miss Cornell's production derives from a refusal of the full swing to the play's cerebral raciness and frank theatre. Not seldom during the performance you note the attempt to glide past some bit of stage trick in structure or dialogue, or to blur effects that, though not high sad art, are yet good, joyous artifice, healthy and strictly theatre. On the same basis the least satisfactory performance is that of Candida's father by Mr. Keye, which cuts down the full, gusty content of the rôle and its business in the whole play.

The abstractions, attributes and heightening given to each of the characters clarify their outlines and make them tend toward types. Thus it is that *Candida* ends by being a play whose rôles are capable of many interpretations and are hospitable to many actors.

As types of what they represent, such rôles are always debatable of course; and in this case it is the poet that heads the debate. Marchbanks is both conventional and unconventional. There are two qualities about him that are true of the poet in general: he responds intensely to things that for most men mean nothing, a sign not of weakness but of strength and significance; he is in the end practical, because he follows what he knows is for him life and reality. The rest of Shaw's poet—not forgetting the persuasive sop of making him the son of a nobleman, which gives another slant to his oddities of course—is a mixture of the Yellow Nineties, with that mauve babble about beauty, plus the stage poet, whose clumsy absurdities make us all feel comfortably indulgent. Thus Mr. Shaw, playing perfectly safe, manages to use Marchbanks to hit the minister—rhetoric, ego, good looks and all—over the head; and while providing a safe happy ending, makes a point for the creative artist by tapping the audience softly on the head with poesy's defense. Mr. Robert Harris' Marchbanks, tormented and comprehending, is well enough, taking the part as it is written.

In fact the casting, directing and playing in Mr. McClintic's production of *Candida* are far above the average. Of all the actresses who have taken the rôle, Miss Mildred Natwick's Prossie must be very likely the surest and best, and the most delicately and profoundly kept within its due scale of comic and pathetic. Miss Cornell's Candida, as in all characters with a type outline, is one of the many versions possible to the rôle. By the same token it is more than usually dependent on the player's own quality. Some of her audience seemed to think Miss Cornell's first moments affected. I did not think so; she seemed, rather, a trifle uneasy, whipped up, as if under some kind of sensitive strain in a casual scene. She could take it more simply. In the last scene she takes up all the word-battle, sermon, self-confident analysis et cetera and turns it into a grace and loving wisdom that is rarely seen on our stage, and that sheer acting, no matter how good, as divorced from personal quality, could never achieve.

RICHARD II

King Richard II. St. James Theatre. February 5, 1937.

THE PERFORMANCE of *Richard II* seems to have made a genuine stir on its first night. It has a quite considerable movement and get-along in the directing. In the acting there are rough edges fairly often; but for this the argument might be made that it tends to help the effect of masculinity and brash events, and to simplify or speed along some of the intricate writing of the play. The casting has been done with a good eye for variety in type; and the individual performances thus take on certain additional aspects of acting, whether the players can act or not. The mere differences in type, for example, between the two leading rôles, the Richard of Mr. Maurice Evans and the Bolingbroke of Mr. Ian Keith, go a long way toward the two portrayals. And many of the more secondary parts came off with a reality that was convincing enough for the play's needs.

Mr. Ian Keith rightly presented a Bolingbroke about whose total quality and final motives you cannot make up your mind, and should not. In Shakespeare's own development of the character later on (see *The First Part of King Henry IV*) we have an extraordinary clarification of the character: Bolingbroke's anxiety lest his dashing son, young Hotspur, will turn out another Richard, without stability, without moral fibre; his desire to show his son the intensity of his concern for England, his confession of his own dissimulation in combatting Richard:

> And then I stole all courtesy from heaven
> And dress'd myself in such humility
> That I did pluck allegiance from men's hearts,
> Loud shouts and salutations from their mouths,
> Even in the presence of the crownéd king.

Shakespeare doubtless thought of some of this long after he had written the play about Richard and as he turned the character of

RICHARD II

Bolingbroke over in his mind; but the germ of the whole portrait is there in this passage, for Mr. Keith to consider.

Mr. Maurice Evans, a competent and well focused player—which is to say he is busy and breathy with, rather than transformed into, the rôle in hand—gave as Richard a performance about on the level with his Napoleon in the recent *St. Helena*. Nothing powerful or searching is achieved and there is a general lack of markings—by markings I mean a certain underscoring of moments where the drama of character and the plot of event touch on crises in the play's pattern. How far Mr. Evans should rub things in, select, stress, is a matter of opinion and for his own discretion in the creation of the Shakespeare portrait of Richard. Certainly one of the remarkable things in Shakespeare's version of Richard is this very uncertainty, a combination of charm, impatience, license, tenderness, weakness, imaginative passion, and in the Greek sense infatuation, which to them signified that you by your obsession invited wreckage from the gods.

We come now to a portion of the production that is out of class, on a different plane, with the acting we have recounted or the agreeable settings, and Mr. Ffolkes' amiable costumes. Mr. Augustin Duncan's John of Gaunt has all the magnificence and reality that is best set down as indescribable. In the death scene with the famous lines to England—this precious stone set in the silver sea, et cetera— Mr. Duncan created a basic effect of actuality, combined with an inmost splendor of style, that could nowhere else on our stage be even approached. I am recording here for, I trust, more than a momentary reading, one of the handful of great intervals in our theatre's long dearth: a reading and soul so grand, so compelling and, in the midst of our current trash, so infrequent and so unwanted, that even to convey it is mere musing in a fool's paradise.

But while these aspects and elements may be of deep regard, they are not all there is to consider. In the light of stage purposes, it will pay anyone truly interested to go over Marlowe's *Edward II*. This play, generally dated as 1593, was no doubt in Shakespeare's mind when he wrote *Richard II*, dated early in 1596. Certain scholars rank Shakespeare's play far ahead of Marlowe's, because of the range and superior plane of the qualities created. The other side of the case, of course, is that Marlowe has selected certain traits and tendencies, full and clear as in Greek drama—and has placed these irrevocably within the substance and development of his play. The form is more consistent, the conclusion more inevitable. There is, as compared with Shakespeare's play, a less delicate and discerning scope; but the sheer form and finality are there, and are in themselves a kind of language. For its intuitive perception, grace of rather more minor understanding, and lyric dispersion, *Richard II* is grouped among Shakespeare's lyric dramas. But Marlowe's play of *Edward II* is miles beyond it as drama. For my part I contend that the march of a bold and inevitable theme surpasses a figure of subtle complexities with regard to character. And I contend that firm lines in the dramatic pattern say more, ultimately, than dainty or passionately cerebral variations in psychology, two-thirds of which sometimes in Shakespeare may consist of pure literary ornament.

Richard II suffers as a play first from the fact that, as every editor of it has remarked for generations, the minor, or perfunctory, scenes are done without much thought or care, though the main effects are ardently searched out. On the other hand there are scenes, admittedly free of all previous sources, Holinshed and the rest, that are Shakespeare's very own. Such a scene—done very well, with Mr. Whitford Kane as the head of it, and with a deep and lovely purity throughout—is that of the gardeners with the Queen. Nobody but Shakespeare would have imagined that, what with its lyric, homely element of growing nature, its symbolism and its visual image. But what the play most seriously suffers from is one single element that derives partly from the epoch, or shall we say the difference between that Elizabethan epoch and our own? It is something that is borne steadily in upon us as the play progresses to its end. I mean the constant elaboration, figures of speech, conceits, fancifications, involutions, not seldom characteristic of Elizabethan writing. When you hear Richard at some important moment twisting and winding, flowering into similes, tropes, birds, botany, music and rhetoric and so forth, while at that very moment something most important is to be swiftly conveyed, you might easily take it to be a case of eloquent weakness, impotent imagination, sensitivity, fatuity, circuitous but keen analytical insights; and you might thus accept Richard as a complicated dear weakling, doomed by his own nature! But when the stout Bolingbroke embroils himself in words and figures, poetical roundabouts and matching variations on straight themes; and all the dukes are perpetually wound up, and the Queen even at a tragic moment goes off with

> Conceit is still deriv'd
> From some forefather grief. Mine is not so,
> For nothing hath begot my something grief,
> Or something that the nothing that I grieve

you can scarcely feel that it is Richard alone who thus gambols from the point, but also the poet and the age.

The fact remains nevertheless that the familiar magic in words and miracles in perception that are Shakespeare's constantly occur in this play, and provide the mind with a literate and often gusty evening. The last moment, with Richard brought in dead, and placed at the foot of the throne, with Bolingbroke looking on him, the silent court around, is a superb stage motif on the part of Miss Margaret Webster in her directing.

It seems unnecessary to note that the whole play gains in occasional appeal by certain rather obvious parallels with recent events in Britain.

THE SEA GULL

The Sea Gull, by Anton Chekhov, translated by Stark Young.
Shubert Theatre. March 28, 1938.

IN THE matter of translation—I shall never be able to say this too often—a strange thing has happened with Chekhov. It is not unique among dramatists or the visual arts, but in this instance it becomes very important in the light of Chekhov's growing fame and influence in our theatre. To be brief, what we have here is a case of a dramatist coming into English with the handicap of the wrong tone bestowed upon him by the translators.

The Garnett translation is the least harmful very likely; it suffers mostly from a lack of theatre knowledge, or shall we say the sense of speakability, without which Chekhov, since he spoke through the theatre, could not be said really to be rendered into English. But that can be, and has been in various productions, somewhat got around by clipping and mending the lines for greater naturalness or plausibility as human utterance. In general, however, the idea holds that Chekhov is something smoky as to the lines, moody, complex, soulful perhaps, certainly very often vague. I once shared this notion. And lately I have been looking into some of those translations with which I began my Chekhov acquaintance, and have searched for instances that might easily excuse or justify such a conception of his style. It is no wonder we have all thought what we did. And it is no wonder that here and there my translation of *The Sea Gull* has been with the kindest and most generous intentions praised as vigorous for modern ears, or as brightening and shortening the text, or as agreeably omitting the literal translation of the original Russian and the Russian idiom. But in many respects these compliments have got the matter upside down. My translation is exactly literal, and most of the Chekhov speeches, taken in themselves, are very simple and straight. So far as I know, I made less than half a dozen departures from the word in Chekhov's text and these always for some practical theatre reason, and always with an acknowledgment in the notes to the published volume. To take one instance only, there is the title. The Russian does not mean sea gull but merely gull, which is obviously impossible for the title in English.

I even tried to keep the mere number of words in any given speech the same as in Chekhov, since the duration *per se* in a stage speech is part of its meaning.

That the translation was otherwise received by those who knew better is evinced by the comment of Dr. Nicholas Rumanceff. He says, "After reading the reviews I might have concluded that *The Sea Gull* had been rearranged for a better understanding and response on the part of American audiences. Knowing the other translations and knowing the play, I could easily have believed that this new version, to be thus successful, must be an adaptation. But such was not the case. I found almost word for word Chekhov's characteristic, it seemed to me, in Mr. Young's translation. The reason the American public loves the play and understands the play is because it is like Chekhov in English." Dr. Rumanceff was formerly Chairman of the Board of Directors of the Moscow Art Theatre.

Mr. Brooks Atkinson said in *The New York Times:* "In view of Mr. Young's discoveries in the tone-deaf and genteel translations of *The Sea Gull*, one begins to wonder how much of the other plays has been lost in opaque translations. But for this one play Mr. Young has produced a version that is clear, brisk and simple and that leaves an impression of mental alertness in the theatre. For the first time we begin to hear the voice of Chekhov as he spoke it in Russian forty years ago."

The fact must always be remembered that *The Sea Gull* is not full-blown Chekhov as to manner and mood. It was written in 1895, and was the first of his plays to get attention. The complete Chekhov quality was to come five years later in such plays as *The Three Sisters* and *The Cherry Orchard. The Sea Gull* is only in spots atmospheric in the sense usually applied to Chekhov; its frame is partly built and accentuated out of the older traditional European drama. Many of the critical clichés so often applied to Chekhov must, therefore, be applied to this play only with the greatest care.

Examining some of these specimens that I have picked out as

examples, I am not surprised that we should have thought Chekhov's lines so complex or hard to translate. As for the Fell translation, one heard, of course, that the author had lived years in Russia and certainly, therefore, knew the language to the last degree; clearly it was conscience alone that made her willing to sacrifice naturalness of effect, ease, even English structure, much less the possibility of the lines ever being spoken by an actor on the stage. Anybody, in sum, would think that these complicated effects must certainly result from a pious effort to render with the utmost accuracy some subtle and complex original. What else would account for these contortions, solemnities, unsayabilities?

I will not try here for any startling effect, but will merely quote some of those speeches that might have misled me to those misty steppes and subtle windings of Chekhov's style as along with so many other people, I had come to imagine it. I will put down the translator's line and after it the straight and nearly always simple line that Chekhov has written.

". . . you can have no inducement to marry a man who cannot even find sufficient food for his own mouth." Chekhov merely asks how one could want to marry a man who can't feed himself.

". . . though what his provocation may be I can't imagine." Chekhov's line is "But what for?"

". . . as if the field of art were not large enough to accommodate both new and old without the necessity of jostling!" Chekhov says, "but there is room for all—why elbow?"

"I am irresistibly impelled toward her." Chekhov says, "I am drawn to her."

"I come back to the conclusion that all I am fit for is to describe landscapes, and that whatever else I attempt rings abominably false." Chekhov says, "I feel that I can write only [of the] landscape, and in everything else I am false and false to the marrow of my bones." Five of the translations refuse Chekhov that repetition of "false."

None of the others is so complicated as this Fell version of *The Sea Gull*. But at that there are wide variations in quality, and such renderings as the two following may crop up almost anywhere. Where Chekhov's manager shouts, "You don't know what a farm means," we find in one translator, "You do not know what the management of an estate involves." Where Chekhov has "Everyone must write as he wants to and as he can," we read, "Everyone must write in accordance with his desire and his capacity."

These instances, though more conspicuously off, are only bits within a larger and impinging general tone that has built up such an idea of Chekhov's lines as would make him frantic and that continue to sicken cultured Russians who encounter it. I could scarcely have been more surprised than I was when I found on coming to Chekhov in Russian that his lines are not complex or difficult at all; they are not even involved. Thinking back over it all, I see now that we should have known better all along. Chekhov's special method, the realistic-psychological, as it is called, should have taught us, I see that now only too clearly. In this method the surface of life is apparently reproduced, natural and familiar; and only by the combinations, the sequences, the underlying associations and implications, are profound meanings created. It should have followed then, if we had kept our wits about us, that his speech would have done a parallel thing. The speech would be simple, on the surface natural and easy; the inner meanings would appear but not through complex or vague lines, not through the muggy, symbolic, swing-on-to-your-atmosphere sort of tone. We should have known that. I for one did not.

Apart from this complete simplicity, the other problems in translating *The Sea Gull* consisted in two things: to get the lines sayable, and thus theatre; to let Chekhov do it his own way, repeat, make images, simplify, whatever he chooses. One may at least try for that. For example when Chekhov organizes a speech where a man says he wanted to become a writer and never became one, wanted to marry and never married, etc., let us not say wanted to become a writer and didn't, wanted to marry and didn't, or remained a bachelor—not one of the six translations allows him his device of repetition here.

The most striking of these cases where Chekhov is shown a better way to do it occurs in the first act of *The Sea Gull,* where Treplev begs his mother's patience and she answers by quoting from *Hamlet*:

> My son,
> Thou turnst mine eyes into my very soul,
> And there I see such black and grained spots
> As will not leave their tinct.

Let us not assume that Chekhov did not know his business when he drew on the lines with which Shakespeare followed that speech of the queen's:

> Nay, but to live
> In the rank sweat of an enseamed bed,
> Stew'd in corruption, honeying and making love
> Over the nasty sty!

Instead of that passage, however, another and quite different one is substituted in whatever productions of this play I happen to have heard of so far, and in four out of the six translations that I have read.

> Leave wringing of your hands. Peace! sit you down!
> And let me wring your heart; for so I shall
> If it be made of penetrable stuff.

That speech is Shakespeare, though transposed, but is not in character for Treplev; it is merely cleverish, and out of place. A fifth translation, if I remember right, gives a fragment of the Shakespeare passage but apologizes and suggests the substitution of the above. The sixth gives the Shakespeare lines verbatim.

But even that is not what Chekhov wants. The brutality of those lines is daring enough for Hamlet to speak before an Elizabethan audience, for all their strong stomachs and open audacity. If Treplev had said them to his mother, it would have brought to the moment something so appalling and obscene that he would have broken up the company gathered there to see his play. What Chekhov does is to paraphrase Shakespeare's lines into, "Nay, but why do you yield to sin, see love in the depths of wickedness?" And in addition to that milder paraphrase, he has the knocking on the floor, the horn sounding, and the play beginning, all of which serve to cut across its impact and draw us adroitly on toward his next impression.

The Sea Gull, as produced by Mr. Alfred Lunt and Miss Lynn Fontanne, and presented by the Theatre Guild, is on the whole the best Chekhov production that I have seen in English. Mr. Robert Edmond Jones' design for the first act was full of a sober, virile style rare indeed in out of door settings. Its one defect was too much light on the side farthest from Treplev's stage, where Chekhov expressly prescribes that the scene be in dusk till Treplev's curtain rises on the lake and the moon. Stanislavsky records that in their first effort to abide by this idea they got the stage so dark that the actors could scarcely be seen. Miss Fontanne in my opinion gave a brilliant performance of the actress. I have in fact the Moscow Art Theatre's Mme. Maria Ouspenskaya's word for it that she thought Miss Fontanne was better than the actress who had taken the part in Russia. Mr. Lunt seemed to me to give Trigorin the right depth, for Chekhov plainly intends him to be only a popular second-rate idol of an author. Miss Uta Hagen played Nina, the young girl, with an admirable lyric ease. Mr. Richard Whorf was at least competent as the young writer, Treplev. And Mr. Sydney Greenstreet as Sorin, the retired councilor, brother of the actress, gave a performance remarkably exact and beautiful; no performance, as Mr. John Anderson said in his *Journal-American* review, either inside or outside the Moscow Art Theatre, could be finer.

Finally there is one thing especially that should be said about Miss Fontanne's and Mr. Lunt's approach to the play: it was what Chekhov productions on our stage very seldom are, and that is an entirely honorable attitude by which there was no changing of lines, no trimming the dangerous corners of some of Chekhov's devices and motifs, no concessions to what might be easier to swallow or more popular.

HEARTBREAK HOUSES

Heartbreak House, by George Bernard Shaw.
Mercury Theatre. April 29, 1938.

I REMEMBER how Mr. Edmund Wilson and I, some years ago in a convivial literary moment, agreed that *Heartbreak House* was probably the best of the Shaw plays. We wondered, I remember, whether in twenty years it might not be the shining light among them. Through the removal of limitations in probability, and through the opening thereby for extravagance, *Heartbreak House* is farce rather than comedy. Nor is that anything against it unless you object to the possibility that farce allows for the poetic or fantastic. The question was whether or not we had begun to be impatient with this larding of social theory and significance on to what essentially was farce, however talented, and would remain so. Mr. Wilson and I must have been thinking that *Heartbreak House* offered a more complete unity of tone than most of Mr. Shaw's plays, and that perhaps the constant effect of assertiveness which was so peculiar to Shaw, and which could get very tiresome elsewhere in his other work, was especially suited to the tone of this particular play. In *Heartbreak House* perhaps this general tone in itself effectively expressed the theme, which is the state of things that was "the cultured, leisured Europe before the War."

It must have been an impression of some different sort that had done the work, for all these reflections went flat on me when I saw *Heartbreak House* produced again these many years after. I had looked forward to seeing the play again not only from curiosity about a work of art, but also, in a way, autobiographically—which is to say curiosity about myself, as to what my state of mind and change might be. For a while, on thus revisiting this drama I took it to be the production at the Mercury Theatre that was at fault. Presently I saw that the production was fair enough—if slightly blurred—with some good performances, especially Miss Phyllis Joyce as Lady Utterwood, but that the play itself was garrulous, unfelt and tiresome.

Evidently the impression from the Theatre Guild production of *Heartbreak House* that had remained so strongly in my mind as the years went by came from the terrace scene and the company talking there in the moonless blue night. It was a long time ago and I had forgotten nearly all they said, but not that haunting tone composed of the scene, the voices, the vibration of characters, the impending blind ruin. And presently there at the Mercury I saw that I had lost even such a response. I was sufficiently concerned to take the book down afterward and read the whole play again, the long preface included. Very likely Mr. Welles' production lacked emphasis to some extent, parts of the play needing to be speeded up, parts slowed down, the pressure lightened here, increased there, for the sake of a more distinct pattern. But at that, the design of *Heartbreak House* proved on this rereading to be no more marked than it is in the production, if as much. Gradually I concluded that there was something very amiable about the willingness of a theatre company to memorize so many lines, and to heed, or seem to heed, so much rather wilted opinion, half point and half patter. An astonishing sort of inner monotony, as it were, was apparent, and had to be coped with. Except for the different voices, you could have shut your eyes and believed not that several people were there, created and expressing themselves, but that one person was describing several people.

Since Mr. Shaw himself goes to some length in the preface to invite more or less comparison of *Heartbreak House* with Chekhov's plays, we may sketch at least the beginning of such a comparison. Chekhov, he says, had produced four dramatic studies of *Heartbreak House,* of which three, *The Cherry Orchard, Uncle Vanya* and *The Sea Gull,* so far as England went, had got as far as a couple of performances by the Stage Society. The audiences had stared and said "How Russian!" To Mr. Shaw on the contrary it seemed that these intensely Russian plays fitted all the country houses in Europe in which . . . et cetera. Such a remark as that seems to me incredibly wilful and silly. The thesis of blind chaos and selfishness and of following the part of comfortable income and securities is a definite thesis. It may readily fit into the motif of a rotting Europe. But Chekhov would have been surprised to learn that his plays were a declaration in advance of all this. The Russian world of Chekhov can be only partially compared to the England that Mr. Shaw has diagrammed in *Heartbreak House*. A great difference arises from the fact that the expressiveness of the Russian temperament, with its gift and power of outpouring the far recesses of the heart, is a far more difficult matter for the English. This is not to say that either one or the other is better, but only that they are different. Where Tolstoy, Mr. Shaw says, was no pessimist and believed in the efficacy of violent measures, Chekhov, "more of a fatalist, had no faith in these charming people extricating themselves. They would, he thought, be sold up and set adrift by the bailiff; and he therefore had no scruple in exploiting and even flattering their charm."

What a patness and charm of persuasion this Mr. Shaw has! But the mere use of the words "flatter" and "charm" give away the British rubbish, or Teutonic conception, behind the idea. The references here are plainly to *The Cherry Orchard*. But no person in it wants to be flattered as to his special idiosyncrasy, nobody in this play is talking with that self-consciousness and varying degrees of egotism or no egotism so common to modest Englishmen. The charm of these people in *The Cherry Orchard,* and often of the Russians we meet is that nobody is thinking at all about being charming; nobody is self-conscious, nobody is affected. That sentence of Mr. Shaw's is a whole commentary on the difference between Chekhov's world and that British world which Mr. Shaw so pugnaciously caters to, rebukes so entertainingly, severely and sincerely, and makes a fortune out of.

The more you know of Chekhov's writing and of him and his life and friends, the more absurd Mr. Shaw becomes on the subject. It is all very well to use a man or a work of art to hit something or somebody over the head with; and certainly the sport is an old one. But nobody could be more astonished than Chekhov would have been to hear of his having no scruples about exploiting the people whose words and little ironic, tender or mad acts, and droll or dark life-patterns he put into plays and stories or left jotted down in his notebook. To "flatter" anything about them would not fit anything in him. What he did with his people was to turn them into theatre, just as Mr. Shaw in *Heartbreak House* turns Chekhov into a sort of literary Hyde Park soapbox dialectic for the theatre.

That such a man as Mr. Shaw could use the life that is presented in Chekhov's plays in Chekhov's way, and even some of Chekhov's ideas and attitudes, is obvious. In spite of the unsuccessful translations of the Chekhov plays into English, a great deal of him comes through; and I should think it possible enough that Mr. Shaw regards his own *Heartbreak House* as being technically related to the three Chekhov plays that he mentions, *The Cherry Orchard* especially. Whether he does so or not, the comparison is inevitable and the relationship plain. On that subject we should have to say that either he boldly exercised his usual independence in the way of doing things, or else he was blind as a bat to Chekhov's technique, stage-effects and spirit. We should be brow-beaten indeed to accept the idea that in *Heartbreak House* there is more than the merest hint or tiny reflection of Chekhov's true method, none of that pure, painstaking economy and drawing, none of that humility of vision, none of that shy certainty of intuition. And Mr. Shaw's play has none of the variety in emotional rhythm that Chekhov has, either in tone or in profound self-revelation among the characters.

Chekhov sees his people as rooted in something, which means that he begins with what they are, their quality, and from this he derives what they will express. Mr. Shaw, for all his prattle about their class, clichés, bogies, culture and complacent, urgent or ironic circumstance, sees his people in the light of their opinions. Such a course makes for certain effective dramatic patterns, for distinct *dramatis personae,* real or not real, and for straw men, to be set up or knocked over at will. But it is, I think, his greatest and his final weakness as a creative artist. And it provides the reason why no intelligent member of the traditional British ruling class has ever needed to fear Mr. Shaw very greatly. Nobody could ever take one of Mr. Shaw's magnates or autocratic ruling class characters as the real thing. They may be arresting or provocative, but—for a while at least—it is their author, not themselves, that is so articulate. The portrayal, however, could be dangerous only when it came from the centre of the character himself. It is this quality of the centrifugal that makes Chekhov different from Mr. Shaw, though centrifugal seems a word too strong for that delicate, moving security and expressive freedom that Chekhov achieves for his people, and the matrix of gentle humor, like that of a wise doctor, within which he sees what they say or do, and for which he brings no compelling benefit or reform.

Taking a work of art as a kind of biological whole, which is the only way it makes any sense, I should say that nothing Mr. Shaw presents in *Heartbreak House* to prove his case could be a better evidence of the decay, if you like, of the English scene than this play itself is, with its lack of any organic unity or exciting technique, its fuzzy lack of power, its exhibitionistic self-assertion, its futile chatter in coquettish monotone about what the first bomb could obliterate or the first ism could make stale.

THE WHOLE TRAGICALL HISTORIE

Hamlet. St. James Theatre. October 12, 1938.

FOR the first time in the American theatre, we have the complete *Hamlet*, not, as some of the news proclaims, exactly as Shakespeare wrote it, the versions having always differed of course, but so far as I could tell from a single hearing, a faithful script that draws on occasion from either the Second Quarto (1604), which is the authority for the text, or from the First Folio (1623), which omits about two hundred lines and adds something like eighty. The passage, for instance, about the actors—"Let them be well us'd," etc., is from the Folio; "And enterprises of great pitch and moment" (not "pith") is from the Quarto.

In general this text, as spoken on the stage under Miss Margaret Webster's direction, is intelligible, which is a good deal to say for any Shakespeare performance. There are only a few cases of the jumpy sort where the actor as he reads seems to be jerking up from his diaphragm things whose meanings have escaped him. I could not agree with the conception of the graveyard scene in Act V, with such a blare of light, the hoar-frost, and the Queen presenting a wreath instead of the usual scattering of flowers that is more effective with the sweets-to-the-sweet motif in the lines. Hamlet's and Laertes' encounters seem to me to be too much blurred. And for that matter, while we are sticking so closely to the text, why not stick to the text's stage directions? The First Folio has "Leaps in the grave," which Hamlet Evans does not do.

With the exception of this whole first part of Act V, which seemed to me to miss the grotesque projection, mystery and tragic power that Shakespeare intended, Miss Webster's direction spread the many scenes of the play into a singularly comprehensive pattern, flexible, never banal and often eloquent. The unobtrusive distribution of her stage movement was remarkable, as was the way in which she managed to leave certain of the obscene passages intact and yet cover them enough with stage business to prevent their sticking out beyond Shakespeare's purpose and thus distracting attention from the true effect. Mr. David Ffolkes' settings, except for the lighting, were something above adequate; and so were his costumes, though they were for the most part poorly worn, and though headdresses and coiffures were almost wholly lacking. It is true that Elizabethan heads were often more or less like the modern, but to hear those intricate Renaissance lines emerge from scene after scene of everyday hair, leads—just as does the casual wearing of the clothes—away from the illusion.

The interpretation of the King (Mr. Henry Edwards) leaves the traditional, or stylized, for the natural, and thus creates, in my opinion, a distinct loss. The advantage in doing the King in the traditional Senecan style—the "tyrant" rôle of Greek drama—is that we get the effect of something strong and imposing, almost monumental, with its own magnetism and power, against which Hamlet, with his sensitive impulse and deep variety of thought, might dash himself out. But as Mr. Edwards plays the rôle, we have merely another agitated person (with the government behind him). Miss Katherine Locke's Ophelia, never haunting, too lowly perhaps for a Councillor's daughter, had, nevertheless, in the mad scenes a certain convincing truth not usual with that rôle. Mr. Whitford Kane did his gravedigger, by now practically a stage classic in itself. Mr. George Graham's Polonius was thinnish and hollow but not so far from Shakespeare's purpose; and Mr. Rhys Williams was curiously outstanding as the Player King.

Miss Mady Christians gave to the rôle of the Queen an air of court breeding and style that contributed to the impression of allure and delicate lushness that she achieved and that helped convince us of the passionate bond between her and the King. It is the first time I ever saw this motif in the play when it was made to count to its full dramatic value.

Mr. Evans brings to his Hamlet the positive virtues of a clear diction, a voice of considerable flexibility and some color, and an approach to the rôle that seems consistently sincere. He gives the appearance, also, of playing honestly with the company around him. Certain more or less direct ideas and emotions he can convey with energetic security. He finds stage positions that are excellently contrived for the moment they serve. Stage movement, however, Mr. Evans has almost none of, none of that intense coördination and flow that makes the actor's body itself a theatre medium of primary importance. Nor does his stage presence do more than faintly suggest the qualities of princely form, the observed of all observers, and so on, ascribed to Hamlet by those around him in the play.

You soon perceive that Mr. Evans aims at vigor in his reading and does achieve a certain impression of it, partly by a very active tempo and a tendency to raise the voice. The result is one that holds the attention as it strikes the main ideas in the lines and simplifies the rest. Many of the subtleties and overtones are thus lost; Hamlet no longer represents so rich an echo or so vast a range in man's experience. These subtleties often lie in the transitions. Mr. Evans' reading is capable to an amazing extent at times of ignoring a transition—for a single illustration take Hamlet's speech to Laertes about ranting, the final sentence: "Nay, and thou'lt mouth, I'll rant as well as thou." Some actors, like the elder Kean, have kept down the rest of the speech as if to set a quietude of contempt against Laertes' ranting and insults: some have taken it head on, in almost a frenzy. But however they took that part, this sentence, with its sudden and profound revelation of Hamlet's inmost habit of mind, marked a transition. Mr. Evans took it in exactly the same tone and pressure as the rest of the speech.

You rarely had in this performance the sense of struggle going on in Hamlet, and this was doubtless what Mr. Evans intended. The purpose behind his approach and method must be to contravert somewhat the idea of Hamlet's feebleness of will, vacillation, and so on, the old familiar theory. In some ways the idea is a good one, for undoubtedly too much has been done, especially in the romantic criticism of the early nineteenth century, to build up such a picture. Shakespeare has definitely provided against such a misunderstanding, but it would seem that his point has gradually been overlooked, partly because of the change in attitude between his day and ours toward ghosts and spirits. A very slight research into the pneumatology of Shakespeare's epoch will make this clear. The existence of ghosts or spirits was not questioned, the problem concerned their goodness or malignity. Up to the middle of Act III (the moment, in fact, when the King stops the play and rushes out), the conflict is by no means wholly concerned with weakness of will, dreams, action, and so on. A great deal of the conflict turns on whether the apparition is really Hamlet's father or a spirit of evil. (Hence the need of the play to prove the King's conscience.) In five separate passages, and from three different speakers, Shakespeare does his best to hammer in this point. The irony, then, is that the actor should lose so many of the finer shades and values trying to do for the character what Shapeskeare has already done otherwise, if the right emphases are given. And a further irony is that the first of these passages expressing this side of the conflict falls to Mr. Donald Randolph's Horatio, whose reading leaves it quite incomprehensible.

Mr. Evans' fundamental mistake, it seems to me, is clear enough, though it is almost impossible to express. It consists of an approach to the words as if he had planned every one of them and intended to put it into action. But the essence of a great deal of Hamlet's utterance is that it is in the nature of improvisation; the words may come to him for his own delight, pouring up from within his consciousness somewhere—who knows how?—his own words leading him, lighting his way, realities themselves within his reality. This, of course, does not alter the fact of the numberless other words, straight or wittily contrived, that he has planned and sets into action.

Another way to put the case would be to say that in speech after speech throughout the play, if Hamlet, in cold blood, had planned and brought into action the words, with all that elaboration, complexity, dilation and ornament, he might be tiresome to think of.

Still another way would be to recognize that the Poetic Style enjoys the license of assigning Hamlet whatever it chooses for him to say, with the purpose of expressing his thought and his will, but over and above that, the quality of his thought, of himself, and of the moment. The actor works finally under the same compulsion.

SAROYAN THEATRE

Love's Old Sweet Song, by William Saroyan.
Plymouth Theatre. May 2, 1940.

THE sum of things said and written about Mr. Saroyan's latest play, *Love's Old Sweet Song*, denies him so far the eternal blazon, despite the fact of the Drama Critics' Circle and the Pulitzer Prize awards that have come to him.

That cool denial seems first of all to be based on the fact that he refuses to use his mind enough—nobody so far, apparently, has decided he has not enough to use. On the whole, though, I think I should start at the other end, put the case another way. Perhaps I should begin by asking him to turn loose on a play that he is writing the full current of his fantasy, imagination, riotous tumult, laughter and disdain, his loving, blowsy double-edged folk observation—that stock of Americana he has up his saucy sleeve—to loose all this in a full stream at the very start and then to see what regulation and final form will accrue to it, either through its own essential quality and needs, as served by him, or through the dressing-down it gets from the harsh world. This would be a kind of sound biological way, as it were, to go about it, especially for an author like Mr. Saroyan. I cannot conceive of his beginning at the mental, or intellectual—whatever that may mean—end, any more than he could begin by being a philosopher, a dietitian or one of Minerva's owls. Seeing how much fifth-rate stuff we have had in the last two decades from the so-called drama of ideas, we could hardly be sorry for that. To be recognized, intelligence does not require statements; it permeates the whole substance of a work of art, the tone, the images, the choice of subject, the theme, the ideal plane. This, I think, is what people mean when they tell, one way or another, Mr. Saroyan to behave himself.

We might add two little bits of advice for him. First: amid the delights and fruits of his teeming exhibitionism, he must look sharp

—the brightest tail feathers are close to the ugliest features in the eagle's, swan's, peacock's, nightingale's—take your choice—anatomy. Second: do the play, or the scene, any way he likes, paying as little or as much attention as he likes to anyone's criticism, but he sure it says in the theatre what he wants it to say. The labor toward that end is his own affair; say it as fully as he can in theatre terms, remembering that the theatre is still a dialect.

Love's Old Sweet Song meanwhile is full of hearty themes, as human or hokum as the creative gift and professional hand behind them may or may not have wrought. The old maid, the medicine man, the migratory workers—"Okies"—the classic family with the grave Greek father and pious bruiser son, and the dénouement's banality—Mr. Saroyan uses banality here as riotously as he uses social justice, love, alcohol or any of the themes just listed.

The migratory wife, her husband, the salesman for *Time Magazine,* the Greek athlete son, with Miss Doro Merande, Mr. Arthur Hunnicutt, Mr. Alan Hewitt and Mr. Alan Reed, had capital performances. Mr. Walter Huston played the medicine man with his familiar lustiness, refinement and sure style. And Miss Jessie Royce Landis, as the old maid, so much entangled with love and "Okies," had a rôle that could easily have been obvious, foolish or sloppy or Freudian. She played it with fine rightness and beautiful taste.

Those grave judgments uttered, I may say that for me *Love's Old Sweet Song* made the most delightfully contagious theatre evening that I have spent in a long time. It is spirited, reckless and overabundant, as if the playwright could turn at any moment he chooses and knock off another play or so. Some of the motivations, like that of the giant son so respectful to his slender old Greek father, are not only tender and exuberant comedy, they are sharply and lovingly observed out of American life. There is so much that is fresh and vibrant about this Saroyan piece that I find myself hoping almost anything from him, if his fates prove kind. Human feeling and a beat of intensity move outward from the core of *Love's Old Sweet Song*; and there is a certain elusive but fine weaving and pressure of rhythms within the whole of it. Whether it is original or not, the word is sure to be applied to this play, which has fulness rather than power, and has flexibility rather than force, but which carries all its varied content with gusto and a kind of open delight in itself. There are many scenes that are recklessly and frankly theatre, frankly sown with tricks and with a relish for the theatre as such; but no harm in that; it is a healthy sign. Whether or not it proves to do so, the fact remains that such writing as this might very well refresh the so-called serious drama nowadays. In something like this sense Mr. Saroyan's play is poetic, far more so than some of the blank-verse efforts that help to give what is called poetic drama a black eye. He has created a plentiful life that pours up constantly; the mind behind the play is rich with curiosity, wide music, variety, an instinct for human color, a patter of human words, and a passion, almost gay, for half-tragic human experience.

The rambling technical defects of Mr. Saroyan's play make good illustrations of the inexorable—you could very well call them biological—exactions of the theatre. The theatre has its distances, physical, mental and emotional, as we have, beyond which nothing can be truly seen or felt. The needs, too, of the actors parallel those of our bodies: just as, for instance, you cannot walk out of a room without legs, so the actor cannot get out of a scene without something contrived for him to get out on.

That practical instinct that is in artists can help Mr. Saroyan to study these matters and consider, with imagination, the laborious imagery and projection special to the theatre. Meanwhile his play furnishes us with an illustration of the artist as distinguished from the craftsman—in any art. Which is to say that the basic, underlying, fecundating and generalizing principle of life is there in him, in his theatre writing; and that the transition to theatrical form is but partially achieved. But it is achieved sufficiently to carry a long way already. Moreover, it should be said—and this will mean very little except to professionals—that at this stage of the game it is a certain innocence in Mr. Saroyan as to what is hackneyed theatre and what is not—this rushing in where the angel playwrights fear to tread—that sometimes lends the play its charming and lovable quality. On the other hand Mr. Saroyan might ask us who these angels are, and make us quite sick. For my part, if he will only keep to it, I should be content with him as our angel.

TWELFTH NIGHT

Twelfth Night. Little Theatre. December 1, 1941.

IN THE presentation of *Twelfth Night* by the Chekhov Theatre Players we have, behind the producing and the devising, a man who was formerly a member of the Moscow Art Theatre Company under Stanislavsky and Nemirovitch-Danchenko, and then himself director of the Second Moscow Art Theatre, an actor and director who has worked in various languages and as many countries. He has made three productions of *Twelfth Night* in three diverse languages before coming to this production in English. He has also directed a company that has worked a long time on the play and has given many performances of it, in its studio theatre at Ridgefield, Connecticut, and on tour far and wide among cities and colleges.

Few productions of a Shakespeare play have such advantages behind them. Most of them are made up of companies got together as God wills, put through three or four weeks of rehearsals, shot around the out-of-town circuit for a bit and then brought in, daring Broadway and hoping for the best and depending largely on the prestige of two or three known players who are—as the saying is—stars. On such occasions there are lovers of Shakespeare who are disappointed, or puzzled, at the inchoate results; others less familiar with his works are pleased to find that he is quite good; and so we go on down—or up or out—to those who think that if there is any deficiency to be found, the fault is Shakespeare's rather than the actor's.

It behooves us, then, to look carefully at this *Twelfth Night* of the Chekhov Theatre Players, and to try and point out what there is in this event that might serve the uses of our theatre, our Shakespeare theatre especially.

Twelfth Night has for its source the Italian novel and—as was pointed out by Shakespeare's own contemporaries—an Italian play or so, and, accordingly, though more remote, of course, Latin comedy,

Attic comedy and the Greek romances. Meanwhile the farcical elements of the *commedia,* ancient and later, are in the offing. Perhaps, even, they underlie the pace and the mixture of every sort of material, mood and motivation that we find in this play. Very likely in the Elizabethan and general Renaissance production of such a piece the solution was ready enough: they merely let it rip—poetry, farce, burlesque, carnival, satire, and the devil take the hindmost. For us that is not so easy. *Twelfth Night* has many jarring combinations—Viola, Orsino, Sir Toby, Sir Andrew, Feste, and so on—not to speak of the cruel shadings to the Malvolio theme, for which we have the cheerful and enthusiastic praise of Shakespeare's contemporaries explicitly recorded as "a good practice," which is to say an excellent invention. All this dramatic matter, which plainly those audiences of Shakespeare's day took in their stride, is less easy for us nowadays to unify and swallow. But as to that, I should say that the fault is not in our stars but in ourselves that we are theatre underlings.

The unfortunate side of the Chekhov production, opening the way for critical objections, or for its ready dismissal as an amateur or school effort, lies in the production, strictly speaking, and in the décor. There are no scenery shifts but merely bits like the prison walls, or chairs, draperies or gates indicated by chords, all changed by means of screens in various satiny colors, manipulated by apprentices, to various degrees of music. The effect as décor is of an idle and worn-out invention, and the result an impression of distracting contrivance, superfluous and much too lively as well as wasteful. There is, too, because of the costumed apprentices, a regrettable impression of some college affair, whereas the company playing is by no means a mere dramatic school; it is better fitted for Shakespeare's play and more profoundly and happily engaged in it than any other company on Broadway has been in who knows when? That business with the screens at the end of the play, the peeping over them and flirting with the footlights, and then the pantomime of several characters, is a case in point. It is bouncy but not gay really; to stick to Shakespeare's text, ending with the song by Feste—of all Shakespeare's clowns the one most worthy of study perhaps—would greatly contribute to the play's lyricism, a quality that is too lacking in this production of *Twelfth Night.*

There is a phrase old in French and at least not strange among us:

the defect of an excellence. We have no way of knowing how much, at this stage of the game, those extraneous touches and motifs, Russian and, if you like, threadbare for us, are the reverse of the free and flowing beauty and accuracy of this version of *Twelfth Night* as a whole, of this wayward, earthy, singing document of the Renaissance that our Broadway audiences now encounter from the Chekhov Theatre Players. That makes it all the more regrettable that the rushing about and the stage archness took time from the text itself, so that a good deal of cutting resulted. We must turn to the positive advantages of the occasion.

Imprimis—first, then, I may record the fact that only here have I, in many years of theatre-going, heard every line of Shakespeare that is spoken make sense—no mouthing, and yet no foolish, vulgar simplification of the speeches to gain a vapid comprehension from the popular audience.

Second: I have never, in a long list of *Twelfth Night* productions, seen certain motifs and themes of the play turn out so clear; I have never heard reading that made them so reckless and irresponsible, as they should be, but yet so exact to the play's intention. The melancholy of Olivia and of Orsino, for example, is usually taken in the declamatory vein, heavy, amatory and unconvincing. But as Mr. Chekhov directs it, the theme is a competition in romantic egotism, in which Viola and her love are delicately included, though Orsino will not have it that she nor any woman can ever love as he does, not any age or inclination equal his despair. Their several loves thus achieve a due placement, sociable, sensible and romantic, so that our hearts shall be wrung by them, musical, elegiac, delirious, as by the lute's playing of some sad, sweet song or by some momentary fading sweetness on the air. In this production we have the delightful experience of finding that what in most productions of the play have been mere dull flats of emotion can take on variety, vigor and something of the rose of spring and all its fatal lovely music.

The reading of the jester's lines turns out mere gibberish in most Shakespeare productions, so much so as to make you wonder why intelligent princes ever had these perky, punning bores around them, as historically we know they did. Here in Feste we hear distinctly the burlesque of philosophic system and thought that Shakespeare intended; grave echoes appear, laments, quips and poignant topsy-turvy. In this case it is entirely right that the clown should be the one who sings, that a story which begins with music should sing itself out with a song.

The motivations for the concluding duel scene, are only a washout in most performances of *Twelfth Night*, but in Mr. Chekhov's hands they are genuinely contrived. In the first place the actors, for a change, can really fence. We see Sir Toby's winey lust for a fight, see Viola's terror of a sword, Sir Andrew's fright, and then Sebastian's entrance, a masculine figure, a fighter, a swordsman who takes Sir Toby's breath away. The shock and stir is such that Olivia coming into it asks the loved young man to go to the chantry near and plight their troth, and young Sebastian, in the whirl of such events, finds it easy and ready to follow her beauty there or anywhere, as easy or as ready as fighting, honor, shipwreck and all mystery and bright life. But the point is that to create this result the actor in the scene must really know how to fence, which is also to say that genuine masculinity must come into the scene. Sebastian, in sum, must have about him what can make us believe the romantic impetuosity of the story at this juncture. In all the productions of *Twelfth Night* that I have seen—among them that of the Theatre Giuld with Miss Helen Hayes' Viola and a Sebastian that seemed equally girlish—this is the only one where the scene makes its proper sense—an amount of making sense, I must admit, that I had not entirely realized until I saw this Chekhov version.

It would hardly be fair to leave unmentioned such admirable performances as the Sir Toby of Mr. Ford Rainey, the Sir Andrew of Mr. Hurd Hatfield, the Viola of Miss Beatrice Straight and so on. At times they lack a certain authority that comes from long experience or from well-tried talents, or from hungry fire, or from a thick-skinned assertiveness or vulgar aggression. At times they afford us the pleasure that comes from purity of intention and intelligent practice and approach. Unfailingly they speak well, and their stage movements are well planned, secure, sometimes brilliant. On the whole, however, the best thing about the performance is, as I have just said, the ensemble playing.

Ensemble—that sounds like the simplest thing in the world. But run over in your mind the Shakespeare performances you have seen these past few years. They may have their good points, but these do not apply to ensemble. They have not had the training, the rehearsing, the playing together, the company organization, for proper results—take the banquet scene in Mr. Maurice Evans' *Macbeth,* for example, in which save for Mr. Evans and Miss Anderson, the rest are mere paper dolls.

Finally there is the baroque element in this Chekhov production of *Twelfth Night.* This is what is really new and fresh about the whole occasion, though it should not be so, since the very soul of the play's whole style lies in the baroque impulse. That performance of Mr. Rainey's as the drunken knight is all in curves, its lines working against the circle, its balances perfect and expert, based on the bodily poise of fencing and dancing. The make-up, too, is good Rubens, is stylized, ruddy and brilliantly executed throughout and exactly right for this particular performance. With the accent of such a make-up, all Sir Toby's speeches seem inevitable and right and there is no whirling of wits or mad flowering of words or allusions that can seem even surprising. What labor and experiment and memory have gone into such a stage execution of this Elizabethan rôle!

The visual production and décor, the Russian, unimaginative jollities and quips of this production could be easily removed, an hour or so of rehearsing and that could be done. We should then see better how all that sound training, precision, diction, sense emphasis and ensemble present a lesson to our theatre. More of Shakespeare's text should be included for their exercise.

M. Elie Faure once said of Renoir's portraits that the silks are like flesh and retain their lightness, the flesh is like silk and retains its weight. That applies subtly enough to *Twelfth Night,* so lovely, varied and accessible. It should be played straight and lustily, in all the rough bravura of its Elizabethan form, heedless, abundant, musical, all the rash elements; and played as if we took the body of the play not as the prison but as the mere shadow, perhaps, of its poetry.

BOOK BASIS

Native Son, by Paul Green and Richard Wright, based on the novel by Richard Wright. St. James Theatre. March 24, 1941.

THE case may be a little different, though not much so, when the author of a novel undertakes a dramatization of it. He has, at least more than does the outside dramatizer, the privilege of doing as he likes with it. In the art of painting, for example, there is obviously nothing new in an artist's turning from one canvas to another, or from canvas to sculpture, and leaving out certain motifs and repeating others. The only esthetic principle necessary, I should think, is that the second piece of art should be, as the first was, complete in itself. Complete in itself is the point.

Many elements from the novel of *Native Son* could not be got into a play; that is obvious. It is equally obvious that various other elements from the novel would have greatly deepened and enriched the play if they had been included. Most of all they might have helped to make it something more like itself and less like the traditional crime, fugitive-from-justice, social-wrong and death-cell plays that we have known so long, and might have served to differentiate it thus from these others, and to allow it more of its own distinction, true substance and innate power.

As matters stand, the play of *Native Son* that Mr. Richard Wright and Mr. Paul Green have written and that we see now produced is entirely recognizable in the modern theatre list of the last two generations or so. That fact is nothing against it of course; the same is true of the greatest masterpieces, if we leave out plane, imaginative passion and rarity. The assets that this particular play at the St. James enjoys over most others of its type are numerous enough, however.

Through dealing with the Negro life, pitted against its own race and the white race, it gains the advantage of a violent and dramatic light and shade in tone and incident, in warmth and gentle strangeness, fear, violence and frustration. The casting for the rôles, too, is for the most part highly astute. To think of Mr. Erskine Sanford for the capitalist father, for example, how many would have done that? There Mr. Sanford is, nevertheless, playing without Times Square punch, without the obvious tycoonery or wealthy insensitivity to the world's wrongs, but with a simplicity of feeling and good taste that could, if the play were written so, intensify the truth implicit in the subject matter. Miss Nell Harrison plays the blind wife with a very right quality, elusive and solitary, which is what it should be. And Mr. Canada Lee brings to the leading rôle a rich and varied gift of imagination, a subtle registration of feeling and poise, and an absence of sloppy self-pity for his man, Bigger Thomas. His is a most admirable performance, sure and steady and varied. It does not depend on the sheer racial vividness and unaccustomed quality—the voice, the movement, the rhythm—that often make performances by Negro players win a critical praise that must discourage many an actor who with labor and long thought has really learned his craft.

Mr. Lee's performance is, in fact, the best I have ever seen in New York from a Negro player. And in admiring it, we must remind ourselves, too, of the obstacles the actor of the leading rôle in this play had to go up against; first of all a certain externality, or objectivity, by which so much of what in the novel goes on in Bigger's mind is left out, and by which—this very objectivity and elimination—so many acting necessities remain, so much is heaped on the actor. And, too, Bigger's lines suffer none too rarely from being over explicit or expected, dull in rhythm, and hampered by semi-stale figures of speech—speeches in which the vital economy has been watered almost to banality, speeches without that passionate centre to spring from by which all words become glowing forms of life and all emotions mere fires of the propelling substance.

In two scenes above all, *Native Son* leaves far behind most plays of this general type: the scene where the girl is smothered by the Negro chauffeur—superbly handled in every way—and the scene before the furnace in which her body is hidden.

Native Son gains also by the thunderous and lurid theatre methods of Mr. Orson Welles. In my opinion Mr. Welles is one of the best influences our theatre has, one of the important forces. I also think the fact that he produced *Native Son* is more important than the fact of the play itself, as the play stands. His talent begins with the violent, the abundant and the inspired-obvious, all of which make for the life of the theatre art, as contrasted with the pussyfooting and the pseudo-intelligent and the feminism that has crept into this theatre art of ours. In *Native Son* he draws on full theatre resources, of light and sound and form, and his statement is almost continuously sonorous and distinct, though it may be at times quite ham, but this is not too dreadful a fault in these soft days.

The thing to ponder here about this directing of Mr. Welles' is that there is no way of telling how far this rushing and plentiful use of the theatre medium *per se* that he is capable of and practices here, cuts down the pathos, or the tragic element, that might have been possible to *Native Son* and its performance. For I must admit that I was from time to time excited rather than moved by the play. I could feel here and there the pull of what was, as it were, a kind of extraneous suspense in moments where everybody in the theatre knew what was going to happen. As a whole, the ten scenes of *Native Son* seemed to me more of a strain than a tragedy.

We should not blame Mr. Orson Welles for that last fact. He has a right to demand that the play supply material that would balance— or even contest—his own contribution to it. And watching *Native Son* scene by scene, I could see that what was not thus supplied him was the subjective detail and the close, loving, ruthless and minute observation and record of Negro details in speech, imagery and thought and habit. We felt most the need of that subtlety and closeness of detail in the first and last scene, where the whole impact depended on this vivid, living poignancy. And there is also the fact that the trial scenes edged off from the sharp issues involved. Mr. Philip Bourneuf spoke his sliding speeches well, and Mr. Ray Collins, who has a lengthy harangue to deliver to the judge, was certainly natural and right—an excellent performance. The speech presented more miscegenation in the theory that was orated than decisions as to what reforms exactly should be instituted; but, as things go in the North and the theatre this is usually the case. No harm could be done to our prestige as intelligent persons if we admitted clearly that the chances taken in *Native Son* are very slight indeed. There is a quiet and tactful suggestion, I am afraid, of business as usual.

Native Son as a discussion of the race problem, as a drama based on the position of a Negro man in the midst of race-prejudice, Chicago politics and mass meetings, justice and minor nationalities, is nothing at all. Beyond a bit of theatre commotion, publicity, sitting in our seats through ten scenes without intermission, and running into waves of intermittent emotion, there is very little remaining with us when the evening is over, though the subject matter of the play concerns one of the most pressing issues in America.

OLD WINE, NEW BOTTLING

A Kiss for Cinderella, by Sir James Barrie.
The Music Box. March 10, 1942.

ON CHRISTMAS DAY, Maude Adams first did *A Kiss for Cinderella,* a trifle more than a quarter of a century ago. It does not seem that long, for the kind of thing Miss Adams presented in the theatre and in such a piece had that kind of freshness that dies but slowly, slowly in people's minds; and those who felt the spell of its enchantment never quite lose, whatever the passing years may be, the memory of such an adored and elusive pleasure and personality.

It must be said, nevertheless, that Miss Adams was of all stage ladies most tricky and projective. She was, to use, as it were, a debased coinage of words, forever on the job. A performance of hers was both a careful science and a complete enchantment. In my entire experience of stage observation, I cannot remember to have seen so expert and attentive a test and formulation of the audiences' reactions. It was all meant to be the Naiad's sure-fire and box-office, clever and detailed, not released too recklessly, not too non-popular, a quality of a nation's sweetheart enchantingly created with good taste, and sold. And at that it should be recorded that the modern theatre has had very little ever which was so unforgettable, evanescent, and which partly unconsciously, partly shrewdly, was so shy, so glittering with woodland shadows in paths that never will grow—to use Tibullus' word—trite with human feet. It was a most commendable method that Miss Adams had, and one that never failed its devoted audience, whose very sweetheart she became.

It follows, therefore, that Miss Louise Rainer's kiss for Cinderella has no little to go up against, traditionally, technically and the devil knows what. I must confess that her performance in this Barrie play is a good deal better than I expected from having seen such of her film performances as that of the late Anna Held in the Great Ziegfeld film. It was a performance that was jerky and banal, over-nerved and much too obvious in its climactic slush. It was exactly what, in sum, the Hollywood Colony would vote to be the outstanding performance of the year.

Miss Rainer, in fact, has won two such Academy Awards for her motion picture performances. As to that one can easily observe the same rot going on this year when the Colony out there decides that Miss Mary Astor's has been the best supporting performance of the year, though what she was supporting was another matter. If they really observed the performance that Mr. Sydney Greenstreet gave in *The Maltese Falcon,* or what he did with the poorly written script of General Winfield Scott in the story of dying with boots on, they should hang their heads in shame for not having given him several or all of the awards. To use one of the finest actors of the modern theater in such a way as he has been used when he might do some of the great rôles better than anyone else is typical Hollywood density. There is no reason, of course, why all this should be doused on the head of poor Miss Rainer; but the point is that many of her defects are either the choice or the fruits, as the case may be, of Hollywood.

A simple way to put the case, no doubt, would be to say that much of the essential trouble with this present production of *A Kiss for Cinderella* may very likely be with the directing—though again, if you know the theatre, you may hazard a guess as to how much this may be quite true. Mr. Lee Strasberg directed it; and the whole course of the production's movement and meaning lacks any great joy or whimsy, which are Barrie's way of covering up and exploiting both the sentiment and the pathos—especially the sentiment, which sometimes, I am afraid, is almost arrant. It might seem to Mr. Strasberg that there is something intellectual in thus muffing the moon and happy sugar in Barrie's writing. We have had plenty of these examples of intellectualism, where the director or the producer or both knew only too well the follies of his author and how to set all that straight. Intellectual though it assumes to be, this attitude is about on a par with the commercial geniuses reducing pork to chicken liver, or changing the flavor of something long eaten with pleasure into what is now to be enjoyed with approval. But there is nothing intrinsically intellectual about all that; it is really a subtle form of the obtuse. Nothing is less functional—to use the high-brow cliché—than the right brain in the wrong skull. There are times when we are well sick of these people in the offing who know better what the author meant than the author himself knew. The sum of all which is to say that it is hard for second-rate people to let anything alone, and equally hard for first-rate people to listen to their inferiors' proposals toward greater perfection. These profound emendations or shiftings of accent may seem to be profound improvements. But such is not the case: to obscure the essential nature of a thing in art is a stupid resolution, false and flat, and so it is. We must make up our minds, crystallize our decisions. There is nothing very distinguished in these improving confusions and these misleading aspirations—they are mostly the results of greedy encroachments. Barrie nowadays, and perhaps from the start of his theatre career, can seem at times a bit too thick to take, what with his stage tricks, his whimsy, sly jokes and shameless coquetry carried off so sweetly and brazenly as to put you out of all countenance; you are really afraid to look your neighbor in the eye. The truth is that playing Barrie has become a very hard problem, as shaky almost as the right handling of Congreve himself, though the comparison of the two is plainly odious.

The right kind of directing for Barrie is to try for some, as it were, innocent stream of playing, in which stream the coy details, the jests, antitheses and dear obvious oddities can take their place easily and in a spirit more or less natural to the whole. Once you have established a current and plane for such writing, everything might bob in and out as it should.

Miss Louise Rainer's playing in *A Kiss for Cinderella* had the same limitations as her playing on the screen, perhaps worse. And Barrie's temptation in the more arch directions only shows Miss Rainer in a sillier light. Mr. Ralph Forbes, as the policemen mentor and lover, gave a fair performance as coquettish, perhaps, as Barrie, but not as shrewd.

OTHELLO

Othello. Shubert Theatre. October 19, 1943.

AN artist like Mr. Robert Edmond Jones, working completely on his own, might have it within his power to give this tragedy of Shakespeare's a full splendor, an audacity and a texture of Venetian Renaissance and wonder. That would mean a brilliant scope in the visual scene and in the costumes, close to the special magnificence of the play.

Such scope was not to happen on this Margaret Webster production of *Othello* that the Theatre Guild presents. A scheme has been adopted of shifting units that serve from scene to scene—palace, seaport, street, castle or bedroom, Venice or Cyprus. The scheme proves effective for some of the play's scenes, confining and concentrating the dramatic action and impact; but for other scenes the limitations are serious. In the death scene, for example, even a bare stage with curtains at the back would have been better than that crowded and ignoble passage of love and death, with its packing and squirming among players and motifs and its scattering realism. The limitation and loss was here most considerable, though it can be said, of course, that nothing can quite defeat the combination of concrete passion and lofty, cleansing abstractions of which this incredible scene is composed.

Mr. Jones' costumes for the most part are cut to the reservations of the scenery, and rather on the Bronzino or Florentine side than the Venetian. Nothing is in bad taste, however, and now and again a costume breaks through this prose discretion into a fine distinction of style. Cassio's costume is an example, as are Othello's, though Mr. Paul Robeson lacks the instinct and phrasing for wearing costumes *per se*. Bianca's clothes are joyous, rich, truly Venetian. Mr. Jones' lighting, meanwhile, is superb, so secure, in fact, that most of the audience must take it for granted. We have no other designer who has so final a use of lighting, so much that is confirmed in terms of light, such right values and dramatic truth. On the whole, however, the fact remains that he is not at his best in this *Othello* décor. It is easily not on the level of the décor we saw in *The Birthday of the Infanta*, for example, *Macbeth, The Saint, Desire Under the Elms, The Jest* and many another production that he designed.

It might be said that this décor for *Othello* has a parallel in the general production that Miss Webster has given it; though we should say, of course, that she has more to contend with among the divers elements that make up the theatre art. Miss Webster is a theatre worker of much ability, honesty and good sense, not to say perseverance, sometimes after success, sometimes after failure—her production, for example, of *The Trojan Women* two years ago was so banal a horror—not to mention Dame May Witty's wholly wrecking the leading rôle in the play—as would have laid most directors low forever. She evinces no bad taste; only, if you like, a quiet absence of taste. Her theatre virtues are solid and respectable; what she lacks is the aesthetic sense to any notable degree. The thing to say about Miss Webster and our theatre, our Shakespearean theatre especially, is that we ought to be thankful that we have her at all, remembering the while the Irish proverb that the least ugly daughter is the family beauty, and the Latin one that in the realm of the blind the one-eyed is king. Her productions are not by any means of the topmost rank—how many productions are?—but they have a good breeding, a good sense, a certain kind of literalness and a sincerity that carry them a long way both as entertainment and as box-office.

There is, however, another aspect of entertainment and box-office to Miss Webster's Shakespearean productions that is not so handsome. This is the heavy cutting and tinkering with the text that she practices. People who are not familiar with the text are thus led to think they have never before found Shakespeare so easy to understand—many have said as much. This, while it seems to do them a favor—and so it might for those who could not follow or swallow it otherwise—does them really a serious disservice culturally. They are misled both as to Shakespeare and as to themselves. In my opinion Miss Webster goes much too far with these simplifications.

Othello must be one of the half-dozen greatest dramas of the world, certainly of the Western world. It has a perfection of structure and content that is the marvel of all study. But so far as modern audiences go, this play has three difficulties to overcome. First of all it exacts, of course, a cerebral response from us that we are by no means accustomed to—democratic principle combined with business methods has led us steadily into the easier and easier, the trashier and trashier even, any way you turn. Second, the conception in this play of woman's position with regard to the male is hard to take, though subconsciously it may be easier for many of us than we choose to think. And, third, the theme of jealousy is the least attractive aspect of sex. The triumph of the play over these difficulties is to a certain extent a measure of its triumph as a work of art.

In the present production a good deal of cutting has gone on in the interest, doubtless, of speed, time, what not, and the whole play has been divided into two acts instead of Shakespeare's five. Together with this, the acting is on the restrained side, if you like to put it that way; the truth is that it does not go in for eloquence, fire or the high tragic style, and no play of Shakespeare's, *King Lear* excepted, has so great a need of these as has *Othello*. A part of its complete excellence is that its content is expressed in its form and its form is entirely inherent in its content. You can do what you deem expedient with this or that play of Shakespeare's, but not with *Othello*. Its perfection, idea, technique and impact are inextricably bound together. Handled otherwise, the play suffers from a seeming incredibility. The melodrama of the situation and the tautness of the dramatic moment are deprived of the right stylistic and emotional support. A part of the greatness of *Othello* resides in its very nearness to the incredible, the forced, the sounding brass. It is perilously near to its own obverse, to what it is not. That may be one way of describing greatness in art.

Miss Webster's performance of Emilia furthers in general the point of the above. She plays as usual very competently and with real intelligence. She should now add two things to her performance, two things for which Shakespeare himself has supplied a more than definite basis: in the scene with Desdemona, when the latter is preparing to go to bed, Emilia should be more bawdy, as her speeches indicate, and in the death scene a little later she should be more noisy and frantic—the very lines she has to speak require that. As Miss Webster does these scenes now, she throws away, in, if you like, the mistaken interest of restraint, the magnificent opportunity that the dramatist so very patently has provided not only for Emilia but also, and especially, for the scene. The crudest actress from a Sicilian company travelling in a cart would know better.

As for the company on the whole, Miss Webster has put a very fair degree of the fear of God into them, so that they read their lines metrically and, since Shakespeare is here at his best, to make sense. The sole exception in this case is Mr. Jose Ferrer's Iago in his first scene, where much is to be set forth and where even a close knowledge of the play left me wondering what on earth those lines were about, as his diaphragm, as if supplanting his brain, went on pumping the words out.

As to Mr. Ferrer's Iago—all Iagos are sure to be praised and, if not so, are blamed at Shakespeare's expense—it could be said that his scenes had poise, stage punch and a determined longevity. I was not surprised, however, when one of our most noted editors expressed to me some wonder as to whether, not having seen the play before, he should take the character of Iago as credible. Iago is credible only to the extent to which we are led to fall in with his cerebral excitement, his non-moral temperament and magnetism and his enjoyment of his own self and his own variety. The most interesting approach to Iago is not to conceive him as wronged in military preferment or in his marriage bed, as to the latter of which you can see from the lines that his inquiry is casual—and therefore burning for revenge. Conceive him as filled with a hatred and resentment of Othello's very self, and looking for reasons to justify it, and then exercising and airing his particular nature toward a mischievous end that engages and absorbs it. Ironically enough, Miss Webster's heavy cutting of Iago's lines, though seemingly in the cause of simplicity, does not make the character easier to understand. Evidently Shakespeare himself, as he wrote, knew better how to analyze and convey it. Mr. Ferrer needs badly and first of all a more distinguished presence, more elegance, more Renaissance Italian. And he should remember that there is no monotony in Iago's brand of evil.

Thanks to Miss King herself, to the director and the costume, Miss Edith King is the first of a number of Biancas I have seen to get the character into its proper dramatic line, its importance in the play's pattern. For all the fluff and insouciance, it would be stupid to take this performance of Miss King's too lightly: we have few actresses indeed who could give the rôle with exactly the touch-and-go weight of folly and pain that we have from her. Miss Uta Hagen —not too happily costumed—with that curiously flexible talent that might carry her far in our theatre, is one of the best of the numerous Desdemonas that I have seen, what with stage and opera versions these many years. Without in herself seeming blind or innocuous, she gives that pearl-like quality that Shakespeare intended. She unfailingly establishes the scene.

That brings us to the portrayal of Othello by Mr. Paul Robeson, a rôle he presented some years ago to London audiences. The fact that the actor in this case is a Negro has no direct bearing on the subject, since Othello was portrayed as black up to the nineteenth century, when critical romanticism changed his color to the Arabian. The Italian original of the story uses the word *negrezzo* to describe him. The subtle values of Othello Mr. Robeson at times conveys, but as often he does not. Othello is voluble but essentially inarticulate; his magnetism must be immense, for everything in the story points to that; he is not stupid; he has the simple human qualities to a magnificent degree—Mr. Robeson conveys no little of that—but all of them wholly and only alive within the tremendous current and blind propulsion of his nature. This drama demands power, for the whole of it is like a storm gathering; and unless we get the sense of an infinity of nature within this superb human creature and of the gathering of forces as strong and distinct as those of a storm, and as distinct and conflicting as those of the classic drama, we end nowhere. No play of Shakespeare's has more tender motifs and exchanges, or a more exact domestic prose and daylight literalness of detail, more surprising lyric immediacy; and yet none is so objective, so remote and complete, so classic in its clarity and motivations. Side by side with the literal and exact in Othello, the humble revelations of life, we have the longer passages of the declamation, the rush forward of his subconscious, with its range and power and tragic capacity.

Mr. Robeson, a singer of distinction, with the benefit of much stage experience, still lacks for this rôle the ultimate requirement, which is a fine tragic method. By virtue of true feeling and intensity of soul he has its equivalent at times; and then he is moving and deep. There are two things that I would suggest. One is that he recast, as it were, his first speeches in the play, and a number of others later on, where he is too aggressive vocally, has too much projection of the tone, gives us the wearing sense of an overworked diaphragm where only the relaxation of dignity and strength are required. In the scenes that call for more emotion or decision his voice is very fine, unrivaled on our stage.

The other suggestion I would give Mr. Robeson has to do with style, the elusive matter of stage bearing, so important in this part. In the scenes of despair he crumples up into a defeat that is far too domestic, gentle and moving though it may be. He must discover for these moments a style that is equally pathetic but more remote.

A GENTLE MRS. STOWE

Harriet, by Florence Ryerson and Colin Clements.
Henry Miller's Theatre. March 2, 1943.

ONE of the critical aspects of the new Harriet Beecher Stowe play is the theatre's relation to historical fact and what the theatre can do with history and has every right to do with it.

When I was a young creature in the South I never saw a copy of *Uncle Tom's Cabin*; it was taboo, no copy on hand, and we were to understand that it had deeply wronged and offended our people and their cause. By some natural process of reasoning, I concluded, accordingly, that everyone in the North read this book and many swore by it. In due time I came North to live. To my surprise, in all these years I have never heard but one person in the North mention having actually read the book itself, though I am sure that, among older people especially, there are people alive who once did so. I have observed that many people from seeing the stage versions or the story in films are under a vague impression that they know *Uncle Tom's Cabin* quite thoroughly. Whereas the sober truth is they have never read it at all. In due course, for definite purposes, I read it through.

Mr. Burton Rascoe of the New York *World-Telegram,* in his very literate review of *Harriet,* says that Mrs. Stowe "happened to write a melodrama, crude and weepy in form and content, which swept the nation and made her famous all over the world." That is exactly true. And to my surprise, when I came to read it, I found *Uncle Tom's Cabin* excessively dated, very much of the epoch—1840, 1850, the early '60's—bombastic, turgid, lurid, something like the Elsie books, derived from the Gothic romances of England, sentimental, gushing, indignant, and laden with the rhetoric of the moral reformers of the time. The death of little Eva, for example, is fantastically absurd, even if you are aware of the Victorian hair theme, in bracelets, brooches and death tokens—the dying child lies there snipping off her curls and handing them out to be remembered by, the most *beautiful*, she says, of all, to *Uncle Tom*, who had been so good, et cetera. It would be an odd sight to see the audience at Miss Hayes' performance if the book and this chapter were brought out on the stage there and read aloud to them.

Nevertheless, we must say for Mrs. Stowe that the great inner gift was there. The book was pretty much made by its fitness to the times; but the author hit on two effective weak points in the slavery system: the fact that one way or another slave families might be scattered, and that the slave might fall into evil hands. To this was added a wordy, emotional, zealous and journalistic impulse and method on the writer's part. All things considered, it is not hard to understand the monumental impact of Mrs. Stowe's book and her enduring reputation.

There is also the Mrs. Stowe who had crying spells and, if I remember right, heard voices after finishing some of her chapters, and was capable of intense and shall we say hysterical states. And we should note at least one other item. There was the Mrs. Stowe who on her visit to England met not only royalty and Dickens and Thackeray but Lady Byron as well. Lady Byron at that time was still eating heartily, and resenting her marital case with Byron, whom scandal, conveyed by her, if by anybody, to the public, had driven to the Continent. Well, Mrs. Stowe came back from England and wrote a whole book about this matter, by then quiescent, of Byron's incest with his half-sister, Augusta, et cetera: a book without humor, meddlesome and resentful. It is a nauseous book, about which I may say that I should hate to have a Freudian analyst turned loose on it. He would do better than Uncle Tom, he would get not a curl but a scalp.

Well, all this would not matter, taking Miss Hayes' play as it stands, were it not for the fact that something in the nature of the theatre art makes the authors, the producer, the actors and even the audience want to think the whole business a great historical click. They subconsciously, if you like, tickle themselves with the idea that they are being scholarly as well as entertained. It is therefore necessary to say that as history this drama *Harriet* has only a pussy-willow, ladies'-magazine relation to history. It is equally necessary, for art's sake, to say that this does not matter at all. Art is long and life is short—*vita brevis*—which is easily proved by the fact that you can, as the play does, misquote Lincoln, muddle the clichés of the Stowe period into modern clichés, puddle up periods as to style, and so on, and still have a most engaging little piece.

Harriet, this new play, is a very agreeable success story, about a charming, sensible, humorous wife who hits on a theme that gets such results as fame, money and acclaim. She marries the vague professor, compared to whom her competence makes her gently superior, manages to get back East from Cincinnati, is catapulted into national importance by some writing done in the midst of family pressures, et cetera. She is dismayed by the effect of her book on the nation and the war. Her talk with Lincoln, whom she had first thought of as an intruder, persuades her of the great cause of freedom and of her book's mission. The play then ends with a speech that Harriet makes to the townsmen—outside the window. The speech is much too long and too obvious; the result would be greatly improved if Miss Hayes would cut it to a few lines.

Since the play goes so pleasantly through history and the historically debatable and takes so syrupy a course, there would be little sense in trying to assert the verity of such portraits as that of the famous and debated Henry Ward Beecher, of Mrs. Stowe's husband and of the other members of the family, much less the violence of the time's issues and their consequences. This play regarded as history is mere nursery rubbish, but it is agreeable enough. Mr. Rhys Williams as the husband gives an almost charming performance. It needs only to be a bit less dull and more wittily absent-minded. Miss Jane Seymour as the dried virgin old-maid sister is excellent. Mr. William Woodson as the suitor for the various sisters' hands is a promising newcomer. Within the limits of the rôle as it is written Miss Hayes acts with finish and skill; there is a security about her work in this play that comes from true study and experience. There is also a good balance of emotion and common sense in all she does. Opinions vary as to Miss Hayes' acting. To my mind she is a sturdy, highly honorable player, capable only of a sensible style and without any great imaginative scope or boldness. At times a part of her solution of stage problems is a certain element of archness which a more intense lover of art would either elevate into seductive style or else eliminate. La Rochefoucauld said that the greatest miracle love can accomplish is to conquer coquetry.

Miss Aline Bernstein's precisely right costume designs, Mr. Lemuel Ayres' settings—handsome and right and never fussy—Mr. Elia Kazan's directing, so clean and expert, and the general good taste with which Mr. Gilbert Miller fuses a production, all help to make an evening in the theatre that is never distinguished but never boring.

SO DIVINE AN AIR

Embezzled Heaven, by L. Bush-Fekete and Mary Helen Fay, based on a novel by Franz Werfel. National Theatre.
October 31, 1944.

THE THEATRE GUILD opens its season with Miss Ethel Barrymore and Mr. Albert Basserman. The vehicle for that distinguished and not unheavenly flourish on the Guild's part is a somewhat dimmish piece in the style, at a distance, of the Spanish Martinez Sierra, in whose *Kingdom of God* Miss Barrymore played, at times with her own grandeur, the abbess a good many years ago.

The warmth and lyricism and true passion of soul that the Sierra play had, that Spanish verity of which Broadway is as incapable as the Bronx might be of the funeral procession of La Bella Simonetta and her fair shadow in Botticelli's *Birth of Venus,* is, as a matter of course, lacking from this new effort on the Theatre Guild's mystical side. The true belief, the pain and fire, the white and black of spirit and body, are not readily amassed for the occasion, however snappy the occasion may be. They are such things as are old and wonderful, bright and dark and elusive, sober and patient, and sweet with wild wings that pass, that pass away. Not even the smartest of deep-art business producers, or elderly Shubert-Bluebird acolytes, or the best of press agents can always summon up such things. Eternity has its jokes as it were. Perhaps the cherubim are not happy in these brisk incubators of Broadway.

I do not know the Werfel novel from which this play is taken, though if the play were more impressive I should feel obligated to do so. Very likely the novel is adept, but I have my doubts about its being profound. At the risk of being more personal than suits my preference, I may say that I have lived in a *convento* in Italy a good many months and more than once. I know something of what is implied in the themes of devotion, sacrifice and shrewdness that this play involves. It would be almost hitting below the belt to say that a very great deal of what inhabits such places is lacking in this play. On the one hand, then, we have the theatre effort, and on the other the grandeur, the unsalable rigor and pattern, the vast heavens of faith and prayer that underlie and support the long days, the repetition and hidden release, the passion and song, the daily hunger and goodness of the Catholic element that the heroine here adduces. I dedicate that sentence to Miss Ethel Barrymore and to what, as we may glimpse through the meanderings of this play, she may truly believe.

The story of *Embezzled Heaven*—a New York title but a poor one as the play is written—tells of a cook who centres on a nephew to represent her in Paradise and thus prepare the way for her eternity of grace. The measly child brought to her by the sister-in-law turns out to be a greedy wretch on whose education she spends all the money she can lay her hands on. Eventually she discovers the deception and in the end finds herself on a pilgrimage to Rome. The Pope, after the right dramatic suspense when it is doubtful whether he will be able to give an audience or not, sees the pilgrims, and she tells him of her aim and sin, her soul's distress. The Pope departs; she dies with his blessing. As for this story, I maintain that only Catholics could truly understand it. Meanwhile, it is as difficult as the most abstruse anatomy and is as simple as the beating of the heart.

The aesthetic deduction from all the above discussion is that we cannot have a truly Catholic source, profoundly searched, for popular appeal along Broadway save only when the story is overwhelmingly right, in essence a true fable. It must discover a living body to carry and reveal it. This play comes close to that verity of form and content; it might well have been a fable in its pattern and rightness, but just misses it.

Embezzled Heaven suffers as a whole, and no little, from underdevelopment in detail. The joy and rippling overtones by which the theatre art swings and goes forward, to our universal delight, is very often lacking nowadays in our plays and in their directing. *Embezzled Heaven* was directed by an admirable man of the theatre, Mr. B. Iden Payne; but there were not enough details and enough realized analysis to create characters with which he could work successfully, or at least to his own full best. That is the same limitation that Miss Barrymore encountered in her first scenes. There was the cook at the castle to be played, and there were the dishes and pots and pans to supply the realistic mechanism, but the vivid intimacy was not at hand. She struggled with broad outlines, not so much false as undeveloped; and but for her own personal splendor, she might have remained quite dull as often as not. In the last act, the audience with the Pope, the confession of her sin, the exhaustion and death, she is beautiful and magnificent. In general, Miss Ethel Barrymore possesses some grand, elusive quality of her own. She is unique and special, not as a performer but as a personage on our stage.

The distinguished Continental actor, Mr. Albert Basserman, had the rôle of Pope Pius XI, the great saint of the First World War. It would have been hard to believe ahead of time that his scene could have been so right, so large, so sophisticated and so compelling. His difficulty with English pronunciation makes no complications here, since the Pope himself is speaking to the pilgrims in a tongue foreign to him and since the scene is short. The greatest compliment I can pay Mr. Basserman is to say that, except for noting the necessary projection that is theatre, it would be as absurd to praise the goodness and mercy and the height of his scene as it would have been to judge that Pope. A new light thus shines in our theatre, a great light and a great technical completeness.

Mr. Eduard Franz gives an excellent performance of the rascally nephew of the cook, her betrayer through the years. Mr. Stewart Chaney's four settings are good; that for the Vatican Reception Hall is very good indeed.

BOSTON LIMITED

The Late George Apley, by John P. Marquand and George S. Kaufman. Based on Mr. Marquand's novel. Lyceum Theatre. November 21, 1944.

WE MAY SAY at the start, and so get the point settled, that *The Late George Apley* is an agreeable evening, if sometimes slow-moving, and that it has some very considerable high lights, due almost entirely to the presence, expertness and taste of Mr. Leo G. Carroll in the leading rôle. That said, we may go on to observe that the occasion is not good enough to warrant a discussion of a play's relation to the novel it is taken from, an analysis of the problems involved in the translation of written fiction into the stage medium. Nor on the other hand is the novel quite worth discussing seriously in this connection.

Taken seriously, this new play at the Lyceum falls, or somewhat vaguely subsides, between two stools. It does not follow the procedure of *Life with Father,* for example, which is also a comedy dealing with a family that lives in a position of security, background and the flavor of a conservative Victorian tradition. *Life with Father* whoops all this up into something like musical-comedy farce values. Its method goes in for speed, for high-lighting and likely emphasis, and for characters, wigs and situations that are round and sure-fire. The whole effect is lively, warm, crotchety and sweet, touched with old things and spiced with something of Dickens. This play of *The Late George Apley* never has a good time like that. It never crackles or sings itself, never suggests the riotous, whimsical or lovably balky, or faded valentines, ribbons, carols and what not. Nor on the other hand does it suggest austerity, a certain elegance that is genuine if thinnish, nor does it contrive strong outlines in each of its characters, whether you admire that special character or not.

There is no reason, in sum, why a person of the class and world the Apleys are supposed to represent should give a second thought to this occasion at the Lyceum as an expression of themselves, though they might perhaps be easy with it as a demonstration of Broadway; they might even conceivably smile at it as at a Christmas pantomime in the servants' hall. That is to speak snobbishly, as it were, or out of the English novels; for it can be said that even where there are servants nowadays they could scarcely constitute the whole rabble of our Broadway first nights. But the point is that the people this play assumes to present could hardly take it seriously. I myself for that matter am not sure there would be much choice between a Broadway version of Boston or a Boston version of Broadway.

This, then, is the whole point about our version of *The Late George Apley*. If it is not going to be gay and speeded up, underscored and full of having a good time with its own self, then it must be a real study, through the comedy medium, of the life dealt with, its distinction, its innate values, its cramped intensities and high discipline. Mr. George Kaufman is not the man to help here. His mood was once relaxed and engagingly successful, full of invention securely theatrical; but in this present case his effort drops into punches where punches are not even funny, first because they are false to the material and second, because they are apt to be mostly common.

As to the direction in which the local truth, quality and humor might lie, I may merely say here that people in the audience who, for instance, find this version of Boston tradition unsatisfactory might naturally fall back on actual explanations: for example, the young lady in her ball gown could not have crossed the muddy back yards; Freud would not have been mentioned in the Apley drawing room in the year 1912, and so forth and so on. These items are valid enough, if you like. But they are not truly the point. The point is that what these dissatisfied people in the audience really would like to say, if they could get it all straight in their minds, is that the inner life is not there; the speech rhythm—even extending into characteristic phrases—and the good solid inherited English language, the subtle, strong heritage of speech, are not there. As speech, the writing in *The Late George Apley* is only good New York Times Square culture or editorial usage. The ear as such is not engaged, and the dramatic infection of true speech is not involved. As character study, plus locale, the play is pleasantly disposed and designed to omit that perfectly natural other side of provincialism, or localism, which is to despise what is outside it. (Mr. Apley, for instance, does not indicate to us of this Broadway audience that, though he may look very benign, he thinks we are all trash.) And this is where, perhaps, it might be said that the Boston Apley tradition, as represented in Mr. Marquand, has often broken down; or is broken down: he does not insist on his own quality or his own heritage or on the integrity of his book to the extent that would risk the loss of whatever gain may lie in the Broadway offing. And thus can every state of society be sold out, we may say.

The story of the play deals with a father and tame mother whose children are bent on making wrong alliances. The son returns to the fold and marries into the clubs and tradition, the daughter elopes—and who among us cares, considering the characters as they are here developed? Of the company we may say that the best casting was that of Mr. David McKay as the Apley son. He had the delicate angularity and austere swish of this sort of young man. It could even be said—and this is a subtle point—that his very lack of talent for acting was an aid to the stuck and inexpressive emotional nature implied in this rôle. Miss Margaret Dale as the troublesome sister and sister-in-law in this aplectomy of things contributed a false note. Her farce method was too insistent and broad for the project, and threw everything around her into a psychological query and mess. Mr. Leo G. Carroll gave his usual smooth and modest and expert performance. Whatever lack in force or emphasis or intensity Mr. Carroll's performance displayed was due to the limpness or canny, commercial vagueness of the dramatization itself.

Mr. Stewart Chaney did a corner at the Berkeley Club for the brief final scene. His main setting for the play, George Apley's house in Beacon Street, Boston, Thanksgiving Day, 1912, offers a New England Georgian drawing-room. It is a handsome setting. As dramatic décor it suffers very seriously from lack of point. The place would need its elegance either sharpened and projected as theatre-conservative elegance, or else cluttered somewhat with photographs, mementoes, Victorian heart gadgets, and slushy slips in taste. This, I mean, if the décor is to be taken seriously as theatre.

THE TEMPEST

The Tempest. Alvin Theatre. January 25, 1945.

MARGARET BREUNING in her introduction to the new Hyperion book of Mary Cassatt, quotes Degas as saying, "I don't admit that a woman can draw so well as that." I confess I am inclined to go old-fashioned and say something of the sort about Miss Webster's production of *The Tempest*. Whatever may be the shortcomings of the occasion, you must be filled with wonder that one little woman, as it were, could pull all this together and send it off with such professional thoroughness. If you read the play again and see the problems involved for its presentation nowadays, you will better understand what is implied by my observation and may even take off your hat to her. Her results with the play are not in the direction of poetry, but do make a good show; and that in itself is something not to be despised.

Whether such is possible today or not, whether any sort of plausibility or absence of artiness could be achieved, is of course highly doubtful; but it is obvious that for *The Tempest* to get much of what Shakespeare intended, the Elizabethan stage is required, or something very like it. There are three points involved. First is the fact that Shakespeare exists and is alive through the words, which, whatever may be his invention in other theatre elements, remain the chief point of supremacy in his genius. Second is the necessity for fluid scenes, no breaks or delays, so that the special lyricism of his form and movement may be achieved. Third is the close contact with the audience, which, if such are to reach us, the speed, the intricacy of expression and the variety in character require.

The matter of the quick changes and flow of scenes Miss Webster has solved well enough. Motley has designed a kind of rock mass on a revolving base that allows easy and continuous shifting of the scene. This is not an impressively imaginative creation, but it serves to good purpose. The first scene, however, of *The Tempest,* that of

THE TEMPEST

the ship's deck in the storm, Shakespeare for some reason has written in lines oddly difficult to speak out or catch the meaning of; at best they might be clear for us by being spoken on an apron stage, smack out among the audience, as the Elizabethan theatre knew how to do. Motley has a painted drop of a fancy ship, in which presently a transparent section shows the commotion on the deck. The scene spoken in the midst of this turns out to be confused, wasted and dull.

If you study the stage history of the play you will see that in divers epochs it was produced with many additions, cuttings and general changes, though the nineteenth century brought it round again closer to the Shakespeare text. Miss Webster has not cut very heavily or ironed matters out of the way until toward the end of the fourth act. There the interlude of the classic goddesses is left out, and the famous speech of Prospero's about our globe and all which it inherit dissolving, and we are such stuff as dreams are made on and our little life is rounded with a sleep, is lifted out and put a whole act forward. Thus the finale of the play is changed from the sunny ending, with everybody happy, to an ending in which the characters go out and Prospero is left alone on the stage with his beautiful philosophic speech from the earlier scene. Whatever Shakespearean students may think of such alterations, the result is most effective, and is more lyric and moody, and thus more modern, than the text is or was intended to be.

As for the words, the character, of course, who most of all has the wings of words on which the play must be borne is Ariel. Miss Vera Zorina understands the rôle and gives herself to its sweet flight and delicacy of presence as perhaps nobody else in our theatre could. She adds to this as a matter of course her expert ballet movement, her beauty and her grace of conception.

Mr. Canada Lee's Caliban spoke often with a good metrical ear though his diction was much too insecure. He was neither malign, evil nor frightening but fitted well enough in the general plane of the occasion, which did not seek perhaps—certainly it did not achieve —poetic intensity or elevation. The two young people, Miranda and Ferdinand, Miss Frances Heflin and Mr. Vito Christi, were young players of an agreeable quality. In the light of the theatre around them on Broadway, we could hardly expect Miss Webster to teach them beautiful speech and style in a few weeks. Mr. Arnold Moss was a dignified and noble Prospero, with a good voice for the lines. And Mr. Paul Leyssac played the difficult and elusive and traditional rôle of the old councillor with his usual distinction, admirable speech and fine tone. The two comics, Trinculo and Stephano, so abundantly supplied with gusty, Elizabethan material by Shakespeare himself, were capitally played by Mr. George Voskovec and Mr. Jan Werich, until lately, we are told, among the prime favorites of the Czecho-Slovakian theatre.

Serious students of *The Tempest* can find many interpretations of its meaning, all kinds of things about power, about freedom, spirit and matter, good and evil, and so on. It is best to begin that discussion merely with noting that *The Tempest* is one of those creations in art that achieve a truly fable form, which means that within it there are infinite implications that may be applied to life one way or another. I may add that on the starry, poetic side, *The Tempest* given by the children of the King-Coit School far surpasses any I know of.

So far as the themes of demons, beneficent spirits, witches and magic are concerned, nobody can arrive at any intelligent approach to *The Tempest* who thinks that either Shakespeare or his audience interpreted these scenes as most people nowadays are apt to do. Such people are likely to read *The Tempest* in the light of their childhood impressions of fairy tales and ghost stories. All that fantasy and naive magic possibility that charmed them had in it little conviction of reality. But this was not the case when *The Tempest* was written. To men of that time, and long before then and after, the spirit world was as close as technology today may be to us. Some of the best minds were concerned with the subject. For a list of books that were written, and an excellent study of pneumatology in Elizabethan drama, we can read Mr. Robert Hunter West's *The Invisible World*, published by the University of Georgia Press.

THE GLASS MENAGERIE

The Glass Menagerie, by Tennessee Williams. The
Playhouse Theatre. March 31, 1945.

OF ALL our actors, certainly of all those who have become
known, Miss Laurette Taylor could not be called the most cultured, the most versatile in divers styles, the most gracious-minded, but few would deny that she is the most talented. She is the real and first talent of them all. She has been largely absent from the stage during so many years that her return is an event and everybody knows it. It turns out, in *The Glass Menagerie,* to be a triumph as well. So is the rôle she plays.

Miss Taylor's rôle in Mr. Williams' play is that of a frowsy, aging woman who lives with her son and daughter, in a flat off a St. Louis alley. It is a far cry from the Deep South, where her girlhood was spent and her memories dwell, and where she has refused the rich planters' sons because she lost her heart to a man who worked for the telephone company and whose smile misled everybody. The daughter is a cripple, too shy and hurt and vague ever to have got through school. She spends her time playing old phonograph records that her father had left behind when he abandoned her mother and went away for good, and collecting glass animals—hence the title of the play. The son is a failure, discontented with his job in the warehouse, vaguely itching to write poetry, and longing to roam the world. The mother worships, nags, scolds and tries to do her best by her children. Finally, when she thinks it is time her daughter got married, she plagues the son into bringing a man home with him; he brings a friend from the warehouse. The visitor, impressed though he is with the daughter, turns out to be already in love and engaged.

In the end the son follows his father's example and goes off to make his way wandering the world. The scheme of *The Glass Menagerie* includes a Narrator, who opens the play and appears between the scenes from time to time (to follow "the part of the sun"). If properly followed, which it is not in the production, this is a very imaginative motif on the dramatist's part, this subtle identification of the father with the son, the son with the father.

This rôle is played by the actor who takes the part of the son. The story, as we see it on the stage, all happens in the son's mind long afterward, and in the last narration, a kind of epilogue, we are told that in the midst of the years and in far, strange places, wherever he goes, he can never lose the image of his sister there at home; all things bring her back to him.

What Miss Laurette Taylor does with these matters can be at least partially imagined if you know the quality of her special gift. This, even after just seeing the play, is almost impossible to convey with anything like the full, wonderful truth. Hers is naturalistic acting of the most profound, spontaneous, unbroken continuity and moving life. There is an inexplicable rightness, moment by moment, phrase by phrase, endlessly varied in the transitions. Technique, which is always composed of skill and instinct working together, is in this case so overlaid with warmth, tenderness and wit that any analysis is completely baffled. Only a trained theatre eye and ear can tell what is happening, and then only at times. Miss Laurette Taylor is capable of a performance so right and perfect that you do not even think of it as a great performance. I do not mean to go into a kind of Seidletz hysterics to make my point about what she does with this rôle in *The Glass Menagerie*, I merely say that it has a characteristic of seeming beyond any contrivance and of a sort of changing rhythm of translucence rarely to be seen in the theatre. The one shortcoming about this portrayal of the mother is that Miss Taylor does not achieve the quality of the aristocrat, however broken down and wasted and lost, that Mr. Williams intended. She is astonishingly Southern, partly due to the writing and partly to her ready intuition of feeling, tone and climax; but in an elusive sense that would be impossible to convey, and that any Southerner of Mr. Williams' class would understand almost automatically, she is not what is implied in the play. No use in wasting time on that point; if she had been so, had been the broken-down aristocrat that Mr. Williams wrote, the effect would have been largely lost on most audiences, and as things went the play got on very well without it.

But true as all this may be of Miss Taylor, we must not let that blind us to the case of the play itself and of the whole occasion. The play gives every one of the four characters that it presents a glowing, rich opportunity, genuine emotional motivations, a rhythm of situations that are alive, and speech that is fresh, living, abundant and free of stale theatre diction. The author is not awed by the usual sterilities of our play-writing patterns. On the other hand he is too imaginative, genuine, or has too much good taste, to be coy about the free devices on which his play is built, a true, rich talent, unpredictable like all true talents, an astute stage sense, an intense, quivering clarity, all light and feeling once the intelligence of it is well anchored—a talent, too, I should say, that New York will buy tickets for in later plays, especially if enough of the sexy is added to things, but will never quite understand.

The Glass Menagerie appears to drag, or go slow, at times, though I am not sure about this and certainly found it less so than a number of people I have heard speak of it. These slow places occur in the Narrator portions and sometimes in the scenes between mother and son. In my opinion this may be almost entirely due to the fact that Mr. Eddie Dowling does not let himself go enough to make you believe that he is the son of such a mother or such a father. We have no ready, or vivid, sense that he longs to wander, to write poetry—I even forgot to remember what he was working at when he sat before the papers on the table, supposed, however, to be bent on a poem. Mr. Dowling speaks his Narrator scenes plainly and serviceably, with the result that they are made to seem to be a mistake on the playwright's part, a mistake to include them at all; for they seem extraneous and tiresome in the midst of the play's emotional current. And many critics will speak of them as such. This is not the case at all. It is curious that an actor of Mr. Dowling's experience and showmanship should pass up thus a rôle where the dramatist's invention is really so striking and, for that matter, so useful to the player. If these speeches were spoken with variety, impulse and intensity, as if the son himself were speaking—which is what happens really, since the play is a dream within his memory —if they were spoken as if they were from a born wanderer and adventurer, a chip off the old block, wild-headed like his father— and like his mother for that matter, for she too had wandered far from home indeed—the whole of the Narrator would be another matter entirely, it would be truly a part of the story. Thus Mr. Dowling does much harm to the play. The fact remains, nevertheless, that he is sure to be praised for his playing of the role, on the basis that it is poised and not exaggerated—such is the irony of the acting art and its observers.

To say, as Mr. Nichols does in his review in the New York *Times* that there are such unconnected things with the story as "snatches of talk about the war, bits of psychology, occasional moments of rather florid writing" is mistaken indeed. The part Miss Taylor plays is, quite aside from her rendering of it, the best written rôle that I have seen in a play for years. All the language and all the motifs are free and true; I recognized them inch by inch, and I should know, for I came from the same part of the country, the same locality and life, in fact, that Mr. Williams does. Such a response and attitude as that Mr. Nichols expresses is the kind of thing that helps to tie our theatre down. It is the application of Times Square practical knowledge, the kind of thing that makes, to take one instance, the writing, the talk, in *The Late George Apley* so sterile and so little like the Boston it assumes to be. One of the things most needed in the theatre is a sense of language, a sense of texture in speech, vibration and impulse in speech. Behind the Southern speech in the mother's part is the echo of great literature, or at least a respect for it. There is the sense in it of her having been born out of a tradition, not out of a box. It has echo and the music of it. The mother's characterization is both appalling and human, both cold and loving. No role could be more realistically written than this, but it has the variety, suddenness, passion and freedom, almost unconscious freedom perhaps, of true realism.

Miss Julie Haydon gave one of her translucent performances of a dreaming, wounded, half-out-of-this-world young girl. Mr. Anthony Ross, as the visitor, for whom the author has written a long and excellent scene, original and tender, with the girl, played admirably.

Mr. Jo Mielziner did the complicated setting for *The Glass Menagerie,* streets at the side, a front room, a back room, a wall shutting them off when needed. The scene is effectively ingenious. But even though the story happens in a dream and vagueness may be called for, I see no reason why the color should be quite so dull.

For example, it was only by a most creditable leap of the imagination that one could make out that the enlarged photograph of the vanished father on the wall was really that of Mr. Dowling, the son. The result was that a notable motivation on the part of the dramatist, which is that the son, the Narrator and the father are all one and the same, was all but lost. Of all places the stage is one of economies in effect, the moment is brief and such a fault as this is serious, practically.

In the Narrator's opening speech Mr. Williams has provided an excuse for music by saying that the play all happens in the memory, and memory always seems to move in music. That idea, or motif, goes well back to the classics: Phoebus replied and touched my trembling ear is Milton, but that in turn was Horace—*aurem vellit*—for the ear was the seat of memory. For *The Glass Menagerie*, therefore, Mr. Paul Bowles has written music that runs in and out of the scenes, sometimes, for a long interval, sometimes less. It seems to be a special gift of his, this writing music for a play that becomes a part of the play, strangely beautiful and strangely right.

MID-SEASON

The Winter's Tale. Cort Theatre. January 15, 1946. Dunnigan's Daughter, by S. N. Behrman. John Golden Theatre. December 21, 1945. The Would-Be Gentleman, adapted from Molière by Bobby Clark. Booth Theatre. January 9, 1946.

NEARLY FOUR DECADES have passed since there were any important revivals of *The Winter's Tale,* and the days of its great popularity in the theatre go farther back into the last century. The Theatre Guild's choice of it may have come as a surprise, but it seems to me an interesting selection and the result is on the whole gratifying and most commendable.

The Guild has backed the production with a very considerable lavishness and pains. The occasion falls in some ways below the standard of those of our older stage, notably in the acting and the reading of Shakespeare's lines; but that is to be expected, since our actors have not had the chance, even if they may have had the desire, at the training in voice and style and at the experience that the actors of those earlier days could profit by. The present occasion excels the former in other ways, in a certain simplification, for example, that is apparently needed for Shakespeare in relation to the modern mind and taste, and especially in the décor—here the general stage design and the technical medium, the stage mechanism, the lighting and so on mark a definite advance. And it is worth recording here that nobody could say that the present production of Shakespeare's play takes your attention away from it any more than those classic productions of the last century were apt to do. The fact is that the Theatre Guild's production of *The Winter's Tale* is less distracting and less at Shakespeare's expense than were the productions of Irving and Mansfield, so lauded in our stage tradition, which I saw as a college student.

As any commentary will tell you, of course, Shakespeare took the story of *The Winter's Tale* from Greene's novel *Pandosto: The*

Triumph of Time, changing the names of characters, combining some of the characters, introducing the rogue Autolycus and divers minor figures, and writing a different ending: Hermione is not dead really and Leontes does not kill himself at the very last, but all are reunited to be happy ever afterward. This change of Shakespeare's is what as much as anything else very likely has served to check the appeal of the play. *The Winter's Tale* was written toward the very end of his career, and the first half of it throughout is as intense, as expert in structure and as searching as *Hamlet,* though on a lesser plane; and then suddenly we are transported to a happy, singing world of young love, flowers, wild bears, shepherds and clowns, and finally, a dénouement, easy, obliging and sure-fire theatrically, where the statue comes to life and love is all for everybody. This divergence in approach and in tone may by some be taken as Shakespeare's comment on young hearts and old hearts, et cetera, but it does not make the appeal of the play any easier. The serious treatment of the first half also makes Leontes' sudden burst into a frenzy of jealous passion none too explicable for many commentators, who have taken pains to explain it either by his being a suspicious, evil tyrant, which he is not, or else by his having fallen into what is a fit of madness. In my opinion all that is beside the point. Shakespeare took the king as he found him in the story, jealousy and all; and the motif of jealous and arbitrary passion, manly honor and the husband's complete authority over his wife, was swallowed by the Renaissance without a quaver. After all, the theme in one of the most admired classics in the Spanish theatre is that the hero's wife, though she has been cleared of every evidence of unfaithfulness, has yet been suspected and so, innocent as she is, must yet die in order that his honor may remain white and perfect. Motivations and themes like that, so alien in their scope and passionate force do not necessarily alter the essential dramatic crux and pressure of the situation, but they may play havoc with our response to it.

Mr. Henry Daniell gave an excellent performance of Leontes, a part that is easily ungrateful. It had not the eloquence and warmth of style by which some one of the old-school actors even when he did not understand the line could still make it count. This is a point worth recording; for it is a fact that many a scene he could not understand the actor of those days could act, where our modern player could understand but not act it. Mr. Daniell, however, brought to the part so much emotional precision and variety and so much understanding that he achieved a kind of fine, subjective rightness. It was a modern, inner approach. The voice is of that dryish British calibre better suited to comedy than to the tragic line's glow and outgoing. The qualities of such a voice function largely as mental comment—which is at least mental and not to be despised. But his intelligence led him to read for the sense-stress in the lines, and since Shakespeare's metrical line is built on the sense, Mr. Daniell's readings were, as verse *per se,* both accurate and telling.

Miss Jessie Royce Landis showed some lapses in the metrical rendering—for a single example, in Hermione's

> Than history can pattern, though devis'd

the metre was lost by not giving the full quantity to the second syllable of "history." Such lapses can be mended by concentration and energy of intention, which from the past stage history of this actress, in spite of all her enormous talent, I fancy, she will not bother with. Miss Landis brought an effective and convincing presence to the part, very necessary to it. And she created, or at least projected, a lofty and admirable seriousness of mood that the dramatist might well be grateful for.

Miss Florence Reed brought her accustomed fire and sword to the part of Paulina. There was a good measure of the old-school Shakespearean in her method, that air of an Olympian hour of ladling it out and letting you have it—come and get your cup of thunder. But this did no harm to one of those ancient high-horse rôles where the lady portrayed is the person in the story who makes things happen and will tell anybody off. Mr. Whitford Kane as the Old Shepherd and Mr. Romney Brent as Autolycus gave really skillful performances in rôles that do not easily make themselves at home with a modern audience. The other rôles in the play, Mr. Colin Keith-Johnson's Camillo, Miss Geraldine Strook's Perdita, Mr. Robert Duke's Florizel, showed various plausible qualities. They all showed the right spirit toward the play. A great deal of the credit for this whole event must go to Mr. B. Iden Payne, who, for a time at least, brought his intelligence and experience to the production's benefit, and to Mr. Romney Brent for their directing.

MID-SEASON

Mr. Stewart Chaney provided *The Winter's Tale* with a sumptuous permanent setting in the tradition of the Bibiena. A happy general tone in stone gray; capitally painted walls and baroque architectural forms, with good perspective; the fore-stage and proscenium arch permanent, with curtain backdrops for certain scenes, and for other scenes variations on the palace rooms, very handsome in their devices, and one a vast cave in the manner of the Renaissance painters. Such a handsome, complex, practical and ambitious stage design is no mean achievement on Mr. Chaney's part. The costumes ranged about in time—they may do so freely, since the play exists in the days of Elizabeth, Apollo, Julio Romano and what not—and many of them are highly effective, a great step forward over the usual Shakespearean costuming. The successful designs, however, are mostly confined to the men's costumes. Some of the lesser ladies came off fairly enough, but Hermione and Paulina were too familiar to our New York eyes; Mme. Paulina Reed's green gown, for example, in the last scene could have come from Fifty-seventh Street. Since Mr. Chaney has got me on such a high plane, I may as well add that the jewelry was mostly all wrong, especially the avalanche of pearls. If we want to follow history, no doubt pearls were worn and some were obligingly painted into portraits, but artificial pearls as we know them did not come in till late in the seventeenth century when Pasquin, of Paris, began to fill beads with iridescent ground fish scales and the ladies with delight. But the historical is not the essential point here: the jewels we see all over *The Winter's Tale* look too much like the shops for raw costume jewelry; it has too much merely vulgar recognizability to be dramatic in such a play. All that is easily avoided. For stage purposes it is not hard to assemble effective dramatic jewels from odds and ends.

Mr. Behrman's new play, *Dunnigan's Daughter,* another Theatre Guild offering, easily merits the harsh and limiting response that apparently it has received from critics and public. It is about an American tycoon in Mexico, his young wife whose father had been jailed, a daughter by a first marriage, a young man from our State Department, and so on and so on. There is a great deal of the personal analysis, of the dainty, half-finicky self and otherwise that underlies the Behrman method, a certain stylish vulgarity, as it were, a sensitivity too delicate to cultivate outside a laboratory—it amounts, in fact, to a gently muddled pathology. This event of *Dunnigan's Daughter* has an assumption, perhaps, of subtlety, or at least some sort of assumption, however hard to describe in any friendly manner, but is full of poor taste and is almost continuously boring.

The entertainment that centers around Mr. Bobby Clark is adapted from various parts of Molière, though assembled into the general framework of *Le Bourgeois Gentilhomme*. It is all gay, if too long, and when it does represent Molière, well represents one side of him: the farce-clowning and buffoonery that Molière retained from his earlier experiences with Italianate farce when he was touring the provinces and was far indeed from the Paris of Louis XIV. And with Bobby Clark to carry that to expert perfection, it would all please Molière more than most of our productions of him would ever have done. At least in this production the line is made clear between Molière as farce and Molière as the most profound of all modern writers of comedy, a profundity that, because of the inherited farce pattern he more or less always retained, has been apt to escape our Anglo-Saxon theatre.

MISS CORNELL'S ANTIGONE

Antigone, adapted by Lewis Galantière from the play by Jean Anouilh. Cort Theatre. February 18, 1946.

THERE SEEMS TO BE a tendency toward apology, or at least an explanation, in the matter of adapting Sophocles' *Antigone* to present uses, but no apology is needed. Every Greek author who touched it wrote the original legend into what served his special purpose—that is obvious. It is also obvious, but a fact more profitable to consider, that men or stories are, as Nietzsche said, heroic to the extent to which their actions take on lasting significance.

M. Anouilh, from whose play Mr. Galantière has made the translation and adaptation which Miss Cornell, in association with Mr. Gilbert Miller, presents, has written a version of the Antigone story that under the very nose of the Nazi censors manages—though that has not a great deal to do with the play as a work of art—to say no little about dictators, individual rights and respect for human instincts.

To accomplish that a good, strong accent would have to be put on Creon, the tyrant. To judge by Mr. Galantière's remarks in a program note, it was, as he considered the play, important that we should hear Creon's arguments. But it was equally important that those arguments have no validity against a higher law which assumes an existence of an immortal soul and commands that priest or rabbi or pastor shall accompany a man to the electric chair as readily as to the field of battle. This has been done, not by taking anything away from M. Anouilh's Creon, but by adding something to his Antigone, his Chorus and his Haemon. I have seen newspaper babble, however, that went further than this and spoke of the play as dealing with the oppressed, which it may be but only incidentally.

This is all very well and perfectly within our rights, so long as we do not get into historical nonsense. We make the story serve what purpose we want it to serve. For what purpose should it be resurrected save for that which Christ gave for His coming, that we may have life and have it more abundantly? But there is no need to fall back on the support of a lot of historical flubdubbery. In the first place, "tyrant" in the Greek scheme does not mean anything about bad government or arbitrary rule; it merely implies that the accession to the throne was not hereditary. And Sophocles was not talking about oppression, not in that society he knew, which was made up of privileged persons and artisans and slaves; he was talking about something far more lasting and innate, as well as less featured on Broadway at this moment—I mean the profound and hidden ties of family devotion and its loving mystery, plus the recoil from a sense of outrage done to our deepest instincts—in this particular case the reverence for the beloved dead and their souls' peace.

Furthermore, the portrait of Creon that we get is not that of Sophocles' *Antigone*. From internal evidence it is plain that this play of his does not follow in the course of an Oedipus trilogy. It is plainly an earlier work, where *Oedipus King* and *Oedipus at Colonos* are products of Sophocles' more mature genius, by which the development of the deeper meaning of Oedipus' suffering and mystical redemption are discovered, and the motif of black craft in Creon's nature is developed. M. Anouilh's conception of the character is a composite of the several epochs of Sophocles plus the modern French conditioning and application. The exposure of Polynices' body after death does not come entirely from Creon's malignity; for all its inhumanity, it ensues partly from Polynices' having invited the seven great captains from Argos to support his royal rights against his brother, Eteocles, and, if need be, to sack the city and wreck it. In the older versions it was the City Council, not Creon, that decreed the shame for Polynices' corpse and was defied by Antigone; who was, we should note, here supported by the Chorus of her Maidens. It was Sophocles who imagined her solitary state; he took away the maidens and left Antigone friendless and alone, with only a chorus of men—a brilliant instance of creative invention as contrasted with some complex and seemingly subtle patter of split-up motivations that often passes for profound. Sophocles dwelt on the motif of her resolution, the single and passionate concentration of her heart, the timid fears of her sister. And it was he who introduced the love motif to Haemon.

MISS CORNELL'S ANTIGONE

In the light of all that, then, we need talk no rubbish or justification, but may use the legend to our own ends, and indeed M. Anouilh has done so.

The production scenically that is given to the play at the Cort consists of curtains and a semicircle of steps, all seen with a quiet not so much classic as elegant by Mr. Raymond Sovey—a soft beige, gray or what you will, according to the lighting—with costumes by Valentina that are perfectly aware of the prose-poetic requirements of the play as, not too boldly, it is given to us.

As to Mr. Galantière's translation, the intention is evident that we are to be idiomatic and natural, in the style more or less of the Nurse, who is to make some coffee in the early morning for the young Theban princesses, one of whom has been out burying her brother and one awake all night in a torture of debate with herself and uneasy doubts. You wipe your nose on your sleeve and say, "Goodmorning, Ismene," or at least you talk our current vernacular. It seemed to me that this effort toward the homely was most effective when the guards were speaking. They were frankly tough characters and their utterances were well written. But the problem of creating the vibration of the vernacular is only a cut below creating that of the great poetic style; John Synge could have told you how for five years he listened on the Isle of Arran before those deathless word-images were born to his phrasing. It is in this respect that the lines Mr. Galantière has written are not by any means first-class. The marvels of the English language—often declared unsingable by those who have studied with German gurglers or Parisian adenoiders—are not too often found in the speeches of this *Antigone*. In the high poetic style there is the beating of the wings, as it were; and in the realistic style, the plain song of our English speech, the homely fire of the pulse. We get touches of both in this adaptation, but not enough of either.

The company of *Antigone* all should be credited with the right spirit, which is much. Some of them spoke very poor English, in voices badly placed and worse employed. Miss Bertha Belmore, with seasons behind her, gave a good performance of the nurse. Mr. George Matthews, as the First Guard, or whatever you call it, was capital in a good part, his cueing was notable and his variations, a kind of counterpoint, as it were, to Antigone's speeches, were something to study as stagecraft—a good actor. Sir Cedric Hardwicke's Creon had an admirable authority and distinctness.

Miss Cornell has lately returned from a tour of the army theatres, where she played *The Barretts of Wimpole Street* nearly a hundred and fifty times. I have heard reports of these occasions from members of the armed forces, so beautiful did they feel the experience to be that she gave them. To many of the men who had never seen a stage play before, it was a great adventure. As to Miss Cornell's Antigone, I can only say it was a wise choice for her. It was a performance that was a little dull and vague but sincerely undertaken, filled with that shimmer and shadow, that stage magnetism, which is essentially hers. If the whole company performance at the Cort is not filled with the height of tragic acting, I can only say that in our Broadway theatre it is not entirely their fault. And I would add that, while various leading exponents of our box-office stage, illustrious stars, so to speak, are getting richer by being cheaper, here is Miss Cornell, who might easily be making more money by being more Broadway, here she is presenting an American version of a French version of a Greek version of something that is at least worth talking about, worth seeing.

There is something about this play *Antigone* as it stands that invites power and intensity of tone but defeats the same. It is thus impossible to direct after a certain point, and Mr. Guthrie McClintic in a sort of cutting-the-corners fashion, has at least done better by it than most directors could have done.

THE OLD VIC

Henry IV, Part I, by William Shakespeare. Century
Theatre. May 6, 1946.
Henry IV, Part II. May 7, 1946.

NOT SINCE the coming of the Moscow Art Theatre more than twenty years ago has there been so notable an advance publicizing as the Old Vic has enjoyed. Travelers returning from abroad have been quoted for their enthusiasm, magazines have printed articles, front pages and laudatory interludes, and there was reason to believe that our somewhat time-thinned shores of art were about to receive a thrill, a reproach for tardy inspirations and dying method, an inclusive fecundation and a pure, full, theatric joy. As a matter of fact, what we have received is an excellent stock company, agreeable, sometimes a bit tame, and blessed in general with quiet good taste and a somewhat more elusive lack of fine style in particular. It is doubtless to be said, however, that the absence of the London housing or atmosphere and, perhaps also a theatre less large and general, makes the company's problem more exacting.

The Moscow Art Theatre was not the equal, in stately form or classic style, of the French theatre in the Comédie Française. But in the field of realism, realism in the final, great sense, this Russian theatre was the last word. It had the authentic pulse and exactitude that we knew already in Tolstoy, with those incredible overtones, deeper than any fact. Fiction like Dostoievsky's opened new possibilities to the Western world. In Gorky and in Chekhov, the Moscow Art Theatre supplied a trend and a passion in contemporary theatre art more immediate and more expert than anything we had. It presented, also, a sense of stylization, definite, founded on solid theory, taste, research and sophistication. There is no stylization, however, indicated in the Old Vic production as we get it now, no insistent theatrical creed, nothing beyond good sense and a mild, second-rate conception of art. Its best element is the human and simply rational and right, with as much appeal as may ensue. Its utmost reliance is on personality, the study of the character and the personality and special traits of its portrayer. To repeat, the best we can say of the Old Vic company is that it is not by a long shot a great art movement or institution, but is an unusually good stock company—an institution more familiar in the old days of the theatre than now; that the continuing experience of playing together gives the company the chance to acquire a certain admirable unity of effect; and that it can boast a certain number of admirable performers.

The Henry plays belong to the earlier section of Shakespeare's career and the verse for stage speaking purposes grows intricate at times and dates itself into the full Renaissance complexity. And Shakespeare's reliance on the chronicles of Holinshed, on old plays and otherwise, does not simplify the statement and impact of his themes or make more portable the burden of his narrative passages. A good deal of the writing of the scenes outside the Falstaff passages is not up to Shakespeare's best by any means and is tedious to listen to. Nothing short of some vast genius in the producer or in the particular performer could force this material into any striking distinction. The selection of the Henry plays is obviously based on character parts, a type of selection characteristic of the British theatre.

Mr. Laurence Olivier, who seems of late largely to have carried the panache for this whole enterprise, or so in our press at least, plays Hotspur in the first Henry play and plays it with a definite charm and poetic fatalism of mind as beautiful as it is rare. In the second Henry he plays Justice Shallow, with an obvious and shivery make-up-impersonation that handsomely belongs in comedy realms—legitimate without being noteworthy. Such a part is, of course, any actor's meat, and only such fine players as Mr. Sydney Greenstreet or some of the Moscow members can reduce it to its last excitement and tragi-comic precision.

In the passages where narrative reading is called for, as so often occurs during *Henry IV, Part I,* Mr. Olivier greatly surprised me at times by mouthing it all away more or less, as many of his fellow actors do, as if they did not know the lines meant anything but the player's self: a sad conclusion, for it ends by meaning nothing at all. The trouble in such cases is basic; which is to say that the phrase or the clause, as existing within the whole sentence, should be studied in each instance for the emphasis, and when the emphases are decided upon, the whole sentence—however precious and ultra—has to be conceived. The second basic point for the reading here is entirely physical: the sense must be gauged with reference to the thought, so that where the proper stress is required there will be the breath to create it and to balance the whole sentence design. Mr. Olivier suggests that he can still learn, and that within him there is a certain noble spirit willing to go forward.

Mr. Ralph Richardson is the Falstaff of these adventures, an actor of great resource, who reads the passages of wit and interthought as if all were in a vacuum of genius, and creates a character that at least suggests the vile wit, the vagary and the dirty grace that Shakespeare intended. This playing of Mr. Richardson's is playing of intelligence and wise values. His speeches are largely prose, and within obvious limits he is an actor more expert than Mr. Olivier, though a figure of less magnetism. Nevertheless, I should not say that his Falstaff is first-rate; it remains in the competent class. The man in the company who really can read verse, noting the sense and the combination of meaning and meter, is Mr. William Monk in the Douglas rôle. Every line he reads has meaning and point. He could teach the whole company how blank verse can have meaning when read aloud. The general defect in this company may well be a seeming obliviousness to the fact that there is such a thing as style or even form in art, style and form fully admitted, shaped and projected.

Not a great deal is done for the women in these Shakespeare chronicles. Doll Tearsheet is there, however and so are her mistress, and the Percy lady and others, all mildly noted and negligible, nobody blessed with any style to speak of or wit or flickering grace. Sometimes their mystery is scored by the sole fact that their performers patter off the verse in such a way that its meaning is completely obscured.

Mr. Gower Parks' scenery is now and again—not always—a triumph of adaptation within simple means. Mr. Roger Furse has contrived some admirable costumes, quite often poorly worn by the players.

THE OLD VIC OEDIPUS

Oedipus Rex, English version by W. B. Yeats.
Century Theatre, May 20, 1946.

AS TO the Old Vic's *Oedipus Rex,* we may say that for people who do not know the story, or who have never read the play, or who have never seen it acted, this occasion of it will arouse a very considerable response and in some cases enthusiasm. The Yeats version is, of course, a great simplification of the Sophocles play, and is written in the beautiful words that belong to this great Irish poet. The complexities of the Greek original are not even attempted; and, if they were, they would be impossible to reproduce in English. The sum and total of the play is thus enormously reduced. The pattern of the myth itself, as found and perfected by Sophocles, is monumental and sure-fire, based on all the technical devices of the Greek genius in drama. The appeal of the Old Vic's *Oedipus* is thus guaranteed for many.

The setting for the play by Mr. John Piper is effective, even dramatically creative in a limited way, though it suggests that the artist's drawing was better than the stage execution of it. It has two columns, suggestive only, with the curtained doorway, a grayish-sky backdrop and some archaic images of Apollo and two other gods such as Pausanias describes as existing centuries later. Once the suppliants arise, however, and Oedipus and others enter and the chorus takes over, the archaism is all over and forgotten. The problem here involves the matter of unity in a work of art—in a theatre production as a whole—not of archaic stylization; for there is no reason the production of this *Oedipus* should necessarily be archaic; it needs only to be a unity. I am anxious to be understood on that point.

The costumes by Miss Marie-Helene Daste are a part of the debacle. They are many and varied. They employ Greek designs, some archaic, some in the more familiar classic modes, and some in the stereotyped manner supposed in the course of time by the theatre to be highly classical. But these costumes were made with so little fundamental conception of costume cutting that they were largely without either historical or—what, of course, is the important point—dramatic value. They were, also, for the most part badly worn, not carried with any style at all by the wearers. Most of the wigs had no style or expertness, and the same was true of the make-ups. Beards were not very frequent, though historically, if we go in for that, the Greeks did not begin to shave till Alexander's time, nearly a century after this play; and esthetically, beards, in the right style, help lessen the effect of familiarity and encourage that of the heroic. Thus Mr. Olivier looked more like a bad Roman coin of the late Republic than an Attic hero or the Cumaean Zeus, the convention of the Periclean theatre. Mr. Olivier further complicated matters by his costume or lack of it. The Greeks knew that even with flowing, kingly robes and with shoes and head-dress that increased the actor's stature, it was difficult enough to give the actor the right heroic presence. Mr. Olivier wore a sort of tunic effect, with his legs bare—handsome legs, if you like, but with a result too youthful and too trivial. It is entirely out of key with the large, type treatment in Sophocles of character, ideas and events. In all this let me say that I am not talking about stylization; you can go in for it or omit it as you please; I am talking about style as implying the significant relation between the thought and the outward, or visual, expression of it.

Mr. Richardson was Tiresias, the seer, in Greek legend a lofty figure touched with the gods' divinity. He played well in relation not to majesty of tone but in relation to the general approach to the play that the Old Vic has followed in its production. In the same manner, Mr. Harry Andrews' Creon was a dignified and excellent performance. Miss Ena Burrill, dressed out in an absurd but becoming costume such as we have seen often enough before this when ladies do classical heroines, was Jocasta, one of the great, subtly motivated and passionate Greek rôles. She was lacking in any tragic quality whatever, and any impact that may have derived from her performance was the sheer result of the deathless impact of words in themselves. And even those words reached us in some airy, semi-nasal jargon. It was not her fault that Sophocles was not completely thwarted.

Mr. Nicholas Hannen, a good actor, did as well as could be as Leader of the Chorus. He was granted a beard; the chorus otherwise was beardless, grimly made up, and with their thin Nordic features looked more like witches than Theban elders. Yeats very wisely has greatly cut down the Chorus' part in the play; but any Greek chorus is by its very nature a stylization of the actuality; and, obviously, having a group of people saying the same words in unison is a form of stylization. In neither of these respects was much done to help matters; and there were doubtless many in the audience who merely charged that off against the poor quaint Greeks.

Taking the Oedipus rôle from the usual point of view, that of heroic tragedy, we must note that Mr. Olivier in the first place has not the voice for it. His voice is fairly light, has small warmth or continuity of tone; his delivery of verse is based very often on a kind of jerky energy. It is a method of reading descended from Sir Henry Irving, who triumphed over having practically no voice at all by throwing it against the bridge of his nose. Mr. Olivier at one point, however, used the celebrated wail, or cry of woe, that Mounet-Sully gave his Oedipus. That wail of Mounet-Sully's, like a stricken animal, human pain, earth pain, was infinitely imagined, infinitely right. Mr. Olivier makes sounds like cries in a boarding-house and gets nowhere at all. At the supreme moment of the play, where Oedipus enters, by his own hands blinded with a buckle from Jocasta's robe, at the realization of the horror laid on him, Mr. Olivier chose to appear in the palace doorway with a change of costume—an unaccountable, medieval-looking, flapping brown garment, made more voluminous by his extended arms. Regardless of history and stage tradition, this was entirely wrong. In the first place, Oedipus' stopping to change his clothes does not accord with the rashness of impulse that Sophocles has already carefully established as a balancing element to the seeming injustice of the curse the gods have put on him. In the second place it does not accord with the violent despair of the moment. The new and very different costume, and such a costume at that, strikes the eye unduly and distracts the eye from the immediate, full impression and shock that Sophocles counts on. Granting the general approach of the Old Vic to the play, however, Mr. Olivier's performance has sincerity, intelligence and a certain degree of semi-projected intensity.

Oedipus Rex in the Old Vic production will, and should, at any rate afford much pleasure to many people in the audience and to some even a degree of exaltation. It marks at least a great advance over another British presentation of the play many seasons ago when Mr. Olivier was in his teens. Sir John Martin-Harvey brought over his company in Gilbert Murray's sighing translation of *Oedipus*. I can still see the hero, in a rather full long skirt, a high metal corselet, with something like Empire sleeves coming out of it and the actor's white arms. He too wore no beard and none of the ambrosial locks of the heroes, but only a slight royal fillet and clustering short hair above a dainty matinee face set sternly to its lofty classical task. The chorus consisted of ten or twelve men with crimpy beards, cloths about their heads, the general lines of their garments like bad statues of Roman matrons or monumental vestal virgins. Their leader, in a full-skirted costume, V-necked, and over it all a kind of thin, floating negligée, stood in the centre and directed their appropriate sentiments and gestures. They swayed and postured with their staffs. The moment came at last when Jocasta, sick with the horror of the doom she saw, ran out; and at this the virgin ballet waggled their beards, shook their wands and seemed about to waltz, while their leader, like the Old Man of the Mountain in an obesity gown, led them on. Oedipus returned; and leaning against a pilaster, he too tried for the Mounet-Sulley cries with three odd, short toots. So much for Sir John.

And so much for at least one treatment of Sophocles. I remember thinking of Nicharchus' epigram:

"Marcus, the doctor, called yesterday on the marble Zeus; though marble, and though Zeus, he will be buried today."

And when it had all subsided and we made our way out of the theatre, I remember thinking of Wordsworth's saying that the gods approve the depth and not the tumult of the soul, and Aeschylus' "All that gods work is effortless and calm."

In the meantime it is worth while to say that the whole of Sophocles' play is one line, splendidly held, modulated with superb emotion, balanced and ordered with due cause and effect, driven forward with the pressure of its own truth. Compared to *Oedipus Rex* there is no play of the Western world so steady and perfect in its progression; no play that has so inevitably found its pattern, story, idea and form together; and no play that contrives to mount and descend with such security, discovering for its climax the greatest image in all drama—those blinded eyes with their bloody stains, that terrible pain, that shudder and dread and shame of life in this world and in the next among the dead. We are completely involved by it—our bodies by the physical reality, our minds by the idea and significance.

THE ICEMAN COMETH
THE NEW O'NEILL PLAY
The Iceman Cometh, by Eugene O'Neill. Martin Beck Theatre. October 9, 1946.

THE ICEMAN COMETH marks the return of Eugene O'Neill to Broadway after an absence of twelve years. The performance of the play runs into two sessions, of about an hour and a quarter before the dinner intermission, and two and three-quarters after. The Theatre Guild, by its own lights, has brought the highest intentions to its production, a large company mostly of experienced actors, plus the décor by Mr. Robert Edmond Jones and the directing by Mr. Eddie Dowling.

The scene of *The Iceman Cometh* is Harry Hope's, a saloon with a back room curtained off, which can pass as a restaurant and run Sundays as well as weekdays, and with lodgers upstairs, which turns it into a Raines Law hotel that can stay open night and day. Among the guests are a former Harvard man; a one-time editor of Anarchist periodicals; a one-time police lieutenant; a Negro, one-time proprietor of a Negro gambling house; a one-time leader of a Boer commando; a one-time Boer War correspondent; a one-time captain of British infantry; a one-time Anarchist; a one-time circus man; a young man from the West Coast, who has squealed on his Anarchist mother; a hardware salesman; the day and night bartenders; and three tarts. They have, the majority of them, fallen from what they once were and now live in a kind of whiskey-sodden dream of getting back: tomorrow will make everything right. The first session of *The Iceman Cometh*—absorbing and in the early O'Neill manner—is taken up with the revelation of the various characters as they wait for the arrival of Hickey, the hardware salesman, who joins them every year at this time to celebrate Harry's birthday with a big drunk. Hickey arrives, greets them with the old affection and surprises them with the announcement that he has left off drink and that he has come to save them not from booze but from pipe-dreams. It is these, he says, that poison and ruin a guy's life and keep him from finding any peace; he is free and contented now, like a new man, all you need is honesty with yourself, to stop lying about yourself and kidding yourself about tomorrow. He hands out a $10 bill to start the party and falls asleep from fatigue.

In the next act Hickey's effect is seen. Harry must go out on the street for the first time in twenty years and see his friends in the ward about the alderman's post they had once offered him; the short-change expert must go back to the circus; the various others back to their old positions in life; the day bartender and one of the tarts must go on and marry instead of always talking about it, et cetera. But now the friendly backwater of sots and wrecks and whores turns into hate, violent rows and imminent fights. Hickey gets them all out, one by one; he knows they will come back again, beaten but free of their pipe-dreams, and so will find peace. They all return, everything has gone wrong, even the whiskey has lost its kick. Hickey, who has confessed to killing his beloved and loving wife, to free her and free himself from a torturing pipe-dream of his reform, turns out to be insane, and this at last, and this only, frees them. All but two, for whom death is the end, go back to their dreams, somewhat gloriously, and the whiskey works again.

Mr. Eddie Dowling has directed *The Iceman Cometh* in his by now well known style. His is a method sure to be admired: it consists largely in a certain smooth security, an effect of competence, of keeping things professional and steady, and often of doing pretty much nothing at all. To this he adds in *The Iceman Cometh* a considerable degree of stylized performance, actors sitting motionless while another character or other groups take the stage. Since there is a good deal of stylization in the structure of *The Iceman Cometh,* this may well be justified. But in my opinion the usual Dowling method brought to the directing of this O'Neill play would gain greatly by more pressure, more intensity and a far darker and richer texture. It was to some extent at least due to this elusively prose, expected, sometimes almost smug, treatment that this new and most profoundly ambitious play of Eugene O'Neill's could scarcely have been said to have had as compelling a quality, as deep a stir and pathetic shock, as were often to be found in the things of his that were done years ago at the Provincetown Playhouse. I am not even sure as to the extent to which I can judge *The Iceman Cometh* after seeing such a production of it.

The same remark applies to the acting. It is a relief to see so many expert actors instead of the usual run of technically indifferent players we so often get on Broadway nowadays. The three actresses who have the tart rôles belong, alas, to this latter indifferent rank; otherwise the acting is notable for its excellence, especially Messrs. E. G. Marshall, Nicholas Joy, Frank Tweddel, Carl Benton Reid and Russell Collins, plus fair enough performances by Paul Crabtree, John Morriott and Tom Pedi. Mr. James Barton as Hickey, a most central character in the entire motivation and movement of the play, plays the part very much, I should imagine, as Mr. Eddie Dowling would have played it, judging from his performance in *The Glass Menagerie* and elsewhere, and from his directing. Which means a sort of playing that is competent, wholly at ease and with a something that appears to settle the matter, to close the subject as it were, so that for the moment at least you are prevented from thinking of anything else that could be done about it. Only afterward do you keep realizing what might have been there and was not. Mr. Russell Collins could have played the rôle of Hickey with much more inner concentration, depth, projection and unbroken emotional fluency. As it stands, he has a smaller part, which he does with a perfection and rightness that shames the whole occasion.

It was these qualities of Mr. Collins' that appeared in Dudley Digges' performance. His Harry, the proprietor, was on a different plane from every other to be seen on the stage at the Martin Beck. It was exact, with the exactness that belongs to all fine art; and full of the constant surprise that appears in all first-rate art whatever, as it does in whatever is alive in our life. It was beautiful, luminous, filled with the witty and the poetic together mingled. 'Twere to consider too curiously to consider so, as Horatio says, and most unfair, perhaps, to wonder what would happen to *The Iceman Cometh* if more of the players could do the same by it. But that would imply no doubt a condition equal to that of the Moscow Art Theatre in Gorki's *The Lower Depths*. How much the play could be cut or not cut then would remain to be seen. As *The Iceman Cometh* now stands, it is a notable play but could certainly be cut.

Mr. Robert Edmond Jones's setting for *The Iceman Cometh* seems to me one of those impalpable evocations of his in the medium of décor, austere, elegant and elusively poetic, and uncannily right for the realistic-poetic quality of this O'Neill drama.

WEBSTER

The Duchess of Malfi, by John Webster, adapted by
W. H. Auden. Ethel Barrymore Theatre.
October 15, 1946.

THE reader may, or may not, have seen the remark (1664) of a French traveler, Samuel de Sorbière, about the English and their drama. "They don't care that it may be only a potpourri, because they look, they say, only at one part of it after another without concerning themselves about the whole" (*san se soucier du total*). This applied to Shakespeare is the best key we could find to the French view of him as barbarous. And it lands squarely on the chief defect and limitation of Webster's famous play of *The Duchess of Malfi*, produced four years, perhaps, and certainly two, before Shakespeare's death. *The Duchess of Malfi* lacks practically all organization; it defeats any attempt to see it as a whole. It runs away in every direction that a richly poetic Elizabethan mind chooses to take. In the fifth act, after the heroine's murder is over and done with, it messes itself up beyond all redemption. To see projected on the stage a play about which so many scholars, critics and poets have written so variously and variably these many years was a genuine privilege.

The version used for this occasion is the play as adapted by W. H. Auden, the poet. It is very often an adaptation indeed, not to mention the very liberal cutting. It transposes scenes and events from this or that act to another, changes about seventy-five percent of the fifth act, writes an entirely new ending that is anything but what Webster had in mind, and introduces what amounts to an innovation in the shape of a Freudian motive for Ferdinand's violent reaction to his sister's love affair. This motive may or may not have been in Webster's conscious or subconscious intention; it remains suspended so far as the lines of the play go; but the fact remains that in *The Fair Maid of the Inn* there is the motive of the brother's infatuation and jealousy with regard to the sister, and on this play Webster collaborated with Ford and Massinger. The very end of the play we see at the Ethel Barrymore is sheer Auden or what you will, with its current clichés about the violence of rulers, the solvent of love, et cetera. In neither of these innovations of Mr. Auden's is the writing convincing as Elizabethan; it butters itself into trash no doubt; but at that I should say that this adaptation has a real talent behind it and has for our present purposes greatly improved the sprawling, excessive Elizabethan drama—*se soucier du total*. Meanwhile, obviously, in improving it we suffer a certain loss in the sense that we cut down its volume and its kind of mad range and disordered power.

Even in this new form the play did not, I was interested to see, come off as living theatre. Its best efforts were the famous purple patches that scholars have hit the public over the head with and poets have swooned over, passages like that of the death of the duchess, the cough-syrup speech and the mine-eyes-dazzle speech. Such passages, doubtless, came off rather furiously in their epoch, with actors acting them to the hilt for audiences who any day might see disemboweled corpses or some headless putrescence hanging at the cross-streets, or gory wax images of the dead borne along to torches and music. But George Rylands, the director, imported from London, where he directed the successful run of this drama last season, has left many elements in it very mild for our consumption. *The Duchess of Malfi* has been almost suspiciously dear to the hearts of professors and graduate students, who are apt to whip up this drama from heated passages rather than from its presentation on the stage. Seeing Webster's play thus, in the theatre flesh as it were, more or less confirms an old impression of mine that it is a drama, often high in import and power, that belongs, for us at least, to the printed page rather than to the stage of a theatre.

Miss Bergner brings a kind of fey gallantry, Berlin-trained, to the effort, but she is not in any respect suited to the part. In the first place her accent, if nothing else, blocks any effect of the central quality of the Duchess, which is a rhythmic liveliness and persuasion of lyric passion. And the besetting impression of female-actress-egotism, whose disturbing mildew Miss Bergner will inevitably bring to any and every part she does, denies that open flower of the heart, that gentle, free sound of the blood, that Webster has written for the heroine of *The Duchess of Malfi*.

Mr. Canada Lee made up in white-face, shall we say, has an admirable energy and sincerity, sustained throughout, for the rôle of Bosola, who is here the villiain of the play. But he has not yet mastered the diction that can serve fully the purposes of such English verse, nor has he as an actor the secure stage projection that is needed for the style required. Whitfield Connor as the Antonio of the Duchess' love and tragedy was better than we might usually hope for in such a rôle. John Carradine as the Cardinal brother played with distinction and a considerable intensity of style.

The scenes by Harry Bennett are well above the average and the costumes by Miles White are both handsome and dramatic.

The contrivance by which the artificial figures of Antonio and the children are shown as if they were dead is practically wasted, without any convincing actuality of horror or of the frank barbarism of which the Elizabethan stage is capable and on which some of Webster's effects depend. Much of the theatre problem of Webster's drama turns on the handling of his violence and complex furor of image and motivation. Before such a torrent we are too often impeded by an inner conviction that Seneca expressed where he says that shallow griefs speak—*curae leves loquuntur, ingentes stupent*—the deep are dumb. This is not necessarily true at all, but there are many moments when Webster shouts us down into believing it.

MARTHA GRAHAM

El Penitente, Letter to the World, Every Soul Is a Circus, by Martha Graham. Various Theatres. 1941–1947.

THE programmes of dance compositions that Miss Martha Graham is repeating, together with the triumphant response from audiences, have been fully reported both from out of town and from New York theatres. *El Penitente,* drawn from the cult of the *penitentes* of the Southwest, is not an imitation of the ritual, but a kind of mystery dance drama; *Letter to the World* deals with the legend rather than the life of Emily Dickinson, using poems or lines from the poems to lead or point the themes, as it were; and *Every Soul Is a Circus* dances some farcical and extravagant fantasy within the soul of a silly woman.

Since I am not a critic of the art of dancing, perhaps the best thing I can do—not staying to comment even on the good work of her two leading dancers, Mr. Eric Hawkins and Mr. Merce Cunningham—is to set down two cardinal points with regard to this dancer's art and the general theatre art in our midst. The first is that Miss Martha Graham in my opinion is the most important lesson for our theatre that we now have. She has come more and more to exemplify some of our stage's chief needs and to illustrate fine possibilities where it may have deficiencies and gaps. Her work can be studied for its search after stage gesture in the largest sense, some discovered and final movement. And it can be imitated in the perpetual revision and recomposing that she does in her search for the right emphases, and the right pressure to be given them, as if she were feeling for the bones of the work's body, within the flowing articulation of the whole. The point here is not that everything we see Miss Graham do is beautiful or perfect; the point is the scraping back to the design, the lyric and almost harsh resolution to be honest toward it. This projection and this firm statement of the emphases are what the ordinary acting to be found in our theatre needs in order to discipline its shiftless inconsequence.

Here endeth the first lesson, and the second is in the matter of conceptions. The conceptions that he has feed and qualify the artist's creative work—the artist in general as distinguished from the practiser in any given art, the actor, painter, poet and so on.

Miss Graham has got her technique to the point now where whatever she says, all she says in fact, is said in terms of dance—a technical completeness rare in any art, and so far so good, regardless of what she has to express. But that is not all. An austere and great light has come behind many of her figures and gradations of imagery. In the three persons of the *penitente* play there is such a sounding out of violent ecstasy, crude and orgiastic, mystical and dark, as is not to be found elsewhere in our theatre, though even this element is surpassed at the climaxes when suddenly the movement stops in exhaustion and passionate fulfilment, and the magnificent drawing marks a climax in the visual design. In the course of *Letter to the World,* the reading of the poetry was imaginatively contrived, as if it were music calling out the movement's soul. The reading itself was none too good, either for the sense stress or the continuity of the metrical line, but that is another matter. The poetry itself was none too perfect. To my mind the range and qualities of tone in the inner and outer experience expressed thus in dancing, the tenderness and freshness of inexhaustible motifs, and the deep statement, inevitable and not falsely romantic, of the dénouement, left many of the lines themselves well behind.

Miss Graham has a sense of stage projection, based on intensity and absorption and strict elimination of the unessential, that is rarely found anywhere in the theatre—Charlie Chaplin has it in the films, of course, but is alone in doing so. Of some of Martha Graham's compositions I can say that they are among the few things I have ever seen in dancing where the idea, its origin, the source from which it grew, the development of its excitement and sanctity, gave me a feeling of baffled awe and surprise, and of wonder and defeat in its presence. By this I mean to imply a contrast with such a dance, for example, as that of Pavlova and Nijinsky in a bacchanal. Beautiful as that was, beyond most things in the theatre of our time, one could easily see how the idea might come from a vase painting, a bas relief, a flash of formal music. This predictability, so to speak, in no way lessened the excellence of that dance. I am only trying to express that other sense, of the wonder at creation and the feeling of an unimaginable origin and concentration.

Tennyson observed that of all things sculpture is one of the most difficult to describe. Dancing is as difficult. We may, with writing talent, find some equivalent in words for the dance we write of. But this is a re-creation of essence. It is not straight description. You could say, in fact, that the more exactly you describe such a dance composition the less you convey it to the reader. I might, therefore, perhaps, be useful by another method.

When I first saw Miss Graham dance I had a feeling of insistent denial that I resented; too many things were cut away that life knows to be enchanting or profound. I thought I saw that this was a dancer who, having heard much of reaching to the heavenly sphere, had brains enough to know that—while all art when it has arrived does indeed move within the heavenly sphere—art must, nevertheless, find first an earth to stand on. In sum, she knew that to look up at the stars you must have and use a head, eyes, neck, backbone and feet, plus the ground under you; it was not a mere matter of your feeling inside you that you were looking up at the stars, as if a feeling were anything significant unless it achieves a form, a body in which it lives. But, in the meanwhile, a great deal too much had been cut away.

There was, then, in Miss Graham's dancing this kind of stubborn elimination. It did show a sincere and genuine nature, but a nature not yet flowered in culture and freedom. There was also too great an absence of movement: the dancer's technique involved steps and positions, but the transition, which is the living element, was close to nil. From this her dancing's early state, all profoundly true to the artist at the time and in that degree right with itself, and moving on a human basis, Miss Graham has year by year progressed. You feel that her art, for all its logic and appeal, has only just begun, and that one of the remarkable things about it is that this fact is even clearer to the artist than it is to you. She very likely knows that, as Cezanne said of his painting, she is a primitive in her own kind of dancing.

There are, as every artist knows, a thousand ways to go forward by means of various cheating surfaces that are void of inner solidity; the refusal of them is the first hallmark of an artist. From this most independent and self-imposed conviction of her present stage of development, proceeds the freshness of Miss Graham's work. She knows that the first young stages of an artist have really no freshness; they have only fresh feeling, or egotism or exhibitionism that is but partially expressed in form that is either casual, traditional or imitative. As the artist's work grows, its freshness is present. Maturity alone brings it alive, into a complete life. Maturity implies not only the freshness and immediacy of feeling or idea—whatever you want to call it. It implies also that the technique to express it is safe, complete. It is possible that Martha Graham has reached her maturity, but she has not passed it. And at that, even, we may say that when maturity is past, an artist may sometimes go on for no little while merely by remembering and repeating these already achieved forms, which, because of their rightness once, carry about them still something of their first desire and light.

It will be worth more to try and put down, rather than a report or attempted picture of Miss Graham's dance, some indication of what one can see in the process of her creation. Her dancing is pictorial, necessarily, since one understands it through the eyes. It is not pictorial in the sense of being representative, but pictorial as in an abstract painting or a pattern in design. She must begin, I should say, not with either a pictorial representational idea (some scene or personage) or with a dramatic idea: her first idea will be more like that of a designer of patterns, lines, angles, rugs, tiles, fabrics, what you will, or like the basic outlay of what will later be a painting. From this pattern or single form there will develop other forms; which in their turn may suggest an idea less visually abstract and more a subject, more a literary or a psychological meaning, and go on from there, perhaps, even to a title for the composition, *Incantation,* say, or *Dolorosa* or *Dithyrambic.* Her dances have been so far both pictorial and dramatic, as music is, not as, for instance, a picture of Velasquez is, or a scene in a play.

There are times when the Graham programme or some number in it seems too long. If you have full faith in the dancer you get an unpleasant sense that, with so much given to it, more must be being said than you are taking in; a sense of inadequacy of perception is laid on you as it were. There are times, too, when the motif and the effect seem over-presented, and you are reminded of Talleyrand's remark that whatever is exaggerated is insignificant. And we may have found not too infrequently an evasion of the dramatic, a concentration on the stark pattern for the design-idea of the composition. The benefits of this—for a period of time, that is—are manifest in the fine cleanness and purity of her dancing. We have the sense that, no matter what has been left out, nothing has entered a composition that has not grown into it organically. It is important to note that in Miss Graham's dancing there is a conscious and even stubbornly urgent sincerity; and that this contrasts greatly with what so often appears in the German dancers—Miss Wigman, for example, or Mr. Kreutzberg—where there is not rarely a kind of false simplification—German theory, in sum, too obviously applied. Stepping out roundly in one sole sweep, for instance, or one lump, is not necessarily simple; in these German dancers it is often the patent application of sheer, not to say raw, psychology, and is often over-elaborate in spirit and in essence impure. It is true, nevertheless, that there is no reason why more of the lyric and dramatic should not—and no doubt will—take their place in the pure form of Miss Graham's art.

We can make another note on Martha Graham's dancing. Certain reiterations are highly manifest: the return of a form, a tone, or a rhythm. This seems to me a very wise tendency. The lack of reiteration is one of the things that send so much modern art off into nothing. There is not only the hypnotic effect of repetition and the satisfaction, as close as our heartbeats, of recurrence; there is the fact that a thing must return on itself as a part of its life process. The dance especially, involved as it is so immediately with life, is gone as soon as it is finished, just as life is gone as soon as it ceases, and so the dance tends to repeat the passion of its vitality. Underlying all that is alive is the compulsion toward return.

INDEX

Academy Awards, 228
Adams, Maude, 227
Adelphi, 157
Adler, Stella, 130
Aeschylus, 123, 132–136, 269
Agamemnon, 135
Aherne, Brian, 148
Alanova, Kyra, 52
Alden, Hortense, 124
Alvin Theatre, 246
American Tragedy, An, 72–75
Ames, Winthrop, 3
Anders, Glenn, 94
Anderson, John, 205
Anderson, Judith, 222
Anderson, Maxwell, 165, 167, 185
Andrews, Harry, 267
Anna Christie, 19, 108
Anouilh, Jean, 259–261
Ansky, S., 67, 69
Antigone, 259–262
Aquinas, Thomas, 86
Aristophanes, 123–126
Aristotle, 190
Arthur, Julia, 100
Ashcroft, Peggy, 188
Ashton, Frederick, 151
Asi Que Pasen Cinco Años, 173
Astor, Mary, 228
Atkinson, Brooks, 201
Attic dramatists, the, 87, 137
Auden, W. H., 275, 276
Autobiography of Alice B. Toklas, The, 150
Ayres, Lemuel, 239

Bacchae, The, 57
Bainter, Fay, 124
Baker, Lee, 137
Barcelona, 105
Barnes, Margaret Ayer, 145
Barratt, Watson, 105

Barretts of Wimpole Street, The, 262
Barrie, Sir James M., 227–229
Barrymore, Ethel, 104, 105, 240–242
Barrymore, John, 8–11, 13
Barrymore, Lionel, 100
Barrymore Theatre, Ethel, 101, 275
Bartlett, Michael, 154
Barton, James, 273
Basserman, Albert, 240, 242
Beck Theatre, Martin, 91, 127, 185, 271
Beecher, Henry Ward, 238
Behrman, S. N., 254, 257
Béjart, Armande, 158
Belasco, David, 3, 19, 43, 44
Belasco Theatre, 145
Belmore, Bertha, 261
Benavente, Jacinto, 169–171
Bennett, Harry, 277
Bergner, Elizabeth, 276
Bernhardt, Sara, 34
Bernstein, Aline, 52, 239
Bible, the, 141
Bill of Divorcement, 21
Birthday of the Infanta, The, 1–4, 16, 231
Bitter Oleander, 169–171
Blair, Mary, 124
Boileau, Nicolas, 158
Bondi, Beulah, 108
Booth Theatre, 254
Boris Gudunoff, 69
Botticelli, 43, 116
Bourneuf, Philip, 225
Bowles, Paul, 175, 253
Bradford, Roark, 119–122
Brady, Alice, 137, 138
Brahms, Johannes, 54
Brent, Romney, 256
Breuning, Margaret, 246
Brothers Karamazov, The, 37, 40, 80–83

283

INDEX

Brown, Charles D., 187
Brown, Maurice, 110
Buck, Pearl S., 140
Burrill, Ena, 267
Bush-Fekete, L., 240
Byron, Lady, 237
Byron, Lord, 57

Caesar, 157
Caesar and Cleopatra, 57–60
Campo Santo, the, 70
Candida, 193–195
Carnovsky, Morris, 82, 131
Carpenter, John Alden, 1, 2
Carr, Joan, 154
Carradine, John, 277
Carrington, Mrs. Margaret, 8, 11
Carroll, Albert, 52
Carroll, Leo G., 243, 245
Carter, Jack, 176
Caruso, 150
Cassatt, Mary, 246
Catholic Church, the, 173
Century Theatre, the, 29, 33, 45, 266
Chaliapin, 16, 69
Chaney, Stewart, 242, 245, 257
Chaplin, Charlie, 279
Chekhov, Anton, 18, 19, 80, 108, 114, 200–205, 207–209, 263
Chekhov, Madame, 38
Chekhov Theatre Players, the, 218
Cherry Orchard, The, 69, 81, 201, 207–209
Ching-Chung Monastery, 116
Christi, Vito, 247
Christians, Mady, 212
Cicero, 137, 192
Clark, Bobby, 254, 258
Clements, Colin, 236
Clurman, Harold, 129
Colbert, Claudette, 94
Collins, Ray, 225
Collins, Russell, 273
Comédie Française, the, 263
Congreve, William, 123, 156, 157, 182, 183, 229
Connelly, Marc, 119–122
Connor, Whitfield, 277
Cook, Elisha, Jr., 104
Copeau, Jacques, 80–83

Coquelin, 16
Cordoba, Pedro de, 147
Cornell, Katharine, 145–147, 187, 194, 259, 262
Cort Theatre, 159, 254, 259
Cosi è (se vi pare), 84–87
Cosi Sia, 33
Cosmopolitan Theatre, 67
Country Wife, The, 181–184
Coward, Noel, 163
Cowl, Jane, 27, 28
Crabtree, Paul, 273
Craig, Gordon, 96
Crawford, Cheryl, 129
Crews, Laura Hope, 76–79
Croce, Benedetto, 86
Cromwell, John, 79
Croue, Jean, 80, 81
Cunningham, Merce, 278

Dale, James, 163
Dale, Margaret, 245
Dane, Clemence, 20–23, 178
Daniell, Henry, 255, 256
D'Annunzio, Gabriele, 33, 171
Daste, Marie-Helene, 266
Daughter of Jorio, 171
Davis, Donald, 140, 179
Davis, Owen, 140, 178, 179
Derwent, Charles, 169, 170
Desire under the Elms, 91, 231
Dickens, Charles, 237, 243
Dickinson, Emily, 278
Digges, Dudley, 82, 95, 273
Diogenes, 190
Dishonored Lady, 145
Don Juan, 57
Dostoyevsky, Feodor, 37, 39, 40, 80–82, 263
Doucet, Catherine Calhoun, 94
Dowling, Eddie, 251–253, 271, 272
Drake, William A., 189
Drama Critics Circle, 215
Drayton, Michael, 175
Dreiser, Theodore, 72–75
Dryden, John, 146, 156, 157, 181
Duchess of Malfi, The, 275–277
Duke, Robert, 256
Dumas, Alexandre (Dumas Fils), 67
Duncan, Augustin, 197

INDEX

Dunnigan's Daughter, 254, 257, 258
Durfey, Thomas, 156, 182
Duse, Eleonora, 29–32, 33–36, 39, 114
Dybbuk, The, 67–70
Dynamo, 91–95

Edward II, 174, 197, 198
Edwards, Henry, 212
El Penitente, 278
Electra, 135
Elizabethan theatre, 115
Elizabeth's Play, Queen, 20–24
Elliott's Theatre, Maxine, 174
Embezzled Heaven, 240–242
Emerson, Hope, 124
Empire Theatre, 153, 185, 193
Esmond, Jill, 163
Eternal Road, The, 189, 190
Ethan Frome, 178–180
Etheredge, Sir George, 156
Euripides, 57, 123, 132, 134, 187
Evans, Maurice, 196, 197, 211–214, 222
Every Soul Is a Circus, 278

Fair Maid of the Inn, The, 275
Farley, Morgan, 74, 75
Farquhar, George, 156
Farrar, Geraldine, 150
Faure, M. Elie, 222
Fay, Mary Helen, 240
Fell, Marian, 202
Ferrer, Jose, 233
Ffolkes, David, 197, 212
Field of Ermine, 169, 170
Fifty-ninth Street Theatre, Jolson's, 15, 37
Fitch, Clyde, 3, 19
Fontanne, Lynn, 82, 204, 205
Forbes, Ralph, 229
Forbes-Robertson, 8
Forty-eighth Street Theatre, 5
Forty-fourth Street Theatre, 48, 150
Forty-ninth Street Theatre, 114
Four Saints in Three Acts, 150–152
Franz, Eduard, 242
From Lorca's Theatre, 169
Fuller, Rosalinde, 12
Furness, Horace Howard, Jr., 123
Furse, Roger, 265

Galantière, Lewis, 259, 261
Gallerati-Scotti, 33
Gamble, M., 50
Garnett translation of Chekhov, 200
Garrick Theatre, the, 88
Gaul, George, 94
Geddes, Norman Bel, 20, 45–47, 97, 124–126, 190–192
Georgia Press, University of, 248
Ghosts, 29, 32
Gillmore, Margalo, 79, 167
Girgenti, Sicily, 86
Glass Menagerie, The, 249–253, 273
Goethe, 174
Golden Theatre, John, 76, 254
Goldoni, Carlo, 37–40
Good Earth, The, 140–144
Goodman, Edward, 74
Gordon, Ruth, 179, 181, 183
Gorki, Maxim, 17, 113, 263, 273
Gozzi, Carlo, 86
Gozzoli, 43
Graham, George, 212
Graham, Martha, 278–282
Graham L., James, 169
Grand Street Follies, 52
Granville-Barker, Harley, 97, 101
Granville-Barker, Helen, 101
Great God Brown, The, 61–64
Green, Paul, 88–90, 127–130, 223
Green Bay Tree, The, 159–164
Green Hat, The, 145
Green Pastures, The, 119–122
Greene, Robert, 254
Greenstreet, Sydney, 124, 205, 228, 264
Greenwich Village Theatre, 61
Group Theatre, the, 127–131
Guild Theatre, 57, 80, 81, 84, 85, 132, 138, 140, 165, 278
Guiterman, Arthur, 153–155

Habima Players, the, 67–71
Hackett, 11
Hagen, Uta, 205, 234
Hairy Ape, The, 65, 92
Hamlet, 8–14, 132, 203, 211–214, 255
Hannen, Nicholas, 268
Harding, Lyn, 98
Hardwicke, Sir Cedric, 262

INDEX

Harriet, 236–239
Harrigan, William, 63
Harris, Jed, 159–163
Harris, Robert, 195
Harris Theatre, Sam H., 8
Harrison, Nell, 224
Harrison, Richard B., 120, 122
Harvey, Georgia, 104
Hatfield, Hurd, 221
Hauptmann, Gerhart, 173
Hawkins, Eric, 278
Haydon, Julie, 252
Hayes, Helen, 221, 237, 238
Heartbreak House, 206–210
Hecataeus, 189
Heflin, Frances, 247
Hegel, Georg, 86
Heggie, O. P., 163, 164
Henry IV, 48–50, 196, 263–265
Hergesheimer, Joseph, 185
Hewitt, Alan, 216
High Tor, 185, 187
Hill, Wesley, 122
Hindu comedy, 52–55
Hines, Altonell, 151
Hogarth, Leona, 63
Holinshed, Raphael, 264
Hollywood, 228
Homer, 87, 132
Hopkins, Arthur, 11, 12, 100
Hopkins, Miriam, 74, 124
House of Connelly, The, 127–131
Houseman, John, 151
Howard, Sidney, 76–79
Hoy, Helen, 143
Hull, Henry, 152
Hunnicutt, Arthur, 216
Huston, Walter, 216

I Pagliacci, 1
Ibsen, Henrik, 7, 29–32, 65, 183
Iceman Cometh, The, 271–274
If Five Years Pass, 173
In Abraham's Bosom, 88–90
India, Hindu comedy from, 53, 54
Invisible World, The, 248
Irving, Sir Henry, 8, 11, 19, 254, 268
Italy, 240
Ivan, Rosalind, 80

James, King, 142
Japan, coronation robes of, 143
Java Head, 185
Jefferson, 19
Jest, The, 231
Jews, 189
Jones, Robert Edmond, 1, 3, 11, 12, 19, 48, 62, 63, 97, 100, 120, 138, 148, 159, 204, 230, 271, 274
Jonson, Ben, 182
Journal-American, The, 205
Journey's End, 110–113
Joy, Nicholas, 273
Joyce, Phyllis, 206

Kachalov, Vassily, 17
Kane, Whitford, 198, 212, 256
Kaufman, George S., 243, 244
Kazan, Elia, 239
Kean, Mr., 213
Kearney, Patrick, 72–75
Keith, Ian, 196, 197
Keith, Robert, 63
Keith-Johnston, Colin, 113, 256
Kelly, George, 5, 7
Keye, Mr., 194
Kilian, Victor, 167
King, Dennis, 26
King, Edith, 233
King Lear, 132, 232
King-Coit School, 248
Kingdom of God, The, 101–105, 240
Kiss for Cinderella, A, 227
Knickerbocker Theatre, 96–100
Knipper-Chekhov, Mme., 15, 17
Korff, Mr., 49
Krauss, Werner, 47
Kreutzberg, Mr., 282
Kruger, Otto, 23

La Dame aux Camelias, 67
La Donna dal Mare, 29–31
La Locandiera, 37–39
La Rochefoucauld, François, 58, 239
Lady from the Sea, The, 29–31
Lamb, Charles, 54
Landis, Jessie Royce, 216, 256
Langner, Lawrence, 153, 154, 155
Larimore, Earle, 137, 138
Lascelles, Miss, 48

INDEX

Late George Apley, The, 243–245, 252
Lawson, Kate, 151
Leacock, Stephen, 81
Le Bourgeois Gentilhomme, 258
L'Ecole des Femmes, 182
L'Ecole des Maris, 155, 182
Lee, Canada, 224, 247, 277
Lee, Robert E., 165
Le Mariage Forcé, 153, 156
Lenihan, Winifred, 22, 23
Leonidoff, 39
Leopardi, Giacomo, 139
Letter, The, 145
Letter to the World, 278, 279
Leung, George Kin, 115
Le Viol de Lucrece, 146
Lewisohn, Irene, 52
Lewisohn, Ludwig, 189
Leysac, Paul, 248
Life with Father, 243
Little Clay Cart, The, 52–56
Little Theatre, 218
Liveright, Horace, 73, 74
Livesey, Roger, 183
Living Mask, The, 48
Livingston, Arthur, 48, 84, 85
Locke, Katherine, 212
Longacre Theatre, 72
Loraine, Robert, 148
Lorca, Federigo Garcia, 169, 171–173
Lord, Pauline, 19, 178–180
Louden, Mr., 49
Louis XIV, 144, 153
Love's Old Sweet Song, 215–217
Lower Depths, 113, 273
Lucrece, 145–149
Lunt, Alfred, 82, 204, 205
Lyceum Theatre, 41, 169, 170, 243
Lysistrata, 123–126

Macaulay, Thomas B., 181
Macbeth, 96–100, 222, 231
Maclaren, Ian, 52
Magda, 162
Maltese Falcon, The, 228
Manetho, 189
Manhattan Opera House, the, 1, 69, 189
Manners, Lady Diana, 45
Mansfield, Richard, 9, 254

Mansfield Theatre, 67, 119, 169
Mariners, 178
Marlowe, Christopher, 174–177, 197, 198
Marquand, John P., 243, 245
Marshall, E. G., 273
Martin-Harvey, Sir John, 269
Martini, Simone, 116
Mason, Reginald, 84, 167
Massey, Raymond, 179
Mather, Sidney, 12
Matthews, George, 261
Matthews, Junus, 52
Maugham, Somerset, 145
McClendon, Rose, 89
McClintic, Guthrie, 195, 262
McGrath, Byron, 187, 188
McKay, David, 245
McKee, Harry, 176
Mediterranean, the, 29, 103, 189
Mei Lan-fang, 114–118, 137
Merande, Doro, 216
Mercer, Beryl, 84, 87
Merchant of Venice, The, 41–44
Mercury Theatre, 206
Meredith, Burgess, 187, 188
Merivale, Philip, 43, 167, 168
Messel, Oliver, 183
Metropolitan Opera House, 29
Michelangelo, 68
Mielziner, Jo, 106, 179, 252
Miller, Gilbert, 181, 183, 239, 259
Miller's Theatre, Henry, 25, 26, 110, 181, 236
Miracle, The, 45–47
Misanthrope, The, 6, 7
Moeller, Philip, 138, 143
Moffet, Harold, 187
Molière, 6, 7, 153–158, 182, 254, 258
Monk, William, 265
Moore, Erin O'Brien, 107
Morgan, Agnes, 52
Morriott, John, 273
Morris, McKay, 104
Moscow, Habima Theatre of, 68–71
Moscow Art Theatre, the, 15–19, 37–40, 69, 80, 113, 114, 144, 201, 205, 218, 263, 273
Moskvin, Ivan, 15, 17
Moss, Arnold, 247

INDEX

Motley, 246, 247
Mounet-Sully, 8, 268, 269
Mourning Becomes Electra, 132–139
Murray, Gilbert, 269
Music Box, The, 227

National Theatre, 20, 178, 240
Native Son, 223–226
Natwick, Mildred, 195
Nazimova, Alla, 137, 142, 143
Neighborhood Playhouse, The, 52, 53, 56, 69, 170, 171, 173
Nemirovitch-Danchenko, 218
New York Times, The, 201
Nicharchus, 269
Nichols, Mr., 252
Nietzsche, 259
Nijinsky, 279

Obey, André, 145
O'Brien, Mr., 12
O'Connell, Richard L., 169
Oedipus at Colonos, 260
Oedipus Rex, 81, 132, 161, 260, 266–270
Ol' Man Adam and his Chillun, 119, 120
Old Vic company, the, 263–265, 266–270
Olivier, Laurence, 164, 264, 267–269
O'Neill, Eugene, 61–66, 91, 93, 132–139, 271–274
O'Neill, Nance, 173
On Trial, 74
Orestes, 135
Othello, 230–235
Oukrainsky, Serge, 2
Ouspenskaya, Mme. Maria, 205

Pandosto: The Triumph of Time, 254
Parks, Gower, 265
Pascal, 4
Pasquin, of Paris, 257
Patriot, The, 98
Pavlova, Anna, 279
Payne, B. Iden, 241, 256
Pedi, Tom, 273
Perkins, Osgood, 154, 156
Peters, Rollo, 26
Philadelphia Theatre Association, 123

Phillips, Stephen, 187
Pinchot, Rosamond, 47
Pindar, 132
Piper, John, 266
Pirandello, Luigi, 38, 48–50, 84–87, 147
Pisa, the Campo Santo at, 70
Pizhova, Madame, 38
Plain Dealer, The, 183
Plato, 161, 190
Plautus, Titus Maccius, 87
Playhouse Theatre, the, 106, 109, 249
Plimmer, Harry, 104
Pliny, 189
Plymouth Theatre, 215
Pole, Reginald, 12
Politics, 190
Pope, Alexander, 184
Power, Tyrone, 12
Primavera, Botticelli's, 43
Provincetown Playhouse, the, 88, 273
Pulitzer Prize, 215

Qualenn, Mrs. James M., 109
Quartermaine, Leon, 113
Quinteros Brothers, The, 28

Rainer, Louise, 227–229
Rainey, Ford, 221, 222
Rains, Claude, 142
Randolph, Donald, 214
Raphael, 68
Rascoe, Burton, 236
Reed, Alan, 216
Reed, Florence, 98, 99, 256
Reed, Paulina, 257
Reid, Carl Benton, 273
Reinhardt, Max, 45, 46, 97, 191, 192
Renoir, 222
Repertory, 114
Rice, Elmer, 106, 107
Richard II, 196–199
Richardson, Ralph, 265, 267
Rickett, Edmond W., 153
Ridgefield, Conn., 93, 218
Right You Are If You Think You Are, 84–87
Roberts, Evelyn, 113
Robeson, Paul, 230, 234, 235
Robinson, Edward G., 82, 84

INDEX

Rochester, Lord, 181
Romanceff, Dr. Nicholas, 201
Romano, Julio, 68
Romeo and Juliet, 21, 25–28
Ross, Anthony, 252
Rovina, Madame Anna, 70
Rubens, 116
Rue de la Paix, 68
Ryder, Arthur William, 52
Ryerson, Florence, 236
Rylands, George, 276

Saint, The, 231
St. Augustine, 191
St. Helena, 197
St. James Theatre, 196, 211, 223
Sands, Dorothy, 52
Sanford, Erskine, 137, 167, 224
Santayana, George, 13
Saroyan, William, 215–217
Savage, Bernard, 99
Savoy Theatre, the, 110
Sayler, Oliver, 15
Schildkraut, Joseph, 47
School for Husbands, The, 153–158, 182
Scott, General Winfield, 228
Scribner's Sons, Charles, 169
Sea Gull, The, 200–205, 207
Seldes, Gilbert, 123–125
Seneca, Lucius Annaeus, 87, 277
Servoss, Mary, 107
Seymour, Jane, 238
Shairp, Mordaunt, 159, 162
Shakespeare, William, 8–14, 18, 19, 26, 40, 41–43, 113, 125, 147, 174, 182, 187, 196–199, 204, 211–214, 218–222, 230–235, 246–248, 254–257, 264, 265, 275
Shaw, George Bernard, 57–60, 65, 193–195, 206–210
Shelley, Percy Bysshe, 136
Sherriff, R. C., 110
Shine, John, 21
Shoemaker, Anne, 63
Shubert Theatre, 200, 230
Shudraka, King, 53, 54
Sicily, 86
Sierra, G. Martinez, 101, 240
Silver Cord; The, 76–79

Simonson, Lee, 93, 142, 153–155
Sir Barnaby Whig, 182
Skipworth, Miss Alison, 5
Sophocles, 123, 132, 134, 135, 161, 259, 260, 266, 267
Sorbière, Samuel de, 275
Sorel, Madame Cecile, 67, 68
Sothern, Edward H., 8
Sovey, Raymond, 83, 261
Spenser, Edmund, 35
Spain, 3
Stage Society, the, 207
Stanislavsky, Constantin, 15, 17, 38, 205, 218
Stanley, S. Victor, 113
Starr, Frances, 169, 170
Stein, Gertrude, 150, 151
Stettheimer, Florine, 151
Stowe, Harriet Beecher, 236
Straight, Beatrice, 221
Strange Interlude, 91
Strasberg, Lee, 129, 228
Stravinsky, 2
Street Scene, 106–109
Strook, Geraldine, 256
Sudermann, Hermann, 162
Sunken Bell, The, 173
Sydney, Sir Philip, 113
Symons, Arthur, 187
Symposium, 161
Synge, John, 261

Tamiroff, Akim, 38
Tarasova, Alla, 40
Taylor, Deems, 149
Taylor, Laurette, 19, 249–252
Tempest, The, 187, 246–248
Tennyson, Alfred, 280
Terence, 157
Thackeray, William Makepeace, 237
Theatre Arts Monthly Magazine, 98
Theatre Guild, the, 59, 60, 81–83, 93, 127, 137, 153–158, 182, 204, 207, 221, 230, 240, 254, 257, 271
Thomas, Harold, 99
Thomson, Virgil, 150, 151
Three Sisters, The, 201
Throckmorton, Cleon, 129
Thucydides, 190
Thy Will Be Done, 33

INDEX

Times, the New York, 252
Tintoretto, 43, 120
Titian, 43
Tobacco Road, 152
Tolstoy, Alexis, 16
Tolstoy, Leo, 80, 208, 263
Tone, Franchot, 130, 131
Torch Bearers, The, 5–7
Tragical History of Doctor Faustus, The, 174–177
Trojan Women, The, 231
Truex, Ernest, 124
Tsar Fyodor, 15–17
Tweddel, Frank, 273
Twelfth Night, 218–222
Tyler, George, 96
Tyndale, William, 142

Uncle Tom's Cabin, 236
Uncle Vanya, 207
Underhill, John Garrett, 169

Valentino, 261
Valley Forge, 165–168
Van Dyke, 116
Van Grove, Mr., 2
Varro, 191
Vasari, Giorgio, 68
Velasquez, Diego, 35
Veronese, 43
Vico, 86
Vollmoeler, Karl, 45
Voltaire, 157
Volterra, 86
Vortex, The, 163
Voskovec, George, 248

Walker, June, 154
Walnut Street Theatre, Philadelphia, 123
Walpole, 183
Warfield, David, 19, 41, 42
Washington, George, 165–168

Webster, John, 275, 277
Webster, Margaret, 199, 211, 230–233, 246, 247
Weidman, Charles, 154
Weill, Kurt, 189, 192
Weissberger, José A., 169
Welles, Orson, 175–177, 207, 224, 225
Wenman, Henry, 113
Werfel, Franz, 189, 191, 240
Werich, Jan, 248
West, Robert Hunter, 248
Wharton, Edith, 178
What Price Glory?, 110, 112
White, Miles, 277
Whorf, Richard, 205
Whitney, Tut, 122
Wigman, Miss, 282
Wilde, Oscar, 2
Wilder, Thornton, 145, 146
Will Shakespeare, 20
Williams, Rhys, 212, 238
Williams, Tennessee, 249–253
Wilson, Edmund, 206
Wilson, Katherine, 74
Wingless Victory, The, 185–187
Winter's Tale, The, 254–257
Witty, Dame, 231
Wood, Philip, 74
Woodson, William, 238
Wordsworth, William, 269
World-Telegram, the New York, 236
Would-Be Gentleman, The, 254, 258
Wright, Haidee, 20, 23, 24
Wright, Richard, 223
Wycherley, William, 156, 181–184

Yeats, W. B., 266, 268
Young, Stark, 200
Yurka, Blanche, 12, 148

Zemach, Benjamin, 189, 192
Zorina, Vera, 247

DATE DUE

FEB 18 '74			
FEB 20 '74			
APR 17 '74			
FEB 25 '75			
MAR 5 '75			
MAR 18 '75			
JUL 23 '75			
FE 9 19 76			
MAR 23 '76			
AP 4 '77			
AP 18 '77			
FE 13 '79			
MAR 4 '86			
MR 18 '85			
MAR 24			
MAR 24 '89			

GAYLORD · PRINTED IN U.S.A.